Rethinking Japanese Feminisms

Rethinking Japanese Feminisms

EDITED BY
Julia C. Bullock, Ayako Kano,
and James Welker

University of Hawai'i Press
Honolulu

Printed in the United States of America

24   23   22   21   20   19   6   5   4   3   2   1

Library of Congress Cataloging-in-Publication Data

Names: Bullock, Julia C., editor. | Kano, Ayako, editor. | Welker, James, editor.
Title: Rethinking Japanese feminisms / edited by Julia C. Bullock, Ayako Kano, and James Welker.
Description: Honolulu : University of Hawai'i Press, [2017] | Includes bibliographical references and index.
Identifiers: LCCN 2017014299 | ISBN 9780824866693 (cloth ; alk. paper)
Subjects: LCSH: Feminism—Japan.
Classification: LCC HQ1762 .R48 2017 | DDC 305.420952—dc23

LC record available at https://lccn.loc.gov/2017014299

ISBN 978-0-8248-6670-9 (pbk.)

Designed by Publishers' Design and Production Services, Inc.

Cover art:
Miki Suizan, Japanese, 1887–1957
Fair Wind (Junpū)
Japanese, Shōwa era, 1933
Panel; ink, color, and mica on silk
241.6 x 191.5 cm (95 1/8 x 75 3/8 in.) Museum of Fine Arts, Boston
Charles H. Bayley Picture and Painting Fund and Museum purchase with funds donated anonymously
2007.813

Contents

Acknowledgments

THIS VOLUME GREW out of a 2013 conference on Japanese feminisms that was supported by Emory University and the Northeast Asia Council of the Association for Asian Studies. The conference offered an unprecedented opportunity to "rethink modern Japanese feminisms" from a broad array of disciplinary, temporal, geographical, and theoretical perspectives, and it generated an overwhelmingly positive response from attendees. This book is the result of that gathering and the enthusiasm of participants.

In addition to the volume's contributors, the editors would like to acknowledge the efforts of the many individuals who contributed time, effort, and intellectual horsepower to the honing of the essays that are included here. They include Jan Bardsley, Laura Dales, Hikari Hori, Ronald Loftus, Dina Lowy, Elizabeth Miles, and especially Vera Mackie, Barbara Molony, and Ueno Chizuko, whose inspiring keynote speeches at the conference are taken up in this volume's conclusion. We would also like to thank Sarah Jiajia Wang, Kirsten Seuffert, and Sumiko Hatakeyama for assistance with the bibliographical sources and for proofreading. The University of Pennsylvania provided financial assistance for image reproduction and producing the index.

In addition, at the University of Hawai'i Press, we would like to thank our editor, Pamela Kelley, for smoothly steering this project through to completion, and Wendy Bolton, for her meticulous copyediting. We are also extremely grateful to two anonymous reviewers who provided excellent feedback that helped us to improve the introduction and helped individual authors to improve their chapters.

Finally, the editors would like to acknowledge all the scholars of Japanese women's studies and feminist studies who have contributed to the creation of these fields, making this volume possible.

Introduction

JULIA C. BULLOCK, AYAKO KANO,

AND JAMES WELKER

T HE GREAT DIVERSITY OF FEMINIST ISSUES and practices represented
in this volume should make it clear why we have opted to write about
"feminisms" in the plural. When the editors of this volume first conceived the idea for a book on modern Japanese feminisms, already more
than a decade into the twenty-first century, it seemed an opportune time
to reassess the many ways that feminist thought and activism have shaped
modern Japanese society, as well as take stock of what work remained for
future generations of scholars and activists.

The chapters in this book work toward the rethinking of Japanese
feminisms in several ways. Some authors throw light on ideas and practices that resonate with feminist thought but find expression through
the work of writers, artists, activists, and laborers who have not typically been considered feminist. These scholars call on us to reconsider,
and perhaps expand, the types of thought and praxis that we generally
include within a feminist rubric. The authors of other chapters revisit
specific moments in the history of Japanese feminisms in order to complicate or challenge the dominant scholarly and popular understandings
of specific activists, practices, and beliefs.

Rethinking Japanese Feminisms draws from and builds on the work of
scholars, activists, and thinkers researching and publishing about "feminisms" since the 1970s, when the field of women's studies emerged worldwide, becoming known in Japan as *joseigaku*. The intervening decades
have seen the repositioning of women's studies as gender studies, followed by gender and sexuality studies, which itself has often incorporated or overlapped with a field now called LGBT/LGBTQ studies or

simply queer studies. These new perspectives have reshaped how we conceive of modern female subjects, and, much as feminist scholarship was instrumental in the development of queer studies, so too has queer studies influenced feminist scholarship—in Japan and elsewhere. Written by scholars who employ methodologies and theoretical perspectives from anthropology, cultural studies, gender and sexuality studies, history, literature, media studies, queer studies, and sociology, the chapters in this volume reflect the influence of these theoretical and methodological shifts. Building on previous scholarship over the past several decades that has explored Japanese culture through the lens of gender and sexuality studies, the essays in this volume apply these insights toward an assessment of the past, present, and future of feminisms in Japan.[1]

The chapters that follow have been organized into sections focused on Activism and Activists, Education and Employment, Literature and the Arts, and Boundaries—specifically, ways feminist activism and thought in Japan have transcended national and cultural borders. Each section is preceded by a brief introduction underlining key points made in each of the chapters and highlighting common themes across the chapters. The conclusion, by Ayako Kano, considers questions of the canonization, nationality, and future of Japanese feminisms, drawing on keynote talks given by leading scholars of feminism, Vera Mackie, Barbara Molony, and Ueno Chizuko, at the 2013 conference. By way of providing context for these chapters, the remainder of this Introduction provides a historical overview of feminisms in Japan.

An Introduction to the History of Feminisms in Japan

While the term "feminism" may sound quintessentially modern, rich premodern veins of discourse empowering women have existed in Japan since the earliest times in the fields of literature, religion, and the arts. Many of the masterpieces of classical Japanese literature—Murasaki Shikibu's *The Tale of Genji* (ca. 1000 CE) being perhaps the best known among many others—were written by women. Recent research continues to push back the origins of "feminist" discourse in Japan as scholars uncover work by itinerant Buddhist nuns, accomplished female poets and artists of the samurai and merchant classes, and peasant women activists who challenged conventional wisdom that a female—whatever her social status—should keep her activities safely confined within the domestic sphere.[2]

Nevertheless, it was during the years of nation building in the Meiji era (1868–1912)—often defined as the beginning of "modern" Japan—that the category "woman" was increasingly understood as cutting across differences in social status, marital status, reproductive status, and age.[3] Women also began speaking out in public on behalf of other women. In this sense, we may trace the beginnings of "feminism" as it is typically understood today to that era.

During the first few decades of the Meiji period, the nature of popular participation in politics was still undecided, creating an opening for women activists like Kishida Toshiko (1861–1901) and Fukuda Hideko (1865–1927) to aspire to prominent public roles. The public speech became a new outlet for women's expression, and though women's formal political participation was increasingly restricted by law from the 1890s, women could publicize their views through writing and circulating petitions.[4] In the 1890s, many of the institutions of the modern Japanese nation-state were founded, and these increasingly inculcated the ideal of "good wife, wise mother" (*ryōsai kenbo*), which sought to redefine women's contributions to family life as a form of service to the state.[5]

But soon Japanese women began pushing against these strictures, as did women in many parts of the rest of the world, where it was still uncommon for the sexes to have equal opportunity for political participation.[6] In 1911 the first feminist journal, *Seitō* (Bluestocking), was founded by Hiratsuka Raichō (1886–1971). This was not the first journal to be edited by a woman—that honor goes to *Fujin no tomo* (Ladies' companion), founded by educator Hani Motoko (1873–1957) in 1906—but it was the first to openly defy existing norms for women's behavior. Members of the collective that produced the journal, the Bluestocking Society (Seitōsha), visited the pleasure quarters and wrote about drinking alcohol, and also discussed controversial issues such as abortion and prostitution.[7] The publication launched the careers of feminist writers such as Itō Noe (1895–1923) and Kamichika Ichiko (1888–1981). Yamakawa Kikue (1890–1980)—discussed in this volume in chapters by Elyssa Faison and Sarah Frederick—was another important feminist who engaged with the Bluestocking Society, and was also a leading figure in the leftist movement.

In the early twentieth century, a confluence of several factors led to a magazine culture focusing on women, including high literacy rates due to compulsory elementary education for both sexes, the rise in publishing technology, women's migration to the cities, access to secondary and higher education and white-collar jobs, and the growth of an urban middle class. These all contributed to what might be called a female public sphere, in which creative experimentation and intellectual debates could take place.[8] The increasing visibility of women in Japanese society was celebrated in the art of Takabatake Kashō (1888–1966), whose work is examined in this volume by Leslie Winston. This era also saw the rise of women's groups such as the Japanese branch of the Woman's Christian Temperance Union (Tokyo Fujin Kyōfūkai), whose activism against concubinage and prostitution was driven primarily by Christian morality and nationalist fervor, but inevitably touched on feminist critique of male prerogatives as well.[9]

The 1920s may be seen as a time of transition, when women were increasingly exhorted to display their "special qualities" as women through contributions to the larger society, not just home and hearth, while simultaneously remaining subordinate to and dependent on men. Women responded to this exhortation in ambivalent and sometimes contradictory ways. On one hand, the decade saw the formation of socialist women's organizations like the Red Wave Society (Sekirankai) and the Eighth Day Society (Yōkakai), encouraged by the rise of proletarian activism and progressive social movements underwritten by an expanded franchise for men.[10] The women's suffrage movement in Japan was also a major locus of feminist discourse and activism in the 1920s, driven by women like Ichikawa Fusae (1893–1981) and Oku Mumeo (1895–1997), who along with Hiratsuka Raichō had formed the New Women's Association (Shin Fujin Kyōkai) in December of 1919.[11] On the other hand, many Japanese women also responded enthusiastically to calls from government bureaucracies to participate in various projects and associations designed to contribute to state goals, such as household savings campaigns, the scientific rationalization of housework and domestic hygiene, and social work activities.[12]

In the early 1930s, government ministries began establishing or taking control of large umbrella organizations in order to channel women's "natural" capacity for nurturing and selfless behavior into gender-appropriate forms of support for the war effort. In addition to the Patriotic Women's

Association (Aikoku Fujinkai), originally founded in 1901, organizations like the Greater Japan Federated Women's Association (Dai Nihon Rengō Fujinkai, 1931) and the Greater Japan National Defense Women's Association (Dai Nihon Kokubō Fujinkai, 1932) sprang up to answer the call for women's public service. Women were encouraged to stage celebratory send-off events for soldiers, to create care packages for soldiers at the front, and to tend to the wounded or sick, among other social welfare projects that constructed women's service to the state as an outgrowth of their primary role within the domestic sphere.[13] Nevertheless, some women continued to resist the dominant ideological presumption of separate spheres for men and women, including progressive educational reformers like Koizumi Ikuko (1892–1964)—discussed in Julia Bullock's chapter—who lobbied for equal educational and employment opportunities for women in spite of their prevailing ideological construction as "good wives and wise mothers."

In the aftermath of defeat in World War II, Japan was ruled for seven years by an Allied Occupation that sought to remake Japan as a democratic nation. Revisions to the Constitution and Civil Code granted its women many of the rights and freedoms that they had long sought—including the rights to vote and run for election, to own property and receive inheritance, to marry and divorce on the same legal footing as men, and to receive an education equal to their male counterparts. The election of thirty-nine women to the Diet in 1946, as well as the creation of the Women's and Minors' Bureau within the Ministry of Labor—whose first head was the aforementioned socialist activist Yamakawa Kikue—signaled the increasing visibility of women in government and attention to women's issues in the postwar period. However, Occupation-era policies toward women were not uniformly progressive, and often had unintended consequences—for example, protective legislation that shut women out of certain types of employment and effectively rendered them second-class employees.[14] The so-called "reverse course" in Occupation policy, a result of Cold War pressures to shift attention from progressive social change toward stabilization of the Japanese economy, further empowered conservative politicians to challenge and mitigate the effects of postwar reforms.

In the decades following the Occupation, the Japanese government moved to re-impose a conservative vision of normative femininity grounded in conventional domestic roles for women. Government-funded women's centers and regional women's associations sponsored "social education" programs to cultivate in married women household skills and traditionally feminine arts like flower arranging,[15] though such skills could also be leveraged for financial self-sufficiency, as illustrated in this volume by Nancy Stalker and Chris McMorran. Formal education for girls, nominally constructed around an ethos of equality of opportunity, increasingly stressed home economics and gendered educational outcomes.[16] As the Japanese economy entered a phase of high economic growth that began in the mid-1950s and accelerated into the 1960s, government and industry collaborated to encourage women to confine their energies to the domestic sphere so that their menfolk could devote themselves wholeheartedly to work outside the home[17]—a division of labor that made the Japanese "economic miracle" possible.[18] On the other hand, conservatism and feminism during this period were not mutually exclusive ideological terrains, and challenges to masculine hegemony could nevertheless be effected through a conventionally feminine or politically conservative rhetorical position—as demonstrated in chapters by Hillary Maxson and Barbara Hartley.

Alongside the continuation of state feminism in the form of the Women's Bureau and other government institutions, the beginning of the 1970s saw the emergence of a new wave of radical feminist activism, widely known as *ūman ribu* (women's lib), that attracted a burst of media attention as well as broad derision in public discourse.[19] Arguably representing the legacy of New Left activism and politics of the 1960s, the university students and other predominantly young women involved in the movement—many of whom themselves had been involved in the New Left—were among the first generation to grow up under *de jure* equality with men as a result of the 1947 Constitution. The *ribu* movement, discussed in chapters by James Welker and Setsu Shigematsu, extended its realm of concern well beyond problems of socioeconomic equality to include women's social and sexual liberation. Rather than rejecting motherhood, *ribu* aimed to build a society in which women might want to have children.[20] While often framed as an import—a Japanese version of so-called second-wave feminism—the *ribu* movement developed as a result of resentment, frustration, and anger at the many contradictions facing Japanese women in the mid-twentieth century. Though they did not attract as much media attention, overlapping with *ribu* in terms of chronology, interests, and membership were other feminist groups such as the

Asian Women's Conference Fighting Against Invasion=Discrimination (Shinryaku=Sabetsu to Tatakau Ajia Fujin Kaigi), which was concerned with fighting Japanese and American imperialism in Asia, as well as multiple forms of discrimination and oppression within and beyond Japan's borders. Resonating with feminist critiques by women in the New Left, women belonging to ethnic and other minority groups seeking social recognition and fighting discrimination in Japanese society would also begin to criticize patriarchal structures within these movements and society at large around this time, an issue taken up in this volume by Akwi Seo.

In response to the United Nations First World Conference on Women in 1975 and subsequent passage of the Convention on the Elimination of Discrimination against Women (which Japan signed in 1980 and ratified in 1985), the government began creating legislation ostensibly to fulfill the aims of the convention—most notably the Equal Employment Opportunity Law (EEOL), enacted in 1986, and the law's subsequent revisions. This legislation has been criticized for being ineffectual, however.[21] The second half of the 1970s also saw the emergence of the field of women's studies (*joseigaku*) in Japan, marked in part by the establishment of the Women's Studies Society of Japan (Nihon Joseigaku Kenkyūkai) in 1977, and the Women's Studies Association of Japan (Nihon Josei Gakkai) in 1979.

While the *ribu* movement itself largely faded by the end of the 1970s, feminist activists and academics as well as artists and writers have continued to focus on issues such as women's reproductive and sexual autonomy and various forms of discrimination. In her chapter, for instance, Kathryn Hemmann examines how these themes have been treated imaginatively in literature. In the mid- to late 1990s, queer theory began to shape the thought of feminist academics in Japan, including cultural and literary theorist Takemura Kazuko (1954–2011), whose writing is explored in this volume by J. Keith Vincent. Around the same time, efforts by public school teachers motivated by feminist beliefs to reform education so that children would feel free from normative restrictions on gender expression—termed "gender free" (*jendā furī*)—sparked a conservative backlash, discussed in this volume by Tomomi Yamaguchi. This era saw both the "gender free" movement and feminists in general fiercely attacked in some circles, and a renewed anti-feminist movement among conservatives that continues today. Since the late 1990s, under the guise of legislation to strengthen the EEOL, conservative lawmakers have also successfully legislated the repurposing of women's centers as "*danjo kyōdō sankaku sentā*," a label that literally translates as "men and women's cooperative participation centers." However, the government uses the term "gender equality centers" in English to give the impression of promoting equality while reframing it as cooperation between the (clearly defined) sexes. While the current conservative government, headed by Prime Minister Abe Shinzō, has called for making a Japan in which women can "take active roles" and "shine" in society, there is little evidence thus far that there will be any policy or legal moves enabling women to participate fully in Japanese society on a genuinely equal footing with men.[22]

Well into the second decade of the twenty-first century, women's status in Japanese society clearly remains a subject of much controversy among the public, among politicians, and among scholars, including the contributors to this volume. As Ayako Kano's conclusion indicates, we are not afraid to disagree with each other in our definitions of feminism, our interpretations of the past, our engagement with the present, and our outlook for the future. But what draws us together, what holds this book together, is our shared commitment to keep rethinking feminisms in Japan, and to invite our readers to think and question and debate along with us.

*   *   *

A Note about Names and Language: In this volume, Japanese and Korean names are written in their natural order of surname preceding given name, except for scholars who publish in English and prefer to use the English order, including all contributors to this volume. We generally follow the Hepburn system of romanizing Japanese and use macrons (ˉ) to indicate long vowel sounds, such as in the word *shōjo* (girl). Major place-names, however, are rendered as English words (e.g., Tokyo, rather than Tōkyō). Finally, we have tried to make this volume as accessible as possible for readers unfamiliar with Japanese. To that end, with the exception of periodical titles, which are often awkward in translation, we generally use translated names for publication titles and group names, with a Japanese gloss for reference. In some cases, however, chapter authors have chosen to retain Japanese names out of respect for their significance.

Notes

1 While an exhaustive listing of previous scholarship would be impossible, the diversity of works cited—including many of the major works in the field—in the introduction and conclusion as well as each of the chapters of this volume suggests the types of scholarship on feminism, women, and gender that have been published in English over the past four decades.

2 See for example the following monographs and essay collections: Gail Lee Bernstein, ed., *Recreating Japanese Women, 1600–1945* (Berkeley: University of California Press, 1991); Anne Walthall, *The Weak Body of a Useless Woman: Matsuo Taseko and the Meiji Restoration* (Chicago: University of Chicago Press, 1998); Edith Sarra, *Fictions of Femininity: Literary Inventions of Gender in Japanese Court Women's Memoirs* (Stanford, CA: Stanford University Press, 1999); Barbara Ruch, *Engendering Faith: Women and Buddhism in Premodern Japan* (Ann Arbor: Center for Japanese Studies, University of Michigan, 2002); Tomiko Yoda, *Gender and National Literature: Heian Texts in the Construction of Japanese Modernity* (Durham, NC: Duke University Press, 2004); Peter F. Kornicki, Mara Patessio, and G. G. Rowley, eds., *The Female as Subject: Reading and Writing in Early Modern Japan* (Ann Arbor: Center for Japanese Studies, University of Michigan, 2010).

3 Ayako Kano, *Acting Like a Woman in Modern Japan: Theater, Gender and Nationalism* (New York: Palgrave, 2001).

4 See Marnie S. Anderson, *A Place in Public: Women's Rights in Meiji Japan* (Cambridge, MA: Harvard University Asia Center, 2010); and Mara Patessio, *Women and Public Life in Early Meiji Japan: The Development of the Feminist Movement* (Ann Arbor: Center for Japanese Studies, University of Michigan, 2011).

5 Koyama Shizuko, *Ryōsai kenbo: The Educational Ideal of "Good Wife, Wise Mother" in Modern Japan* (Boston: Brill, 2013).

6 See Jan Bardsley, *The Bluestockings of Japan: New Woman Essays and Fiction from Seito, 1911–16* (Ann Arbor: Center for Japanese Studies, University of Michigan, 2007). A similar observation might be made about men and masculinity, as men at this time were correspondingly defined as soldiers, regardless of class or social status, through conscription laws. See Sabine Frühstück and Anne Walthall, eds., *Recreating Japanese Men* (Berkeley: University of California Press, 2011).

7 Abortion was made illegal just before the start of the Meiji era but practiced clandestinely, and prostitution was legal and regulated by the state but opposed by many social reformers. For more information on the abortion debates from the Meiji period to the present, see Ayako Kano,

Japanese Feminist Debates: A Century of Contention on Sex, Love, and Labor (Honolulu: University of Hawai'i Press, 2016), 64–103, and for more on prostitution see ibid., 29–63.

8   See Sarah Frederick, *Turning Pages: Reading and Writing Women's Magazines in Interwar Japan* (Honolulu: University of Hawai'i Press, 2006); and Kano, *Japanese Feminist Debates.*

9   Elizabeth Dorn Lublin, *Reforming Japan: The Women's Christian Temperance Union in the Meiji Period* (Vancouver: UBC Press, 2010); Sharon L. Sievers, *Flowers in Salt: The Beginnings of Feminist Consciousness in Modern Japan* (Stanford, CA: Stanford University Press, 1983).

10 Vera Mackie, *Creating Socialist Women in Japan: Gender, Labour and Activism, 1900–1937* (Cambridge: Cambridge University Press, 1997). Universal male suffrage was granted in 1925, an issue discussed by Elyssa Faison in this volume.

11 For an overview, see Sievers, *Flowers in Salt*; and Barbara Molony, "Women's Rights, Feminism, and Suffragism in Japan, 1870–1925," *Pacific Historical Review* 69, no. 4 (2000). On Ichikawa, see Fusae Ichikawa and Yoko Nuita, "Fusae Ichikawa: Japanese Women Suffragist," *Frontiers: A Journal of Women Studies* 3, no. 3 (October 1, 1978); and Ichikawa Fusae and Ichikawa Fusae Kinenkai, *Ichikawa Fusae shū*, 8 vols. (Tokyo: Nihon Tosho Sentā, 1994). On Oku, see Narita Ryūichi, "Haha no kuni no onnatachi: Oku Mumeo no 'senji,' to 'sengo,'" in *Sōryokusen to gendaika*, ed. Yamanouchi Yasushi, Narita Ryūichi, and J. Victor Koschman (Tokyo: Kashiwa Shobō, 1995); and Akiko Tokuza, *The Rise of the Feminist Movement in Japan* (Tokyo: Keio University Press, 1999).

12 See chapter four of Sheldon Garon, *Molding Japanese Minds: The State in Everyday Life* (Princeton, NJ: Princeton University Press, 1997).

13 See chapter five of Vera Mackie, *Feminism in Modern Japan: Citizenship, Embodiment and Sexuality* (Cambridge: Cambridge University Press, 2003).

14 Maho Toyoda, "Protective Labor Legislation and Gender Equality: The Impact of the Occupation on Japanese Working Women," in *Democracy in Occupied Japan: The U.S. Occupation and Japanese Politics and Society*, ed. Mark E. Caprio and Yoneyuki Sugita (London: Routledge, 2007).

15 Miriam Murase, *Cooperation Over Conflict: The Women's Movement and the State in Postwar Japan* (London: Routledge, 2006).

16 Atsuko Kameda, "Sexism and Gender Stereotyping in Schools," in *Japanese Women: New Feminist Perspectives on the Past, Present and Future*, ed. Kumiko Fujimura-Fanselow and Atsuko Kameda (New York: The Feminist Press, 1995).

17 Andrew Gordon, "Managing the Japanese Household: The New Life Movement in Postwar Japan," in *Gendering Modern Japanese History*, ed. Barbara Molony and Kathleen Uno (Cambridge, MA: Harvard University Press, 2005).

18 Mary C. Brinton, *Women and the Economic Miracle: Gender and Work in Postwar Japan* (Berkeley: University of California Press, 1993).

19 On state feminism, including various incarnations of the Women's Bureau, see Yoshie Kobayashi, *A Path Toward Gender Equality: State Feminism in Japan* (New York: Routledge, 2004). On *ūman ribu* and postwar women's writing, see Julia C. Bullock, *The Other Women's Lib: Gender and Body in Japanese Women's Fiction* (Honolulu: University of Hawai'i Press, 2010).

20 On *ūman ribu* and the New Left, see Setsu Shigematsu, *Scream from the Shadows: The Women's Liberation Movement in Japan* (Minneapolis: University of Minnesota Press, 2012), 47.

21 On this legislation, see Joyce Gelb, *Gender Policies in Japan and the United States: Comparing Women's Movements, Rights, and Politics* (New York: Palgrave Macmillan, 2003); and Stephanie Assmann, "Gender Equality in Japan: The Equal Employment Opportunity Law Revisited," *Asia–Pacific Journal* 12, issue 45, no. 2 (November 10, 2014), http://japanfocus.org/-Stephanie-Assmann/4211/article.html.

22 Helen Macnaughtan, "Womenomics for Japan: Is the Abe Policy for Gendered Employment Viable in an Era of Precarity?" *Asia–Pacific Journal* 13, issue 12, no. 1 (March 30, 2015), http://japanfocus.org/-Helen-Macnaughtan/4302/article.html.

PART I

Rethinking Activism
and Activists

THE CHAPTERS IN THIS SECTION work to shed new light on activism by women in Japan at different points in the twentieth and early twenty-first centuries. While not all activism by women has been classified as feminist, the issue of women's activism opens up a number of key questions related to feminism. Foremost among these: which activists and which movements should we consider "feminist"? Moreover, how do these activists and movements position themselves vis-à-vis culture, society, and the state? To what extent have specific activists and movements promoted the interests of all women in Japan? To what extent have they prioritized the needs of particular groups of women at the expense of others? Ultimately, how should we assess the goals and successes of their activism and their ideologies? The first three chapters help us rethink feminisms in Japan by variously addressing these questions in relation to women's activism and activists, while the fourth enriches our understanding of Japanese feminisms by focusing not on feminist activism but at the pushback against it.

First, Elyssa Faison's chapter reexamines socialist feminist Yamakawa Kikue (1890–1980), who in prewar decades criticized the socialist movement for failing to address the low status of women workers, and criticized women's rights activists for pursuing issues, including the right to vote, that she felt would be of little benefit to ordinary women. Her staunch postwar support for equal rights has been read by some as inconsistent with her prewar views, but Faison challenges this assessment. In comparing Yamakawa's positions on women's political status before and after the war, Faison provides a richer understanding of Yamakawa as a feminist thinker and activist. In the next chapter, Hillary Maxson focuses on the Mothers' Congress of 1955, in which mothers from around Japan gathered as part of an effort to redefine motherhood, which had for the first half of the century been closely aligned with the goals of the state. In particular, the Mothers' Congress rejected the ideal of the "stoic, tearless . . . martial mother" who sacrificed her children for the Japanese nation, a move that, Maxson argues, ideologically realigned these women with mid-century feminists. Then James Welker looks at lesbian feminism, which emerged at once within and, in part, in opposition to *ūman ribu* (women's liberation) in the 1970s. The *ribu* movement has long been remembered as an unwelcoming environment for lesbians. Some women who openly expressed their same-sex desire felt invisible or shunned within the *ribu* movement, for instance. And yet, as Welker shows, attention within *ribu* to women's sexuality, as well as the very existence of the *ribu* movement facilitated the emergence of lesbian feminism in Japan. Finally, rather than focusing on feminist activism, Tomomi Yamaguchi examines the recent conservative backlash against both state policies perceived as feminist and local gender-equality legislation. She also turns a critical eye toward how feminists have understood and reacted to conservative motivations and strategies. In so doing, Yamaguchi offers a fuller picture of anti-feminist conservatives in Japan, as well as of the local politicians, ordinary citizens, and feminist activists working to counter this backlash.

—JW

CHAPTER 1

~

Women's Rights as Proletarian Rights

Yamakawa Kikue, Suffrage, and the "Dawn of Liberation"

ELYSSA FAISON

I N THE FIRST POSTWAR ISSUE of the newly resuscitated journal *Fujin kōron* (Women's forum), the essayist and socialist feminist Yamakawa Kikue offered her assessment of newly granted women's suffrage rights for postwar Japan. In "Standing at the Dawn of Liberation: An Historic General Election and Women's Suffrage," Yamakawa anticipated with great hopefulness the upcoming general election of 1946, which was to be the first in which women would be allowed to vote and stand for office.[1] In this essay Yamakawa, who would soon be named the first director of the Women's and Minors' Bureau of the newly created Labor Ministry, celebrated women's suffrage and the general election, saying that "equal political rights will translate into social and economic equality for women. Inequality in education, work, and the family system will be abolished."[2]

On the face of it, such an optimistic statement might seem to contradict the prewar position of the socialist and communist left in which Yamakawa had been active since the 1910s. That is, the prewar left (and Yamakawa working within it) had argued that only through the abolition of the capitalist system could full human rights for all peoples be achieved, while her 1946 statement expressed hope that political rights for men and women would translate into social and economic equality. How, then, could Yamakawa now celebrate not the abolition of capitalism, but the extension of political rights even if, as she noted in her essay, most women would probably end up voting for conservative parties that did not advocate for women's interests?

Understanding this apparent tension in Yamakawa's prewar and postwar positions with regard to the possibilities of true liberation for women through the granting of women's suffrage becomes possible by considering her holistic and historicist theory of the state and of human rights—a theory in which she refused to trade off considerations of class for those of gender, or vice versa. Her contemporaries in the women's suffrage movement typically eschewed class analysis, and were dedicated to a program of expanding rights within the existing framework set by the Meiji Constitution and its associated laws. While proponents of women's suffrage like Hiratsuka Raichō, Oku Mumeo, and Ichikawa Fusae lobbied for revision of the Civil Code, which subordinated married women to male heads of household, and against laws that prevented women from attending political meetings, they did not identify deeper structural problems in the character of the state. By examining Yamakawa's work alongside that of women's suffrage leaders like Ichikawa and the policies and proposals of the Women's Suffrage League (Fusen Kakutoku Dōmei) that Ichikawa co-founded and helped lead, it becomes clear that Yamakawa's pre- and postwar assessments of the importance of women's suffrage are largely consistent with her overall view of the prewar state as fundamentally authoritarian and anti-democratic in both its legal and economic nature. For Yamakawa, the collapse of the authoritarian state— even though it took place as a result of defeat in war rather than through class struggle—allowed for the possibility that human rights could be attained. Additionally, I argue that Yamakawa—usually described as a theorist rather than an activist—needs to be placed back into discussions of women's and workers' rights activism. While she was a prolific writer and a gifted theoretician, she was also an activist in both women's and socialist organizations from the time she finished her higher education through her service to the state bureaucracy.

The Reluctant Suffragist

Leaders of Japan's women's suffrage movement worked successfully to overturn a legal ban on women's right to political assembly in the 1920s, and continued through the end of the war to push for changes to Japan's Civil Code, which dictated the legal rights and responsibilities of women and men within a highly patriarchal family structure. Such efforts represented the interests of an almost exclusively middle-class suffragist movement with the specific goal of a particular type of political enfranchisement—namely, the addition of women to the category of Japanese imperial subjects who would hold the rights to vote and stand for office in a political system defined by the Meiji Constitution. Yamakawa challenged the very foundations of that political system, while maintaining throughout her life a pragmatism that kept her from charges of ideological extremism, and which always took the actual material conditions of Japanese women into consideration.[3]

The basic outlines of Yamakawa Kikue's contributions to the development of feminism in prewar Japan have been amply noted in historical literature.[4] As a founding member of the Red Wave Society (Sekirankai), Japan's first socialist women's organization, and as one of the most visible socialist women in prewar Japan, Yamakawa is among the most heavily cited socialist women of the early twentieth century, in part because she was also one of the most prolific. She is perhaps better known for her engagement with liberal women's rights activists, who she debated in a range of women's magazines throughout the 1910s and 1920s, since those debates took place in the newly emergent popular press. But her participation in male-dominated socialist organizations and her interventionist writings on behalf of women within those organizations directed toward her male socialist peers were equally substantial. She argued continually and passionately with her male colleagues, trying to force them to recognize that the concerns of proletarian women could not be separated from those of proletarian men. And while she did not always succeed in convincing them to adopt her proposals, she shifted socialist discourse in significant ways that forced a consideration of women and their relation to class. Additionally, Yamakawa's popular nonfiction writings, including an important study commissioned by the famous ethnologist Yanagita Kunio on the nature of Tokugawa-era samurai families and women's position within them, found a substantial audience throughout the prewar and wartime years.[5]

Yamakawa's postwar life and activities have been largely ignored, despite the important role she played as the first director of the Labor

Ministry's Women's and Minors' Bureau, and her ongoing engagement with women's and workers' rights activism. She was especially active in the years immediately following the end of the war. In March 1946, she joined with other women's rights activists from across the political spectrum to form the Women's Democratic Club (Fujin Minshu Kurabu) "to promote the participation of women in politics" in this crucial time before women would be allowed to cast their first votes in Japan the following month.[6] A year later she founded the Democratic Women's Association (Minshu Fujin Kyōkai), an organization affiliated with the short-lived Democratic People's Federation (Minshu Jinmin Renmei) formed and led by her husband, the prominent leftist intellectual Yamakawa Hitoshi. She held the position of founding director of the Women's and Minors' Bureau from 1947 to 1951, beginning under socialist prime minister Katayama Tetsu. That she stayed in this position after Katayama stepped down in 1948 and served under two prime ministers from the conservative Liberal Democratic Party suggests how effective she was. The historian Takemae Eiji claims that due to her strong leadership of the Bureau, "women subsequently were appointed to head other Ministry bureaux as well."[7] She also continued publishing, with *Japanese Democratization and Women* (*Nihon no minshuka to josei*) and *For the Women of Tomorrow* (*Ashita no josei no tame ni*) appearing in 1947, a new journal called *Women's Voice* (*Fujin no koe*, affiliated with the Women's Division of the Socialist Party) founded in 1951, and an autobiography titled *A Record of Two Generations of Women* (*Onna nidai no ki*) published in 1956.[8]

Yamakawa was born only one generation after the abolition of the samurai class, as the daughter of a scholarly and progressive-minded samurai family. She attended Tsuda Women's College starting in 1908 and early in her life expressed an interest in working for the betterment of women.[9] In 1916 she married the communist activist and theoretician Yamakawa Hitoshi, founder in 1922 of the short-lived prewar Japan Communist Party, and a leader of the Labor-Farmer faction within the Japanese communist movement. She is best known for her position in debates on prostitution and motherhood, in which she consistently challenged liberal feminists (who she termed "bourgeois feminists") on the possibility of women achieving full rights within a capitalist system.[10] While Yamakawa never actively advocated for suffrage rights, understanding her position with regard to the issue of formal political rights for women is crucial to understanding the continuity of her pre- and postwar writings.

An examination of two key moments in the movement for expanded suffrage rights in Japan allows us to better understand Yamakawa's historicist critique of liberal efforts to expand civic rights within the framework of what Andrew Gordon has referred to as Japan's prewar system of "imperial democracy."[11] These were the passage of a Universal Manhood Suffrage Law in 1925 and the acquisition of women's suffrage that came with the promulgation of the postwar Constitution in 1946. Although Yamakawa generally supported expanded civic rights for women including suffrage, she never believed that suffrage rights in and of themselves would create class or gender equality. For this reason, and to better comprehend the scope of her arguments about women's rights as proletarian rights and proletarian rights as women's rights, we must often rely on her broader arguments on topics that do not always address the issue of suffrage directly.

Suffrage and Proletarian Rights

The Universal Manhood Suffrage Law, passed in 1925, abolished tax requirements and allowed males over twenty-five years old to vote and run for office in local and national elections. The first elections held after this significant expansion of voting rights took place in 1928, and included colonial peoples, especially the large proportion from Korea, as new voters and as candidates in local elections. By 1932 a Korean named Pak Chungum, with close connections to the Japanese police regime, became the first Korean elected to the Japanese House of Commons, marking the emergence of Koreans resident in Japan as a visible constituency in national politics. As the historian Matsuda Toshihiko has argued, Koreans had been legally able to vote in local elections since at least the passage of the Common Law of 1918. Yet, politicians who debated the Universal Manhood Suffrage Law seemed unaware of the existing legal status of Koreans with regard to suffrage, and similarly unaware of any impact the bill for expanded suffrage would have on the resident Korean population.[12] The law regarding eligibility to vote in local elections before the passage of the 1925 Universal Manhood Suffrage Law, in addition to fairly substantial tax requirements, stated only that eligibility was restricted to male imperial subjects living in Japan (*danshi taru shinmin*) and said nothing about ethnicity or nationality. Thus, when the tax requirements were lifted after 1925, the number of eligible Korean voters increased significantly.[13]

For reasons that demand further attention by scholars, there do not seem to have been debates in Japan centering around what U.S. historian Allison Sneider has called "suffrage imperialism." Sneider argues that in the late nineteenth century, American suffragists increasingly pointed to the real or potential extension of voting rights to non-white men and other minorities (such as men from new American territories such as Hawai'i and Santo Domingo, and Mormons in Utah) as a threat to the continued hegemony of white political power. She further notes that they used white fears about the enfranchisement of men of color as part of urgent appeals to grant suffrage to white American women, which would thus bolster white political supremacy.[14] Despite a similarly expanding imperium in early twentieth-century Japan made up of the newly incorporated prefectures of Hokkaido and Okinawa, formal colonies including Taiwan and Korea, and a number of protectorates, I have not found evidence in their writings to suggest that Japanese women's suffrage advocates concerned themselves with arguments about the (non-)desirability of allowing non-ethnically Japanese men to vote before Japanese women could do so. Perhaps this was due to the fairly small numbers of non-Japanese men who were actually eligible to vote, or the even smaller number of those who successfully stood for office in local or national elections.

Yamakawa articulated her position on the 1925 Universal Manhood Suffrage Law and the issue of civic rights for Japan's colonized peoples within the context of political organizing efforts taking place within the proletarian and communist left. "Special Demands of Women," published in the *Hōchi shinbun* newspaper in October 1925, formed one of Yamakawa's most important and visible interventions in male-dominated socialist political organizing, and it came as part of a larger socialist response to the 1925 expanded male suffrage law. Leftist organizations united to plan for the creation of a mass proletarian party in anticipation of the first election to take place after the law's promulgation, scheduled for February 1928.[15] Unions and proletarian organizations, including the leadership of the recently disbanded Japan Communist Party and its successor group the Japan Labor Union Council (Nihon Rōdō Kumiai Hyōgikai, known simply as Hyōgikai) met to discuss draft proposals for such a mass party at the Proletarian Party Preparatory Council held in September 1925.[16]

Responding to these platforms in a document that elicited debate among proletarian movement leaders, Yamakawa first expressed great satisfaction that the various party platforms under consideration seemed to be largely in agreement on significant practical and ideological points, and delighted at the prospect that a mass proletarian political party might soon be formed. But in her "Special Demands of Women," she identified only three items out of the party platform proposals submitted that directly related to women. These included demands that all men and women over the age of eighteen be granted voting rights; that overtime, night work, and dangerous work for women and children be prohibited; and that women be granted paid maternity leave before and after childbirth.[17]

The suffrage plank in these platforms proposed a substantial reduction of the age of eligibility for voting rights from the current twenty-five years down to eighteen; and, equally as significant, they proposed that women as well as men have voting rights, a proposal that may possibly have reflected Yamakawa's influence within the movement to that point. Yamakawa agreed strongly with this promotion of civil political rights for men and women, which after all formed the basis of the desire among leftist organizations to create a mass political party in the first place; that is, in expanding the franchise to men and women, and to younger men and women than could currently vote, the movement hoped to mobilize mass support for proletarian rights and sustain a mass movement that had not as yet materialized within Japan.

Suffrage and Women's Rights

The expansion of suffrage after 1925 had in fact been the impetus for the original party platforms to which Yamakawa found herself responding. But instead of engaging at length with the issue of suffrage, Yamakawa used the dearth of additional provisions that spoke to women's concerns as an opportunity to not only offer additional demands for women, but also to use those demands as a vehicle for theorizing women within Japanese Marxism. Quoting the draft platform of the Political Studies Association, she said:

If we are to go beyond the statement "Completely removing feudal remnants and completing the bourgeoisification of society are necessary in order to follow the path of socialism," we must also recognize that demands for democracy that are closely bound up with the daily lives of women are also "necessary in order to follow the path of socialism."[18]

The additional demands proposed by Yamakawa and the Women's Division of the Political Studies Association (an organization headed by prominent communists like Sano Manabu and affiliated with the Labor Union Council) that she believed were necessary for any new mass proletarian party "in order to follow the path of socialism," included the following:

1. The abolition of the head-of-household system.
2. The abolition of all laws relating to the [political] incapacity of women regardless of marital status; equal rights of men and women in marriage and divorce.
3. Equal opportunities of education and employment for women and peoples of the colonies with that of Japanese (*naichi*) men.
4. The implementation of a standard living wage without regard to ethnicity or sex.
5. The implementation of equal wages or salary without regard to occupation for people of the colonies and for men and women.
6. The provision of break rooms for women with nursing infants, and the allowance of at least thirty minutes every three hours for nursing.
7. The prohibition of the practice of firing women for reasons of marriage, pregnancy, and childbirth.
8. The complete abolition of licensed prostitution.[19]

In the first two points Yamakawa shared much with her women's suffrage colleagues. Both Yamakawa and the leadership of the Women's Suffrage League argued throughout the prewar period that Japan's legally codified family system, which designated a usually male head-of-household and excluded other family members (including wives) from owning property, denied women legal decision-making capacity. These provisions of the Civil Code and its related laws became even more a target for

Ichikawa Fusae and other suffrage leaders in 1931, when a limited suffrage bill that would have allowed women to vote and, with the permission of their husbands, stand for election in local offices passed the lower house of the Diet. This gave hope to suffrage proponents that a full suffrage law might be enacted in the following Diet session.

In points three, four, and five, Yamakawa differed substantially from her Suffrage League colleagues, for whom issues of equality and inclusion for Japan's colonized peoples had no bearing in consideration of suffrage or other rights for Japanese women.[20] Her final three demands represent the heart of her concern for women's rights as workers' rights. By pointing to the most basic issues affecting working-class women—their access to continued employment even during and immediately after pregnancy, and their susceptibility to the unfree conditions placed upon women in the licensed prostitution system—she emphasized the importance of waged and other paid work for proletarian women.

In the same year Yamakawa presented her arguments for the special demands of women, she also authored a manifesto arguing for the creation of a women's bureau within the Labor Union Council (Hyōgikai). Arguing in her "Thesis on a Women's Bureau" (1925) that female factory workers "are the key to Japan's labor movement," she suggested a direction for the labor movement that would alleviate their poor working conditions.[21] This focus on female factory labor as the basis for much of her theorizing on women's issues as well as her critique of Japan's specific manifestation of capitalist development distinguished Yamakawa from her liberal feminist colleagues. While by no means monolithic in their own views, women's suffrage activists focused their attention on those features of Japan's political system such as the Civil Code that prevented women from exercising political rights.

Yamakawa focused on female factory labor and its relation to the recently codified family system to argue that capitalist leaders were entangled in a feudal "master/slave" relationship. That is, industrialists took the feudal family system of the agrarian countryside and extended it to their own factory dormitories, thus controlling female factory workers by restricting their bodily movements (*jinshin kōsokuteki ni shihai suru*).[22] This relationship also controlled female factory workers internally, having transferred the custom of familial servitude to the factory and depriving them of the consciousness that their labor was being sold cheaply. As a result of this lack of human self-consciousness, their awareness was not that of a "modern working class." However, Yamakawa argued that men also suffered this lack of self-consciousness. Men extended to their social consciousness their own feudal view of the family and of women that constructed women as things they could possess, rather than as people whose life experiences had a similar class basis. Men in the socialist movement, she argued, needed to recognize that women's issues, like men's, were fundamentally class-based, and must be thought of as important issues related to the labor movement as a whole. Thus, creating class consciousness among female factory workers would destroy the feudal family relationship and the feudal relationships obtaining between the sexes. In short, her "Thesis" argued that men who did not realize or accept that women were the comrades of men fighting on the front lines of the class war were themselves "class traitors."

Women's Rights and Wartime Mobilization

Scholars working in the field of Japanese women's history have undergone several shifts in how they view the wartime actions and writings of Japanese women's rights activists. By "wartime" I mean the period beginning with the Manchurian Incident of September 1931, which prompted a significant expansion of Japanese military presence on the continent, and after which it became increasingly difficult for women, and indeed anyone, to openly criticize the state. The first postwar generation of women's historians gave little attention to women in wartime. Instead, scholarly attention went toward excavating an early history of women's activism, beginning with the Popular Rights Movement of the 1880s and ending with the failure of the women's suffrage movement after the Manchurian Incident pre-empted further attempts to press the Diet for full women's suffrage. By the time women's historians began examining the wartime period—marked as it was by the consolidation of women's organizations and the mass appeal of state-sponsored groups such as the Patriotic Women's Association (Aikoku Fujinkai) and the Women's National Defense Association (Kokubō Fujinkai)—they found that the most prominent women's rights groups and their leaders seemed to have been coopted by the state during the country's period of mass mobilization. By the 1980s, several of the most vaunted figures in twentieth-century women's history, including the most prominent leader of the women's suffrage movement, Ichikawa Fusae, became the targets of

; that they had willingly and knowingly supported the
its policies of imperialism and militarism.[23]

ts were part of a broader postwar analysis of *tenkō*, or
term *tenkō* was originally applied to Japanese com-
er the duress of imprisonment and often torture, had
rty and its ideals in favor of a pro-state nationalism for
te war. Eventually the term came to be applied more
e variety of social groupings and even to "the masses"
achers and students, workers, union members, mem-
arties, and even women's rights activists appeared to
ositional stance and embrace nationalism and state-
ing wartime.[24]

tenkō, however, has never adequately explained what
a sudden and complete reversal of ideological commitments among those, like promoters of women's suffrage, who had
throughout the 1920s been the most vocal opponents of the state. Recently
historians have offered a more complex analysis of what had previously
appeared to be a "conversion" among women's rights advocates. Narita
Ryūichi has argued compellingly that in the case of Oku Mumeo, the
prewar colleague of Ichikawa Fusae and co-founder of consumer rights–
focused women's rights organizations, it is not so much that Oku changed
her position from one of state opposition to state support, but rather that
the wartime state came to adopt a number of positions she had held all
along. Narita demonstrates that Oku's primary concern before 1930 had
been with women as mothers and family managers, and that she promoted forms of cooperativism among women and families. Therefore,
when the state began to promote such cooperativism and to valorize
motherhood and the position of the housewife as part of its wartime
mobilization policies, it should not come as a surprise that Oku quickly
became a backer of state policies that now appeared to support the very
policies toward women she had championed all along.[25] Barbara Molony
has made a slightly different argument, but one that performs the similar operation of rendering visible an internal logic and consistency of
thought and action in what has been interpreted by others as an aban-
donment of principle by women activists who supported the militarist
state. Molony suggests that a suffrage movement based on the demand
for more institutionalized recognition of national belonging and state-
based rights inevitably aligned suffragists with state interests. Or as she

has put it, "the possibility of feminist support for heinous state policies was always embedded in the liberatory rhetoric of full civil rights."[26]

Such analyses of women's complicity with the wartime state and willingness to embrace its goals have helped us better understand the nature of the women's suffrage movement and women's reform movements in the years before military mobilization. While people like Ichikawa never abandoned their hope for full women's suffrage, the creation by the state of nationalist women's organizations, cooperative associations, and increased protections for women during wartime gave many women's rights activists enough of a sense of full subjecthood within the imperial state that they were willing to defer other goals for the duration of the national crisis.

Yamakawa was one of the few prewar women's rights activists who did not support state actions or the state mobilization of women during the war. Despite increasingly harsh censorship and the threat of police persecution, she published when she could during the late 1930s and early 1940s, and what she published was frequently of an apolitical nature.[27] Her participation in a roundtable discussion published by the conservative-leaning journal *Bungei shunjū* in 1937 illustrates the way she negotiated the need to appear in print to support herself economically, and the constraints put upon what she could say publicly in a political environment increasingly hostile to criticism of the state. In "A Roundtable Discussion on the Problem of Women During Wartime," Yamakawa appeared with other prominent women and men long involved in advocating for women's rights, including Hiratsuka Raichō, Tatewaki Sadayo, Okada Junko, and Katayama Tetsu. Published only months after the China Incident of July 1937 that launched Japan's all-out war on the continent, and only months before Yamakawa's own husband, Hitoshi, was arrested for his involvement in the Popular Front Movement that sought to create a united front within Japan against fascism, the roundtable revolved around the perception of drastic (and presumably positive) changes for women as a result of national mobilization by the state. While never explicitly criticizing the war, time and again throughout the roundtable Yamakawa challenged her colleagues' assertions to point out that women had been working in these capacities long before state mobilization. Only now with the intensification of new forms of nationalist ideology, she argued, did many women possess a consciousness of the kinds of changes that had been taking place for women in Japanese society for some time.[28] While some scholars have pointed to her participation in this roundtable as evidence of wartime complicity, my own reading suggests more of what Ienaga Saburō has referred to as a form of "passive resistance," wherein a number of writers and leftists kept from being prosecuted under the provisions of the Peace Preservation Act by not criticizing the war, but nonetheless refused to actively or explicitly support it.[29]

The Dawn of Liberation

After the war, one of the first essays Yamakawa published was the 1946 piece cited at the beginning of this chapter, titled "Standing at the Dawn of Liberation: An Historic General Election and Women's Suffrage."[30] A brief introduction of its contents here will help demonstrate the consistency of Yamakawa's thought from her early works such as "About the Special Demands of Women" and "Thesis on a Women's Bureau" from 1925, through the period of the Occupation. Even in 1946, Yamakawa continued to debate her fellow women's rights activists like Ichikawa Fusae, who she mentions by name.

In "Standing at the Dawn of Liberation," Yamakawa reiterates her long-standing criticisms of Japan's prewar and wartime state that was to her characterized most significantly by authoritarianism and militarism. And in keeping also with her assessment that women's issues are always also men's issues, she stressed that,

> This is a general election that has historic significance not only for women, but for men too. This is because men too are now able to express their political will for the first time without heavy-handed interference from the government. What does it mean to have voting rights in a country with no freedom of speech, where there does not exist the power of the will of the people to be expressed through government, and where a deliberative assembly is no more than window dressing (*keishiki*)?[31]

Her critique of the wartime state would have resonated with readers experiencing the first years of foreign occupation after a devastating defeat, and suffering through food shortages, starvation, and massive loss of housing that resulted from Allied fire and atomic bombings.

Referring obliquely to the foreign-imposed postwar Constitution that granted women full political equality with men, including suffrage, Yamakawa points out, "Women's suffrage did not come about by coincidence, but was mixed with the blood of our husbands and sons who died in foreign lands. With their blood, the military dictatorship fell from its self-imposed wounds. Japan's democracy is a result of this, and women's suffrage is one part of that democracy."[32]

Engaging yet again with Ichikawa and leaders of the suffrage movement, she insisted that the high rates of abstention among women voters about which Ichikawa had expressed concern in the lead-up to the general election were more an indication of the penetration of democratic ideals than, as Ichikawa argued, a fundamental problem of a lack of civic education among women. That is, Yamakawa saw abstention from voting itself as an act of volition and an exercise of an individual's political rights. Political education, she argued, is a very personal process. It would be in the process of participating in a democracy that a sense of political autonomy would be created among women. Further, because women now have political rights, men, she said, were beginning to see women as full human beings.[33]

Conclusion

Yamakawa is famous for having worked relentlessly to critique Japan's prewar socialist movement for its lack of attention to women's issues. Her impassioned argument for the creation of a Women's Bureau within the leadership organization of the proletarian political organizing committee, the Labor Union Council (Hyōgikai), reminded her male colleagues that women's rights were also proletarian rights that male workers would do well to engage with for their own sakes. The "Special Demands of Women" of the late 1920s inspired an impassioned debate and put women's issues once again before the eyes of a largely male socialist leadership that often seemed ready to abandon working women as irrelevant to the cause of socialist revolution. No other single woman in prewar Japan was able to put women's issues on a national socialist agenda as Yamakawa did.

In addition to her continual presence in person and in print as an oppositional figure operating simultaneously at the margins and the center of Japanese socialist political and organizational activities, during the same decades she offered similarly relentless critiques of what she considered "bourgeois" women's groups and their pursuit of liberal political rights like suffrage that would benefit primarily elite women. Her 1946 essay extolling the "dawn of liberation" that she believed would follow women's newly acquired suffrage rights notwithstanding, she was highly ambivalent during the prewar period regarding the importance of advocating for women's suffrage. But with the end of the war, and thus the end of the authoritarian and militarist state against which she had fought her entire adult life, Yamakawa could embrace the cause and the reality of suffrage without hesitation. This also marked the start of her willingness to try to effect change from within the political system as a bureaucrat, even as she continued to agitate for women's and workers' rights. What other Japanese women would do with their new political rights was up to them. For Yamakawa, this was truly the "dawn of liberation."

Notes

1 For more on the 1946 election, which doubled the eligible electorate from what it had been before the end of the war thanks to the new enfranchisement of women and the lowering of the voting age, see Takemae Eiji, *The Allied Occupation of Japan*, trans. Robert Ricketts and Sebastian Swan (New York: Continuum, 2003), 263–266.

2 Yamakawa Kikue, "Kaihō no reimei ni tachite: Rekishiteki sōsenkyo to fujin sanseiken," in Suzuki Yūko, ed. *Yamakawa Kikue hyōronshū* (Tokyo: Iwanami Bunko, 1990), 220. This essay originally appeared in *Fujin kōron* in April 1946.

3 Jennifer Shapcott has noted that in her contributions to the 1918 "motherhood protection" debates that took place in the pages of the journal *Seitō*: "[Yamakawa] pointed out that both the women's suffrage movement and the motherhood protection debate had originated in Western society and criticized the artificial transplantation of western feminism to the different social conditions of Japan." See Jennifer Shapcott, "The Red Chrysanthemum: Yamakawa Kikue and the Socialist Women's Movement in Prewar Japan," *Papers on Far Eastern History* 35 (1987): 8.

4 In English, see for example, Shapcott, "The Red Chrysanthemum"; E. Patricia Tsurumi, "The Accidental Historian, Yamakawa Kikue," in *Gender & History* 8, no. 2 (August 1996); Vera Mackie, *Creating Socialist*

Women in Japan: Gender, Labour and Activism, 1900–1937 (Cambridge: Cambridge University Press, 1997); Indra Levy, "Against Essentialist Identity Politics: The Status of Difference in the Critical Writings of Yamakawa Kikue," in *Across Time and Genre: Reading and Writing Women's Texts: Conference Proceedings*, ed. Janice Brown (Alberta: University of Alberta, 2002). In Japanese, see Sugaya Naoko, *Fukutsu no josei: Yamakawa Kikue no kōhansei* (Tokyo: Kaien Shobō, 1988); Hayashi Yōko, "Seikatsu to rekishi o musubu mono: Yamakawa Kikue ron," *Dōshisha hōgaku* 50, no. 4 (February 1999); and Yamakawa Kikue Kinenkai, *Ima josei ga hataraku koto to feminizumu: Yamakawa Kikue no gendaiteki igi* (Tokyo: Rōdōsha Undō Shiryōshitsu, 2011).

5 Yamakawa Kikue, *Buke no josei* (1943; Tokyo: Iwanami Shoten, 1983), published in English as Yamakawa Kikue, *Women of the Mito Domain: Recollections of Samurai Family Life*, trans. Kate Wildman Nakai (Stanford, CA: Stanford University Press, 2002). This ethnological study of samurai life is based largely on interviews with people Yamakawa knew from her own childhood and from the reminiscences of family members.

6 Takemae, *The Allied Occupation of Japan*, 265.

7 Ibid., 329.

8 Yamakawa Kikue, *Ashita no josei no tame ni* (Tokyo: Masu Shobō, 1947); Yamakawa Kikue, *Nihon no minshuka to josei* (Tokyo: Sankō Shorin, 1947); Yamakawa Kikue, *Onna nidai no ki* (1956; Tokyo: Heibonsha, 2001).

9 E. Patricia Tsurumi, "The Accidental Historian," 260.

10 On these debates, see Barbara Molony, "Equality Versus Difference: The Japanese Debate Over Motherhood Protection, 1915–1950," in *Japanese Women Working*, ed. Janet Hunter (New York: Routledge, 1995); E. Patricia Tsurumi, "Visions of Women and the New Society in Conflict: Yamakawa Kikue Versus Takamure Itsue," in *Japan's Competing Modernities: Issues in Culture and Democracy, 1900–1930*, ed. Sharon A. Minichiello (Honolulu: University of Hawai'i Press, 1998), 336–340; and Sarah Frederick, *Turning Pages: Reading and Writing Women's Magazines in Interwar Japan* (Honolulu: University of Hawai'i Press, 2006), 47–55.

11 Andrew Gordon, *Labor and Imperial Democracy in Prewar Japan* (Berkeley: University of California Press, 1992).

12 This law was meant to consolidate the different legal spheres that had developed in colonial Korea and Taiwan since the Meiji Constitution was put in place and permit them to work more smoothly. See Matsuda Toshihiko, *Senzenki no Zainichi Chōsenjin to sanseiken* (Tokyo: Akashi Shoten, 1995), 15.

13 Even so, residency requirements of at least one year at the same address continued to limit the number of proletarian men, both Korean and

Japanese, who were eligible to vote. Matsuda Toshihiko estimates that
only about 10 percent of the resident Korean population was actually
eligible to vote after 1925. See Matsuda, *Senzenki no Zainichi Chōsenjin
to sanseiken*, 36. For this same reason, the true "universality" of male
suffrage rights even among Japanese men has tended to be overstated
among historians.

14 Allison L. Sneider, *Suffragists in an Imperial Age: U.S. Expansion and the
Woman Question, 1870–1929* (New York: Oxford University Press, 2008).

15 George M. Beckmann and Okubo Genji, *Japan Communist Party, 1922–
1945* (Stanford, CA: Stanford University Press, 1969), 149.

16 Beckmann and Okubo describe the three proletarian parties that were
created from this process and their respective characteristics: the Japan
Labor-Farmer Party (Nihon Rōnōtō), a centrist organization that claimed
independence from the Comintern; the Social Democratic Party (Shakai
Minshutō), an anti-communist organization on the right; and the Labor-
Farmer Party (Rōnōtō) on the left. See Beckmann and Okubo, *Japan
Communist Party*, 98–99.

17 Yamakawa Kikue, "'Fujin no tokushu yōkyū' ni tsuite," in *Yamakawa
Kikue hyōronshū*, ed. Suzuki Yūko (Tokyo: Iwanami Bunko, 1990),
127. Ellen Carol DuBois notes that by the 1907 meeting of the Second
International, women's suffrage had been accepted as "a non-contingent,
fundamental demand that socialist parties must pursue 'strenuously.'"
Protective labor legislation also became a classic socialist demand
during the time of the Second International, but often it served to "keep
women in a separate and unequal sector of the labor force." See Ellen
Carol DuBois, "Woman Suffrage and the Left: An International Socialist
Perspective," *New Left Review*, no. 186 (March–April 1991): 31–32.

18 Yamakawa, "'Fujin no tokushu yōkyū' ni tsuite," 126. The draft statement
cited by Yamakawa refers to the Marxist theory of history, in which a full
socialist revolution can only happen after the completion of a bourgeois
revolution that does away with the feudal system.

19 Ibid., 128.

20 As Vera Mackie has noted, however, "while Japanese people have a
gender and a class, colonised people are featureless, without gender or
class in [Yamakawa's] writings." See Vera Mackie, *Feminism in Modern
Japan: Citizenship, Embodiment and Sexuality* (Cambridge: Cambridge
University Press, 2003), 88. The scholar Song Youn-ok has also pointed
out that while Yamakawa supported colonized peoples and in particular
Korean women in their efforts to gain rights, she was never able to
adequately grasp the ways and degree to which Japanese feminists
benefited from Japan's colonial policies. See Song Youn-ok, "Shokuminchi

Chōsen ni okeru josei kaihō no kokoromi," in Yamakawa Kikue Kinenkai, ed., *Yamakawa Kikue no gendaiteki igi: Ima josei ga hataraku koto to feminizumu* (Tokyo: Rōdōsha Undō Shiryōshitsu, 2011), 47–52.

21 Yamakawa Kikue, "Fujinbu tēze," in *Yamakawa Kikue hyōronshū*, ed. Suzuki Yūko (Tokyo: Iwanami Bunko, 1990). For an excellent analysis of Yamakawa's "Fujinbu tēze," which has influenced my own reading of that essay, see Itō Akira, *Nihon Rōdō Kumiai Hyōgikai no kenkyū: 1920-nendai rōdō kumiai no kōbō* (Tokyo: Shakai Hyōronsha, 2001), 290–293.

22 This is not unlike arguments made by historian Tōjō Yukihiko, although he uses the terms "modern" and "contemporary" (*kindaiteki* and *gendaiteki*) to describe characteristics of the labor market that Yamakawa defines as "feudal" and "modern." Tōjō juxtaposes what he calls the restrictive "modern" wage labor market system in which female textile labor operates without free individual agency and is instead restricted by families and by companies (what Yamakawa refers to as the feudal elements), with a "contemporary" (*gendaiteki*) labor market that operates on the basis of individual worker agency. See Tōjō Yukihiko, *Seishi dōmei no jokō tōroku seido: Nihon kindai no hen'yō to jokō no "jinkaku"* (Tokyo: Tōkyō Daigaku Shuppansha, 1990).

23 See Tsurumi, "The Accidental Historian"; and Barbara Molony, "From 'Mothers of Humanity' to 'Assisting the Emperor': Gendered Belonging in the Wartime Rhetoric of Japanese Feminist Ichikawa Fusae," in *Pacific Historical Review* 80, no. 1 (February 2011): 6–10, for discussions of these historiographical trends.

24 For some of the foundational treatments of the concept of "conversion," see Fujita Shōzō, *Tenkō no shisōshiteki kenkyū* (Tokyo: Iwanami Shoten, 1975); and Tsurumi Shunsuke, *Tenkō kenkyū* (Tokyo: Chikuma Shobō, 1976). See also Patricia G. Steinhoff, "Tenkō and Thought Control," in *Japan and the World: Essays on Japanese History and Politics in Honour of Ishida Takeshi*, ed. Gail Lee Bernstein and Haruhiro Fukui (London: MacMillan Press, 1988); Germaine A. Hoston, *Marxism and the Crisis of Development in Prewar Japan* (Princeton, NJ: Princeton University Press, 1990); and chapter five in Gordon, *Labor and Imperial Democracy in Prewar Japan*.

25 Narita Ryūichi, "Women in the Motherland: Oku Mumeo Through Wartime and Postwar," in *Total War and "Modernization,"* ed. Yasushi Yamanouchi, J. Victor Koschmann, and Ryūichi Narita (Ithaca, NY: Cornell University East Asia Program, 1998), 147.

26 Barbara Molony, "Women's Rights and the Japanese State, 1880–1925," in *Public Spheres, Private Lives in Modern Japan, 1600–1950: Essays in Honor of Albert M. Craig*, ed. Gail Lee Bernstein, Andrew Gordon, and Kate

Wildman Nakai (Cambridge, MA: Harvard University Asia Center, 2005), 258.

27 A good example of this is Yamakawa, *Onna nidai no ki.*

28 Maruoka Hideko, ed., *Nihon fujin mondai shiryō shūsei,* vol. 8: *Shichō 1* (Tokyo: Domesu Shuppan, 1976), 646, 653. Yamakawa Hitoshi was arrested in December 1937 and held in jail until his trial in 1941, at which time he was sentenced to five years in prison for violation of the Peace Preservation Law. See Richard H. Mitchell, *Janus-Faced Justice: Political Criminals in Imperial Japan* (Honolulu: University of Hawai'i Press, 1992), 147.

29 Saburō Ienaga, *The Pacific War* (New York: Pantheon Books, 1979). Ueno Chizuko has pointed to this roundtable as evidence of Yamakawa's wartime complicity in her *Nationalism and Gender* (Melbourne: Trans Pacific Press, 2002), 39–40.

30 Yamakawa, "Kaihō no reimei ni tachite."

31 Ibid., 212.

32 Ibid., 221.

33 Ibid., 223–224. Sugaya Naoko suggests that Ichikawa's insistence on the importance of vigorously mobilizing women's votes and preventing voter abstention and Yamakawa's equally strong appeal to the importance of fostering women's free will and critical powers regardless of whether this resulted in women's votes, animated political debates between these two important women's rights activists throughout the postwar period. See Sugaya Naoko, *Fukutsu no josei: Yamakawa Kikue no kōhansei* (Tokyo: Kaien Shobō, 1988), 13–14.

~

CHAPTER 2

From "Motherhood in the Interest of the State" to Motherhood in the Interest of Mothers

Rethinking the First Mothers' Congress

HILLARY MAXSON

SHORTLY AFTER 3:45 on the morning of March 1, 1954, radioactive ash rained down on the Lucky Dragon tuna boat crew. The boat had the misfortune of drifting near Bikini Atoll, the United States' hydrogen bomb test site. All of the Lucky Dragon's crewmembers experienced symptoms of radiation poisoning, but the shocking death of Kuboyama Aikichi, the Lucky Dragon's radio operator, inspired waves of protest throughout Japan.[1] In a seemingly unrelated development, one month after Kuboyama's death—in an effort to place the concerns of Japanese women on an international platform—prominent feminist Hiratsuka Raichō began organizing an international women's rally comprised of mothers from around the world. Irrespective of "ideology, creed, race" and class, Raichō proposed to convene what she called a Mothers' Congress (Hahaoya Taikai) to "protect the lives of children from the dangers of nuclear war."[2] This new women's movement aimed to promote the interests of women and children in a violent, nuclear age. A little more than a year after the Lucky Dragon Incident, in June and July of 1955, large numbers of women gathered in Tokyo for Japan's first Mothers' Congress and, at the insistence of Raichō and Japanese women activists, in Lausanne, Switzerland, for the first World Congress of Mothers. The Lucky Dragon Incident galvanized many Japanese women into political action, and in a matter of months Raichō and her colleagues managed to harness public outrage surrounding the incident into national and international women's movements.

Japanese historians who have discussed the Mothers' Congress have typically treated the state's wartime policies toward women as aberrational.[3] But this has obscured the Congress' significance by disconnecting it from the wartime era, resulting in a narrative that characterizes the Mothers' Congress as a movement that reinforced the state's prewar maternal policies rather than as one that challenged wartime policies. By positioning the Mothers' Congress in conversation with the wartime regime, this chapter serves two interconnected purposes: first, to function as a reminder that the state hijacked motherhood during the war; and second, to highlight the fact that the Mothers' Congress was a vehicle by which postwar Japanese women reclaimed historical agency by seeking to liberate mothers from the wartime state's hegemonic construction of motherhood. Additionally, this chapter examines the broader feminist significance of the Mothers' Congress, arguing that Japan's June of 1955 Mothers' Congress and the subsequent July of 1955 World Congress of Mothers—or what I will call the "summer of mothers"—can be interpreted as a truly historic summer that laid the foundation for a postwar "matricentric feminism."[4]

Wartime Motherhood

Nakajima Kuni insightfully characterized Japan's treatment of women during the war as "motherhood in the interest of the state."[5] State slogans like "Be Fruitful and Multiply for the Prosperity of the Nation" urged mothers to have numerous children and to do so at increasingly younger ages.[6] Although abortion had been banned since 1880, additional pronatalist policies were newly established during wartime.[7] The 1940 National Eugenics Law, for example, supported sterilizing people who had hereditary diseases and banned birth control for the healthy, placing women's reproductive bodies under the state's control.[8]

Beyond this, however, the state also sought to control women's minds and bodies in another way—namely, in its construction of an ideology of "martial motherhood" that required women to send their sons off to war without public displays of distress or anxiety. The stoic, tearless, and child-sacrificing *"gunkoku no haha,"* which I translate as the "martial mother," had been the state's ideal mother since as early as 1905. Japanese citizen-subjects were first introduced to the martial mother in national ethics textbooks, with stories like "Mother of a Sailor" (*Suihei no haha*) in which a mother wrote a letter to her son serving in the navy. In this letter, she called her son a coward for not fighting in battle and told him that she prayed at a Hachiman shrine every day in hope that he would actually fulfill an admirable purpose while away at war. Wartime films brought the martial mother to life in a new medium.[9] In a scene from *Sea War from Hawaii to Malaya* (*Hawai Marē oki kaisen*, 1942), a mother states that her son is no longer a member of her family after he leaves for military training, insinuating he was already dead to her.[10] This constructed and widely circulated gender ideal, however, did not represent the actual feelings of most mothers. During the Pacific War, many mothers felt pressured to adopt a martial mother persona in public; but privately, they feared the imminent death of the sons they sent off to war. Many mothers spoke to pebbles, as if these objects were their soldier sons, expressing the unspoken fears that the state had forbidden them to utter and that their local communities might feel compelled to condemn.[11] Motherhood was a thoroughly male-dominated institution during the war—a fact encapsulated in the phrase "motherhood in the interest of the state."

The Mothers' Congress and the World Congress of Mothers

Following the Lucky Dragon Incident in 1954, Raichō used her position as vice president of the postwar international women's organization, Women's International Democratic Federation (WIDF; Kokusai Minshu Fujin Renmei; founded 1945), and her friendship with the president of the WIDF, French scientist and women's rights activist Eugénie Cotton, to present an appeal for the creation of a World Congress of Mothers.[12] At a meeting held in Geneva on February 22, 1955, the WIDF listened to the appeal of five Japanese representatives: Hani Setsuko, Maruoka Hideko, Tsurumi Kazuko, Kōra Tomi, and Takada Nahoko. Raichō could not attend the meeting for health reasons, but informed Cotton about the Mothers' Congress of Japan in a letter.[13] The appeal raised concerns about a global nuclear arms race and warned the WIDF against forgetting the terror of World War II. "Those who plan for war do not ask for the opinions of mothers," the appeal stated. "For this reason we need to raise our voices."[14] The representatives were successful: the WIDF endorsed the first World Congress of Mothers and set the dates for its realization as July 7 to 10, 1955.[15] In sum, the influential power of Raichō and Japanese women activists was fundamental in the creation of the World Congress of Mothers.

Before the World Congress of Mothers convened, Japanese women held their own Mothers' Congress. On the muggy morning of June 7, mothers lined up outside of Toshima Hall in Tokyo in anticipation of the Congress' first day.[16] A diverse group of women, from as far away as Hokkaido in the far north of Japan and Kagoshima to the south, attended the convention. This included childless, unemployed, and impoverished women, middle-class housewives, and even survivors of the atomic bomb.[17] While the organizers arranged a temporary nursery for the attendees, some women carried their young children on their backs. The rally's organizers distributed newspapers that welcomed all of the attendees and encouraged them to share their ideas as well as their struggles.[18] On the first day, the Congress assembled in one large group. Then on June 8 the attendees broke up into eleven subcommittees to discuss three issues: "the protection of the happiness of children," "the protection of the livelihood of women," and "the protection of peace."[19] On the final day of the rally, the women met in a large group once again to conclude some of their discussions, especially ideas relevant specifically to mothers.[20] All of the attendees were allowed to speak about issues concerning women, children, and war. Rather than merely repeating the common phrase *"sensō wa iya desu"* (war is detestable), the women of the Congress engaged in discussions of how war actually harmed the lives of women and children.

Economic independence and stability for mothers was a common concern voiced at the conference. During the last year of the war, and even after the end of the war in 1945, most Japanese suffered from poverty and malnutrition. Despite the efforts of the Japanese government and the American Occupation forces in the latter half of the 1940s, the average Japanese person still struggled to meet their basic needs, such as food, clothing, and shelter.[21] While severe conditions gradually improved, during the 1950s Japan was still in a period of economic recovery.[22] The myriad economic problems that plagued the women who attended the rally reflected the ongoing obstacles that many Japanese faced during the mid-1950s. Attendees discussed issues such as childhood poverty, malnutrition, unemployment, child suicide, and the prostitution of young girls.[23] Beyond this, childless working women demanded affordable childcare so that they too could become mothers. Other speakers addressed the issues of maternity leave and the need for more part-time employment options for housewives.[24]

The women of the Mothers' Congress gave speeches, elected committees, and by the end of the rally on June 9, composed a collective manifesto. The language of the manifesto signified a strong response to the state's construction of wartime martial motherhood. Members of the Mothers' Congress rejected the wartime state's hijacking of motherhood:

> Because of the war, the pride and joy of being a mother has been shattered. Mothers were even forbidden from expressing the reasonable feeling that they felt in their hearts: that war was detestable. We were not even allowed to shed tears of farewell while we sent our children off to war; we just gritted our teeth.[25]

As expressed in this manifesto and verified in the accounts of wartime mothers, many mothers felt they could not express their true feelings. The manifesto of the Mothers' Congress rejected this emotionless, state-constructed ideal of motherhood—that is, the martial mother—and committed themselves instead to redefining the role of mothers.

The women of the Mothers' Congress defined motherhood ultimately as an act of pride and joy shared by mothers from all walks of life. Observing that some mothers struggled with poverty or unemployment, and others were widowed or single, the Congress refused to construct a unitary image of mothers based on class, race, age, marital status, or occupation. After all, some mothers worked in the home as full-time homemakers, while others grew rice for their communities even though they frequently could not even afford to feed their own children. But most importantly, the Mothers' Congress insisted mothers were no longer "scattered and weak" individuals.[26] Mothers, they suggested, were no longer relegated to the role of national icons constructed by male bureaucrats. Instead, they were now real women engaged in public discourse to define their own identity. This is not to say that women had not harnessed any maternal agency prior to the Mothers' Congress, but rather that mothers achieved greater visibility following the Mothers' Congress. Together, the women of the Mothers' Congress transformed motherhood into a public, political force deployed by women.

The Mothers' Congress was not the first occasion where women publicly discussed motherhood together. Some of the "New Women" of the Taishō era (1912–1926) also debated the ideal relationship between mothers and the state.[27] Hiratsuka Raichō, Yamakawa Kikue, Yosano Akiko, Yamada Waka, and others engaged in heated exchanges, published in magazines and newspapers from 1915 to 1919, that have commonly been referred to as the "motherhood protection debate" (*bosei hogo ronsō*).[28] During the Mothers' Congress, Maruoka Hideko, a social commentator involved with the Mothers' Congress who wrote prolifically about women's issues, argued that the motherhood protection debate had not merely resurfaced but had been repurposed. To her mind, the discussions held at the conference were not just reminiscent of the motherhood protection debate of the Taishō era, but initiated a broader debate over the place of motherhood in society.

The Mothers' Congress produced a total of thirteen resolutions, demonstrating that the participants felt impelled to demand certain actions from the state. The language found in the manifesto articulated a major shift in power between mothers and the state. Based on the language of the resolutions, it was quite clear mothers would no longer raise their children for the state. Instead, mothers expected the state to help them raise their children. Some of the resolutions included demands for medical insurance, social security benefits, nurseries for working mothers, increased educational budgets, and special-leave provisions for women. Mothers also addressed perceived threats to the family in their resolutions. For example, attendees called for the prohibition of prostitution. They also opposed unfair firing practices and the revival of the patriarchal family system. As part of a united Mothers' Congress, members felt empowered—and they defined this moment as "the turning of a new page in the history of mothers in Japan."[29]

This newly constructed idea of motherhood caught the attention of the media. During wartime, mothers achieved public recognition by behaving as ideal martial mothers. The Mothers' Congress, however, rebuked the state-constructed ideal of martial motherhood in its manifesto and reimagined an empowered, pacifist, and politically engaged motherhood. As Maruoka wrote, the voices of mothers could not be heard anywhere until the Mothers' Congress. The Mothers' Congress produced a united voice for mothers that the state neither constructed nor controlled. "Before and after the day of the Congress," Maruoka wrote, "if you opened the newspaper, you would see articles about the Mothers' Congress. If you turned on the radio, you would hear the voices of mothers. If you went to the movies, you would see news about the Mothers' Congress projected on the screen."[30] Mothers had become visible political activists and had done so on their own terms.

Maruoka stressed that the women of the Congress walked away feeling compelled to act. She believed that as political actors the women of the Congress now shared responsibility with the government to correct society's inequalities. To accomplish this, insisted Maruoka, women could start by altering the everyday language that they used to express their place in society. Instead of referring to her husband as "master" (*shujin*), a woman could call him "husband" (*otto*). Women could avoid phrases like "take a wife" (*yome wo morau*) and say "marry" (*kekkon suru*) instead. Women could stop merely listening to their husbands' ideas and start thinking for themselves first. Maruoka suggested that women remember to stop treating their daughters differently from their sons, and that they create an atmosphere in the home of social equality.[31] Not every woman who attended the Mothers' Congress embraced these ideas. But, as Maruoka argued the following year, the Mothers' Congress empowered Japanese women to envision the home as a political space where their daily acts of defiance had significance.

The spirit of the Mothers' Congress of Japan was one of idealistic inclusivity, but in practice this was an uphill battle, as the selection of delegates to the World Congress of Mothers in Lausanne, Switzerland, soon revealed. The selection committee included thirteen Japanese women who held a series of six meetings. Maruoka, one of the members of the selection committee, revealed that some of the committee members were prejudiced in their selection of delegates. Maruoka suggested Tsuchikawa Matsue as a representative but was voted down by everyone on the committee. When Maruoka inquired about the reason, the others responded that they thought Tsuchikawa's "*zūzū-ben*," a term for the Northeastern dialect, would be a problem. The committee also worried that Tsuchikawa might wear rural work clothes to the conference. Maruoka argued that Tsuchikawa's rural voice and dress would be a welcome addition to the delegation, and, after a long meeting, won a majority vote for Tsuchikawa. When Tsuchikawa met the elite women who attended the World Congress of Mothers with her, she purposely spoke in her Northeastern dialect.[32]

By July of 1955 the Mothers' Congress had selected fourteen Japanese delegates to travel to Lausanne for the World Congress of Mothers.[33] Women of different ages, races, and economic backgrounds attended the Congress in an international call for "the defence of their children against war, for disarmament, and friendship between the peoples."[34] Altogether the Credentials Commission registered 1,060 participants from 66 countries, spanning every continent.[35] Of these participants, 653 had never taken part in an international meeting. Many of the women were selected to represent their countries in elections held in local neighborhoods, factories, and schools. This international "revolt" of mothers, as Cotton described it, was a reaction to the creation of arms capable of destroying large numbers of people with little concern for whether they were "soldiers or civilians, children or old people."[36] In her opening speech entitled "The Mothers Who Gave Life Want to Defend It," Cotton, as president of the Women's International Democratic Federation, specifically mentioned the appeal of Japanese women and credited them for making the "whole world realize the horror of atomic bombs."[37]

Although the World Congress of Mothers met just that once, the Mothers' Congress of Japan continued to meet annually, and at times more than once a year. Attendance in subsequent years ranged from 4,000 to 34,000 people.[38] Immediately following the first Mothers' Congress, the Ministry of Education strengthened the women's bureau and increased its budget. The Liberal Democratic Party also followed suit and reinvigorated its policies toward women. Gradually the Congress transitioned from discussions to demonstrations as they later protested the US–Japan Security Treaty in 1960.[39]

Did the Mothers' Congress presume all women were mothers? It is impossible to speak for all the attendees, and certainly some may have conflated womanhood with motherhood, but Raichō, often referred to as the creator of the Mothers' Congress, did not.[40] In 1958, for example, Raichō encouraged the establishment of the Society of Japanese Women Scientists (Nihon Josei Kagakusha no Kai).[41] In a letter to Saruhashi Katsuko, one of Japan's first prominent women scientists, Raichō related her desire for women and mothers to work together with female and male scientists to abolish nuclear weapons.[42] Raichō, a woman of ideological breadth, was conscious that women were not just mothers, and in the 1950s Raichō helped create different organizations for women that did not revolve around motherhood—although mothers could certainly belong to these organizations as well.[43] At the hundred-year-anniversary celebration of Raichō's birth in 1986, Maruoka spoke about Raichō's views on motherhood. Maruoka made the point that Raichō believed motherhood was a right in need of protection, not a blessing—meaning that Raichō viewed motherhood as a human rights issue rather than as an essentialized and romanticized characteristic of womanhood.[44] This leaves us with a complex picture of the Mothers' Congress. The Congress often used maternalist language, but many attendees, like Raichō and Maruoka, also supported equal rights feminism.

Rethinking Modern Japanese Feminisms: Rethinking Global Feminisms

While the Mothers' Congress was certainly a popular women's movement, Japanese historians have pondered its place in the history of Japanese feminism, usually characterizing it as a maternalist women's movement.[45] By rethinking the definition of the term "feminism," I believe we can shed new light on the Mothers' Congress and better assess its feminist significance. Historian Karen Offen's take on feminism has particular resonance in this case. She explains that feminists in male-dominated societies tend to fight to instate a "balance of power between the sexes," and argues that a common denominator found in all definitions of feminism is that the movement in question must challenge masculine domination.[46] The Mothers' Congress did exactly this by challenging the Japanese wartime state's appropriation of "motherhood" as a male-dominated institution. In this sense, following Offen, the Mothers' Congress was feminist because it represented a pivotal historical moment at which women from across Japan gathered to reclaim motherhood from the state and to redefine motherhood for themselves. We can see this broadly as a shift from the wartime concept of "motherhood in the interest of the state" to a new postwar notion of motherhood in the interest of mothers. This was a significant moment in Japanese history and labeling it simply as a maternalist movement does not give it the credit it deserves.

Recent scholars have argued against critics of maternal movements and have repositioned mothers' movements back toward the central narrative of the history of feminism. Critics of maternal movements have argued that they reinforce gender essentialism and gender difference, concluding that maternalist politics are a form of activism to which women resort only when they cannot do any better.[47] Patricia Hill Collins argues, however, that this type of thinking sets up a "hierarchy of feminisms" and portrays women involved in these movements as "politically immature."[48] Other recent scholars have recognized that motherhood movements have even increased in number globally in the twenty-first century. In *The 21st Century Motherhood Movement*, Andrea O'Reilly states that motherhood activism can absolutely be feminist and applies the term "matricentric feminism" to twenty-first-century movements. O'Reilly's matricentric feminism is broadly defined as a "mother-centered standpoint" that combines elements of maternalism, equal rights feminism, and feminist care theory.[49] O'Reilly's discussion is exclusively limited to the twenty-first century; however, I believe we can also apply this useful term to earlier movements like the Mothers' Congress of Japan.

The Mothers' Congress of Japan can be interpreted as a matricentric feminist movement because—in keeping with O'Reilly's definition—it was a mother-centered movement that combined maternalist thought, equal rights feminism, and feminist care theory. The manifesto of the Mothers' Congress contained maternalist language, but simply labeling it as maternalist diminishes the diversity and complexity of thought it encompassed. As mentioned above, the movement fought for economic gender equality, arguing that working mothers needed maternity leave, affordable childcare, and health care. At the rally, attendees also discussed how they could make their homes gender-equal. Furthermore, the pacifist and anti-nuclear stance of the Mothers' Congress resonates with feminist care theory—the theory that caregiving can be a central, rather than a peripheral, political practice. The Mothers' Congress of Japan fits the definition of matricentric feminism, albeit an early form of this feminism, because it employed these three frameworks; but most importantly, it was a movement that empowered mothers.[50] It is also worth stating again that the Mothers' Congress shifted motherhood from a male-dominated discourse to one that included the voices of mothers.

By reexamining the labels that scholars have placed on women's movements—in the case of the Mothers' Congress, a "maternalist" label—and focusing instead on their broader historical contexts, we can rethink not only our interpretations of modern Japanese feminisms, but also global feminisms. In the twenty-first century social critics have often called motherhood the unfinished business of feminism, but I think instead that matricentric feminism has been largely ignored, underappreciated, and understudied.[51] As Collins has suggested, mother-hood alone may have enough symbolic significance to empower women in certain communities or parts of the world.[52] It makes sense, then, that matricentric feminism might have a longer history in some communities and parts of the world than in others. In the case of the World Congress of Mothers, Japanese women conceived and executed the idea to hold the Congress, demonstrating not only that matricentric feminism has a long history in Japan, but that Japanese women also sought to spread their feminist vision to other parts of the world during the "summer of moth-ers."[53] The World Congress of Mothers was the first instance in which Japanese women became international feminist leaders, and they did so through the language of matricentric feminism.[54] Applying Collins' and O'Reilly's views on motherhood and Offen's definition of feminism to Japan contributes to our rethinking of modern Japanese feminisms by highlighting the Mothers' Congress' significance not only in Japanese history, but in global history. Rethinking Japanese feminisms forces us to rethink global feminisms.

Conclusion

An event from the life of Raichō encapsulates the intertwined nature of war, motherhood, and feminism not only in Japan, but also globally. As a feminist opposed to the existing patriarchal family system, Raichō refused to marry her partner and the father of her two children, Okumura Hiroshi. In August of 1941, however, Raichō married Okumura to regis-ter her children as legitimate. Raichō did this because she feared her son, Atsubumi, would be drafted. If the military drafted Atsubumi while he was an illegitimate son, he would have been unable to become an officer. Raichō knew that if her son became an officer, he would have a much better chance of surviving the war.[55] In February 1942 Atsubumi was called up. Because of Raichō's decision to marry Okumura and register Atsubumi as legitimate, Atsubumi became an engineering officer, never saw the front line, and returned home safely.[56]

Interpreting this moment in Raichō's life has proven quite difficult. Did the wartime regime force Raichō to sacrifice her feminist convictions by not allowing her to simultaneously be the feminist she wanted to be and a mother concerned with the life of her child? Initially I thought this to be the case, but reflecting on the significance of the Mothers' Congress has pushed me to reinterpret this significant decision in Raichō's life as a feminist one. The most important thing the state demanded from a mother during the war was the life of her child. Raichō did all she could to subvert state demands by keeping her son alive. What was feminist for Raichō during the prewar period (her refusal to marry) changed during wartime, prompting her to marry to save her son's life, which demonstrates how feminist motherhood is unstable and can change based on historical context.[57]

Raichō's story clearly highlights the connections between the wartime state, the Mothers' Congress, and feminism. If historians do not acknowledge the experiences of mothers like Raichō under the wartime state in analyzing the postwar Mothers' Congress, the Congress' feminist significance is lost. The Mothers' Congress feared an imminent revival of the wartime regime and did all they could to prevent the state from hijacking motherhood again through motherhood in the interest of the state. Ten years prior to the Mothers' Congress, the state told mothers who they were and demanded their stoic obedience to the state. At the Mothers' Congress, mothers told the state who mothers were and began making demands of their own.

Notes

1 James Joseph Orr, *The Victim as Hero: Ideologies of Peace and National Identity in Postwar Japan* (Honolulu: University of Hawai'i Press, 2001), 47.

2 Nihon Hahaoya Taikai, "Ayumi no Nenpyō," http://hahaoyataikai.jp/04_ayumi/nenpyou/index.html, accessed January 9, 2016.

3 Scholars who have examined the Mothers' Congress include Kathleen S. Uno, "The Death of 'Good Wife, Wise Mother'?" in *Postwar Japan as History*, ed. Andrew Gordon (Berkeley: University of California Press, 1993); Vera Mackie, *Feminism in Modern Japan: Citizenship, Embodiment and Sexuality* (Cambridge: Cambridge University Press, 2003); Mari Yamamoto, *Grassroots Pacifism in Post-War Japan: The Rebirth of a Nation* (London: Routledge Curzon, 2004); and Tatewaki Sadayo, Hasegawa Ayako, and Ide Fumiko, *Sengo fujin undōshi* (Tokyo: Nihon Tosho Sentā, 2005).

4 "Matricentric feminism" is a term I borrow from Andrea O'Reilly; I engage further with this concept below. See Andrea O'Reilly, "Introduction," in *The 21st Century Motherhood Movement: Mothers*

Speak Out on Why We Need to Change the World and How to Do It, ed. Andrea O'Reilly (Toronto: Demeter Press, 2011).

5 Nakajima Kuni called discourse in this period "motherhood in the interest of the state" in Nakajima Kuni, "Kokkateki bosei: Senjika no boseikan," in *Onna no imēji*, ed. Joseigaku Kenkyūkai (Tokyo: Keisō Shobō, 1984).

6 Yoshiko Miyake, "Doubling Expectations: Motherhood and Women's Factory Work Under State Management in Japan in the 1930s and 1940s," in *Recreating Japanese Women, 1600–1945*, ed. Gail Lee Bernstein (Berkeley: University of California Press, 1991), 271.

7 Uno, "The Death of 'Good Wife, Wise Mother'?," 300.

8 Miyake, "Doubling Expectations," 278.

9 Monbushō, "Suihei no haha," in *Jinjō shōgaku tokuhon*, vol. 9 (Tokyo: Monbushō, 1922).

10 *Hawai Marē oki kaisen*, directed by Yamamoto Kajirō, Japan, 1942.

11 Ohara Tokuji, *Ishikoro ni kataru hahatachi: Nōson fujin no sensō taiken* (Tokyo: Miraisha, 1964).

12 Hiratsuka Raichō, *In the Beginning, Woman Was the Sun: The Autobiography of a Japanese Feminist*, trans. Teruko Craig (New York: Columbia University Press, 2006), 314; Hiratsuka Raichō, *Genshi, josei wa taiyō de atta: Hiratsuka Raichō jiden*, vol. 4 (Tōkyō: Ōtsuki Shoten, 1971), 182–187. For more on the Women's International Democratic Federation (WIDF), see Francisca de Haan, "Continuing Cold War Paradigms in Western Historiography of Transnational Women's Organisations: The Case of the Women's International Democratic Federation (WIDF)," *Women's History Review* 19, no. 4 (2010).

13 Hiratsuka, *Genshi, josei wa taiyō de atta*, 186.

14 Kokusai Minshu Fujin Renmei Hyōgikai Hahaoya Taikai Junbikai, "Sekai Hahaoya Taikai o hiraku tame no apīru," in *Shiryō shūsei gendai Nihon josei no shutai keisei*, vol. 3, ed. Chino Yōichi (Tokyo: Domesu Shuppan, 1996), 153.

15 Hiratsuka, *Genshi, josei wa taiyō de atta*, 187. The representatives were in Geneva from February 9 to 13, Nihon Hahaoya Taikai Renrakukai, *Nihon no okāsantachi* (Tokyo: Awaji Shobō Shinsha, 1961), 297; Tatewaki, Hasegawa, and Ide, *Sengo fujin*, 72–73.

16 Maruoka Hideko, *Inochi e no negai: Nihon no haha no koe* (Tokyo: Yomiuri Shinbunsha, 1956), 49.

17 Tatewaki, Hasegawa, and Ide, *Sengo fujin*, 74–76; Ronald Loftus, *Changing Lives: The "Postwar" in Japanese Women's Autobiographies and Memoirs* (Ann Arbor, MI: Association for Asian Studies, 2013), 118.

18 Maruoka, *Inochi e no negai*, 50.

19 Ibid., 53; Nihon Hahaoya Taikai Renrakukai, *Nihon no okāsantachi*, 260; Wakita Haruko, *Bosei o tō: Rekishiteki hensen* (Kyoto: Jinbun Shoin, 1985), 242.

20 Maruoka, *Inochi e no negai*, 53.

21 John Dower, *Embracing Defeat: Japan in the Wake of World War II* (New York: W.W. Norton & Company/The New Press, 1999), 94.

22 Laura Hein, "Growth Versus Success: Japan's Economic Policy in Historical Perspective," in *Postwar Japan as History*, ed. Andrew Gordon (Berkeley: University of California Press, 1993), 112.

23 Tatewaki, Hasegawa, and Ide, *Sengo fujin*, 75.

24 Ibid., 76.

25 Nihon Hahaoya Taikai, "Dai ikkai Nihon Hahaoya Taikai ketsugi, sengen," in *Shiryō shūsei gendai Nihon josei shutai keisei*, vol. 3, ed., Chino Yōichi, 157. A full English-language translation of the manifesto is available in Fujioka Wake, *Women's Movements in Postwar Japan* (Honolulu: East–West Center, 1968). (The translation in this chapter is my own.)

26 Fujioka, *Women's Movements*, 81.

27 See Laurel Rasplica Rodd, "Yosano Akiko and the Taishō Debate over the 'New Woman,'" in Bernstein, *Recreating Japanese Women*; Barbara Molony, "Equality Versus Difference: The Japanese Debate over 'Motherhood Protection,' 1915–50," in *Japanese Women Working*, ed. Janet Hunter (London: Routledge, 1993); Mackie, *Feminism in Modern Japan*; Hiroko Tomida, *Hiratsuka Raichō and Early Japanese Feminism* (Boston: Brill, 2003); and Dina Lowy, *The Japanese "New Woman": Images of Gender and Modernity* (New Brunswick: Rutgers University Press, 2007).

28 Molony, "Equality Versus Difference," 126.

29 Fujioka, *Women's Movements*, 81.

30 Maruoka, *Inochi e no negai*, 49. Hiratsuka Raichō wrote a similar description about the visibility of mothers in Hiratsuka, *Genshi, josei wa taiyō de atta*, 188.

31 Maruoka, *Inochi e no negai*, 54.

32 After Tsuchikawa returned to Japan she toured the Northeast as a public speaker, giving more than two hundred public lectures. Maruoka Hideko, "'Seitō' kara kokusai fujin nen e," in *Hiratsuka Raichō to Nihon no kindai*, ed. Ōoka Shōhei (Tokyo: Iwanami Shoten, 1986), 20–22.

33 Nihon Hahaoya Taikai Renrakukai, *Nihon no okāsantachi*, 300.

34 Credentials Commission of the World Congress of Mothers, "Report of the Credentials Commission," *World Congress of Mothers for the Defence of Their Children Against War, for Disarmament and Friendship Between*

the Peoples, World Congress of Mothers (N.p.: Women's International Democratic Federation, 1955), 10.

35 Ibid., 11.

36 Eugénie Cotton, "The Mothers Who Gave Life Want to Defend It," in ibid., 4.

37 Ibid.

38 Nihon Hahaoya Taikai, "Ayumi no Nenpyō."

39 Loftus, *Changing Lives*, 81–82. For personal accounts of women involved with the Mothers' Congress from 1955 to 1960, see Tanaka Sumiko, "Nihon ni okeru hahaoya undō no rekishi to yakuwari," in *Josei to undō*, ed. Sōgō Joseishi Kenkyūkai (Tokyo: Yoshikawa Kōbunkan, 1998); and Tsujimura Teruo, *Sengo shinshū joseishi* (Tokyo: Kaseikyōikusha, 1978).

40 Yanbe Kazuko, "Kyō ni uketsugu hahaoya undō," in Ōoka, *Hiratsuka Raichō to Nihon no kindai*, 22.

41 "The Society of Japanese Women Scientists," Society of Japanese Women Scientists, http://www.sjws.info/english/index.html, accessed January 9, 2016.

42 Hiratsuka Raichō, *Hiratsuka Raichō chosakushū*, vol. 8 (Tokyo: Ōtsuki Shoten, 1983), 59.

43 Ide Fumiko, *Hiratsuka Raichō: Kindai to shinpi* (Tokyo: Shinchōsha, 1987), 269.

44 Maruoka, "'Seitō' kara kokusai fujin nen e," 22–23.

45 Uno, "The Death of 'Good Wife, Wise Mother'?," 307; Sheldon Garon, *Molding Japanese Minds: The State in Everyday Life* (Princeton, NJ: Princeton University Press, 1997), 201; Mackie, *Feminism in Modern Japan*, 134–135.

46 Karen Offen, "Introduction," in *Globalizing Feminisms, 1789–1945* (London: Routledge, 2010), xxix–xxxi.

47 Some critics of maternal politics include: Julia Wells, "Maternal Politics in Organizing Black South African Women: The Historical Lessons," in *Sisterhood, Feminisms, and Power: From Africa to the Diaspora*, ed. Obioma Nnaemeka (Trenton, NJ: Africa World Press, 1998); Patrice DiQuinzio, "The Politics of the Mothers' Movement in the United States: Possibilities and Pitfalls," *Journal of the Association for Research on Mothering* 8, nos. 1–2 (Winter/Summer 2006); Heather Hewett, "Talkin' Bout a Revolution: Building a Mothers' Movement in the Third Wave," *Journal of the Association for Research on Mothering* 8, nos. 1–2 (Winter/Summer 2006); and Michelle Moravec, "Another Mother for Peace: Reconsidering Maternalist Peace Rhetoric from a Historical Perspective, 1967–2007," *Journal of Motherhood Initiative* 1, no. 1 (Spring 2010). For

larger discussions of this debate, see Patricia Hill Collins, *Black Feminist Thought: Knowledge, Consciousness, and the Politics of Empowerment* (New York: Routledge, 2000), 192–194; and Andrea O'Reilly, "Introduction," in *The 21st Century Motherhood Movement.*

48 Collins, *Black Feminist Thought*, 194.

49 O'Reilly, *The 21st Century Motherhood Movement*, 24–27.

50 Ibid., 8–11.

51 Ibid., 25.

52 Collins, *Black Feminist Thought*, 194.

53 It is important to note one additional "summer of mothers" historical incident that occurred around this time. In August of 1955, just one month after the World Congress of Mothers, a fourteen-year-old African American child, Emmett Till, was kidnapped, violently tortured, and murdered by two white men. In one of the most important maternal acts in modern history, Emmett Till's mother, Mamie Till Bradley, held an open-casket funeral for her son. She wanted to show the whole world what had happened to him. See Collins, *Black Feminist Thought*, 194.

54 Kobayashi Tomie, *Hiratsuka Raichō* (Tokyo: Shimizu Shoin, 1983), 204.

55 Tomida, *Hiratsuka Raichō*, 348–349.

56 Ibid., 349.

57 I would like to thank Tomomi Yamaguchi and Pamela Scully for helping me to reinterpret this part of my chapter.

~

CHAPTER 3

From Women's Liberation to Lesbian Feminism in Japan

Rezubian Feminizumu *within and beyond the* Ūman Ribu *Movement in the 1970s and 1980s*

JAMES WELKER

I N CONTRAST WITH THE MID-2010S, in which LGBT issues have become increasingly visible in Japan, in the 1990s groundbreaking lesbian (*rezubian*) activist Kakefuda Hiroko bemoaned the lack of attention given to lesbian issues within mainstream Japanese feminism. The feminist movement then, she observed, was oriented toward issues related to heterosexual women.[1] Around the same time, activist and translator Hara Minako denounced the fact that lesbians were sometimes seen within the feminist community in Japan as a sexual threat to straight women. Some heterosexual feminists viewed lesbians as potential sexual predators— akin to men—and were clearly uncomfortable "participating in support groups or staying overnight in the same room at a women's conference" with openly lesbian women, Hara explained.[2] While these particular critiques date to the 1990s, efforts in Japan to garner attention for lesbian issues among feminists and in society at large were by no means novel at the time. Also not new was the marginalization or overt rejection of those issues—as well as of lesbian-identified women themselves.

Indeed, two decades prior, similar frustration was expressed by lesbians in regard to *ūman ribu* (women's liberation), a radical feminist movement that coalesced in Japan in the middle of 1970.[3] And yet, the rejection of lesbians and lesbian issues would seem to run counter to principles espoused by *ribu* activists. One notable aspect of *ribu* was the significant

attention given within the movement not just to women's social independence but also to the liberation of eros (*erosu no kaihō*)—that is, wom-
en's sexual autonomy.[4] In discourse circulating within the movement
as well as commercially produced publications written or translated by
individuals linked to *ribu*, practical information on women's sexual and
reproductive health, along with avenues for women's sexual pleasure—
including sex outside marriage and masturbation—were treated as vital
components of this new wave of activism. Further, the institution of
marriage and the normative family model were sharply critiqued and
sometimes outright rejected by *ribu* activists.[5] However, within the *ribu*
movement, which peaked in the first half of the 1970s, and within the
arguably less radical feminism and women's studies that followed on
ribu's heels in the late 1970s and into the 1980s, one potential avenue for
women's sexual and romantic fulfillment was conspicuously neglected:
the company of other women. Just as Kakefuda and Hara criticized the
feminist community of the 1990s for its insensitivity to lesbian issues,
two decades earlier the *ribu* movement had likewise been indicted by
women who felt silenced or ostracized from feminist circles because of
their same-sex attraction, as I will discuss below.[6]

As marginalized as lesbians were in the *ribu* and feminist spheres
of the 1970s and 1980s, in this chapter I propose that the *ūman ribu*
movement helped set the stage for the emergence of lesbian feminism
(*rezubian feminizumu*) in Japan both through the centrality of women's
erotic subjectivity—and of women's subjectivity in general—within *ribu*
discourse and activism, as well as through the creation by *ribu* women
of spaces in which women could figuratively and literally step outside
many aspects of patriarchal society. In the remainder of this chapter, I
proffer a rethinking of the historical relationship between lesbian activism and feminist activism in Japan by drawing attention to the development of lesbian feminism within—rather than merely opposed to—*ribu*
and other feminist activism in the 1970s and 1980s.

Ūman Ribu Activism, Lesbian Activists, and Feminist Translation

Anecdotal evidence as well as the scarce references to lesbian experiences in published *ribu* discourse makes it clear that the *ribu* sphere was,
on the whole, not a welcoming space for lesbian-identified women—nor

for women merely considering the possibility of romantic or sexual relationships with other women. Among open lesbians participating in *ribu*
activities were women who were aware of a romantic or erotic attraction to females prior to joining the *ribu* movement, sometimes from a
young age. For instance, Asakawa Mari, who was involved in *ribu* almost
from its outset, became involved in late October of 1970 in the small but
influential Group of Fighting Women (Gurūpu Tatakau Onna), led by
ribu's most visible activist, the highly outspoken Tanaka Mitsu. Asakawa
soon moved into the tiny, cramped apartment that served as the group's
home base, joining a communal life with around nine other *ribu* activists. Before long, however, the openly lesbian Asakawa was told by one
member that the women there didn't like sleeping next to her because of
her attraction to women. The discomfort caused by that situation, com-
pounded by Asakawa's dislike of what she perceived as Tanaka's authoritarian leadership style, quickly led Asakawa to leave the group and to
leave behind the *ribu* women she had thought were her comrades.[7]

Another lesbian-identified woman, Amano Michimi, who became
involved in Group Fighting Women around 1972, was also quite open
about her sexuality from the beginning, yet she herself did not feel she
was treated poorly because she was a lesbian. Like Asakawa, however, she
also had a personality clash with Tanaka, who forced her out of the group
around six months after she joined. Unlike Asakawa, Amano remained
connected with *ribu* activism for the next several years.[8] In 1974 she
would produce what was perhaps the first translation by a self-identified
lesbian of lesbian feminist writing to be commercially published (discussed below). This translation represents an important move toward
rectifying the near absence of discussion of lesbians—translated or otherwise—in *ribu* publications.[9]

While locally produced writing dominated *ribu* discourse in general,
translations of writing from the United States and Europe also played a
key early role in some areas, particularly in regard to women's health and
sexuality. Given the dearth of locally produced writing about lesbians in
the 1970s—and the fact that, at the time, most existing writing about lesbians was produced by and for men—translations of even highly culture-
specific writing by and about lesbian women abroad served as invaluable
resources for lesbians in Japan.

In that regard, the translations of two collections of groundbreaking
feminist writing from the United States, *Women's Liberation: Blueprint*

for the Future and *Our Bodies, Ourselves* (published in Japan in 1971 and 1974, respectively) were opportunities lost.[10] The translators of each work omitted chapters focused on the place of lesbians within society in general and within feminism specifically.[11] That *Women's Liberation* was translated by a group of scholars lacking a strong connection to the *ribu* movement is evident in both the chapters they chose to include or omit, and in the way the primary translator, Takano Fumi, framed the collection.[12] On the other hand, *Our Bodies, Ourselves* was translated by women philosophically and personally connected to *ribu* activism.[13] Thus, the beliefs and priorities that guided the choices they made might be said to more closely reflect the *ribu* movement itself.

While the translators of *Women's Liberation* do not explain why they included some chapters and excluded others, the women who rendered *Our Bodies, Ourselves* into Japanese are overt about the many choices they made in creating their translation. The three translators, who came together specifically for this project, had planned to translate a mimeographed version that had been informally circulated. Before they made significant progress, however, a commercial edition was published that had been substantially revised and expanded, including the addition of a number of new chapters. Among these new chapters was the controversial and groundbreaking chapter "In Amerika They Call Us Dykes."[14] As the translators explain in their afterword, while they still wanted to translate the whole volume, they realized they needed to abridge it to make the book affordable. Guided by the structure of the older version, the translators decided to concentrate on what they felt to be the "topics of greatest urgency" to women in Japan: women's bodies, birth control, pregnancy, and childbirth.[15]

Although the translators did not include the new lesbian chapter, in a broader chapter on sexuality they did include a short section on homosexuality from the earlier edition that had been cut from the commercial edition.[16] It is clear then that they did not completely disavow the topic of female homosexuality itself. This renders more credible their justification for the "unfortunate" omission of the lesbian chapter: namely, that it was written by a lesbian group not otherwise connected to the Boston Women's Health Book Collective, the group who put together *Our Bodies, Ourselves*. The translators also direct "those who are interested" to the translation already published in the new commercial *ribu* journal *Onna erosu* (Woman eros, 1973–1982).[17] Although she had no connection to any lesbian groups in Japan at the time, one of the three translators, Akiyama Yōko, later noted that she was concerned about leaving the chapter out but felt satisfied that it had been introduced to a lesbian group to translate.[18] The lesbian "group" turned out to be the aforementioned Amano. Funamoto Emi, one of the founding editors of *Onna erosu*, had invited Amano to help produce the journal, and specifically asked her to translate the lesbian chapter for the magazine, which Funamoto thought would be a shame not to make available in Japanese.[19]

In approaching "what it means to be a lesbian" in American society, the chapter's authors included the experiences of four individuals narrated in the first person—a perspective women in Japan (and in the United States) were unlikely to get elsewhere.[20] The authors—members of a "Gay Women's Liberation" group[21]—do not identify their mission as specifically "lesbian feminist," yet they foreground women's personal experiences and the effects of patriarchal restrictions on lesbian lives, which would clearly resonate with the experiences of lesbians in Japan. While it is difficult to assess the influence of this translation within and beyond the *ribu* movement as a whole, encountering the article and its mere use of the term *"rezubian"* was a startling and memorable experience for future lesbian feminist Kagura Jamu. Kagura would later become a founding member of the lesbian group Regumi no Gomame.[22] Kagura was not specifically searching for information about lesbians when, by chance, she stumbled across one of the few issues of *Onna erosu* in which lesbians were prominently discussed.[23]

Had Kagura been seeking information on being a lesbian, her odds of finding reference to lesbians in noncommercial *ribu* publications—where the vast majority of *ribu* discourse and debate was being carried out—may have been worse. One well-known forum for discourse within the *ribu* sphere was the *minikomi* (newsletter/zine) *Ribu News: This Straight Path* (*Ribu nyūsu: Kono michi hitosuji*), published out of Ribu Shinjuku Center (1972–1977) and distributed to *ribu* groups nationwide.[24] Three of the four references to lesbians I found in the roughly 250 pages of *Ribu News* printed over its four-year run between 1972 and 1976 are passing references to lesbians in the United States. In a 1972 article introducing the two-year-old Los Angeles Women's Center, for instance, there's a paragraph on the Lesbian Feminists (described as a *"resubian kaihō gurūpu,"* or lesbian liberation group), which notes that "[American] lesbians have a sense of guilt forced on them within Christian culture, which makes it easy to fall into self-loathing," but this group is working to help people affirm their own "homosexuality" (*dōseiai*) and is engaging in activities to expand dialogue around the country between those who are homosexual and those who are not.[25] A 1973 article notes that in Chicago there are individuals not yet formally organized who have begun activism aimed at "eliminating social pressure against homosexual [men] and lesbians."[26] A third reference, in 1974, is in a translated article by two radical feminists in the United States, who note that there are women separatists, "many of whom are radical lesbians."[27] By contrast, the final piece referring to lesbians I found in *Ribu News*, also published in 1974, is a full-page dialogue between two women in Japan, "Bi" and "Su" (from the word "*resubian*," an earlier pronunciation of "*rezubian*"), with the former asking the latter about being a lesbian. Even here, the United States is a point of comparison: Su notes that in the United States women are fired if it is discovered they are lesbians, whereas in Japan, if women are openly lesbian the only work they would be able to find is in a lesbian bar. Bi remarks that "lesbians occupy a relatively large position in the American (women's) liberation movement," which would be "unthinkable in Japan."[28]

Lesbian Activism beyond *Ribu*

Over the next two years, a number of things unthinkable in 1974 began to happen within the *ribu* movement. One of them was the withdrawal of de facto leader Tanaka Mitsu. As official and unofficial delegations of women from Japan headed to the 1975 United Nations First World Conference on Women in Mexico City, Tanaka and a few other *ribu* women from Ribu Shinjuku Center headed for North America, with Tanaka and others using it either as an opportunity to network and to learn firsthand about feminist movements in the United States or to simply drop out of the ribu movement.[29] Tanaka's departure from Ribu Shinjuku Center created both a void and opportunities. As a result of the consequent dramatic changes, 1975 is sometimes associated with the end of the *ribu* movement, or at least the beginning of the end. Those who stayed behind in Tokyo changed the organization of Ribu Shinjuku Center; some stepped down their activism for various, sometimes personal reasons. Those living in the center moved out within a year and the center itself closed in 1977.

Asakawa believes that Tanaka's absence made it possible, or at least easier, to organize what were to be called the "wonderful women" (*subarashī onnatachi*) surveys to find out about lesbians within the *ribu* movement.[30] Between 1975 and 1976 four lesbians involved in *ribu*—including a few with ties to Wakakusa no Kai (Young Grass Club, 1971–1985), a group with no stated "feminist" goals, established to provide a space for lesbians to meet one another—created several surveys to find out more about the other lesbians they were certain were in the *ribu* movement. They circulated the surveys among *ribu* women at meetings and via *ribu* group membership lists and other channels. The first survey asked "female homosexuals" (*josei dōseiaisha*) about issues such as when they became aware of their desire for women; the other was a survey of those in the *ribu* movement in general and other interested women and men. The fifty-seven responses they received to the lesbian survey led to three roundtable discussions between March and May 1976 and then the creation of the first—and ultimately only—issue of a *minikomi*, called *Wonderful Women* (*Subarashī onnatachi*), published in November of that year.[31] The seventy-two-page booklet contains a combination of general reflections on life for lesbians in Japan, including a nearly twenty-page roundtable discussion involving seventeen women as well as single-author pieces on *ribu* and on what it means to be a lesbian.

Wakabayashi Naeko was another Ribu Shinjuku Center member who combined the Mexico City conference with an extended sojourn in North America. But unlike Tanaka, who used her departure as an opportunity to withdraw from the *ribu* movement, Wakabayashi used her time abroad to network with and learn from foreign feminists, and came back recharged and ready to engage again in local activism.[32] She also came back with a new lesbian feminist identity, an understanding of herself she came to after spending a significant amount of time working with radical feminists in the United States—including a stint working at the Feminist Women's Health Center in Oakland, California, where most of her coworkers were lesbians. Prior to getting involved in the *ribu* movement, Wakabayashi had held a negative impression of lesbians based on images circulating in public discourse in Japan, including pornography. Through her work as a translator for *Ribu News*, she was exposed to writing from lesbian feminists abroad; and within the movement she met lesbian-identified women in Japan, and her prejudice against lesbians "quickly disappeared."[33] Nevertheless, prior to living in the United States she did not think women loving women had anything to do with her. But at the women's health clinic, for the first time in her life, she became romantically attracted to a woman, leading her to the realization that liking women was the same as liking men had been for her in the past.[34] When Wakabayashi returned to Japan, the women who had put together the "wonderful women" surveys were still working on a *minikomi* based on discussions about the results, and she immediately found herself working on that project. Her contribution to *Wonderful Women* was the translation into Japanese of an article by a foreign woman living in Japan.[35] In an oral history taken in 2007, Wakabayashi acknowledges that within the community she is considered an "ideological lesbian" (*shisō-ha rezubian*), that is, someone who is a *rezubian* for "ideological" reasons. This, she knows, positions her differently from someone who grew up attracted to other women.[36]

As lesbian activist Izumo Marou recalls, those who were *rezubian* as a "political choice" (*seijiteki sentaku*)—which she links to the influence of American feminism—had not experienced the same kind of anxiety about or rejection for being *rezubian* and, consequently, were not adequately sympathetic toward the needs of those for whom being a *rezubian* was not experienced as a choice. These needs included speaking and writing about negative issues in order to address the wounds they had incurred from going against or feeling forced to comply with social norms.[37] In her study of this period, Sugiura Ikuko makes a distinction between the women involved with *Wonderful Women*, who came to the project from *ribu* or Wakakusa no Kai, and women who made the political choice to be a *rezubian* under the direct or indirect influence of American lesbian feminism.[38] Yet, Izumo's recollection of her involvement in the project, as well as Wakabayashi's experience, noted above, suggest no clear line can be drawn at this pivotal moment in the development of lesbian feminism. Izumo recounts that some women in the *Wonderful Women* project harshly rejected the expression of ideas and experiences that contradicted the notion that lesbians are "wonderful women," and Izumo was ridiculed and criticized for talking about her own struggles, leading to her withdrawal from the group and longstanding resentment.[39]

In 1977 Sawabe Hitomi—who had herself traveled to the United States in the mid-1970s to network with lesbian feminists there—and several women who had come to *Wonderful Women* from Wakakusa no

Kai formed the group Everyday Dyke (Mainichi Daiku), which produced two issues of its own *minikomi*, *The Dyke* (*Za daiku*, 1978).[40] Its mission statement defined Everyday Dyke as a "women's group centered around lesbians who are seeking independence and liberation." They "oppose[d] all discrimination and oppression against lesbians" and women in general, as well as "male roles" (*otokoyaku*) and "female roles" (*onnayaku*) within lesbian relationships, and sought to engage in activities such as exchange and dissemination of information to support this mission.[41] Differences of opinion led Sawabe to split off and form another lesbian feminist group, Shining Wheel (Hikari Guruma), which produced an eponymous *minikomi*.[42] In spite of their differences the two groups continued to cooperate, however. Everyday Dyke, for instance, promoted the premier issue of *Shining Wheel* in *The Dyke*.[43] While both groups positioned themselves as *rezubian feminisuto*, Sugiura points out that lesbianism as an explicitly political choice was central to neither.[44]

In 1981, however, members from each group joined together to start the Lesbian Feminist Center, which was guided in part by the belief that lesbianism is a rational political choice for feminists.[45] Activities organized by the groups using the center included holding consciousness-raising workshops, throwing dance parties with an attendance of between fifty and sixty women, and providing support to lesbians from around the country who sent letters to its post office box. While the facility was repurposed into a rape crisis center in 1983,[46] around the same time, several women organized what they called the Sisterhood Club (Shisutāfuddo no Kai) and began producing a *minikomi* called *Lesbian Communication* (*Rezubian tsūshin*). At a rented space near Waseda University in Tokyo, the group presented a slideshow put together by lesbians in the United States called "Women Loving Women." Afterward, five of them, including Wakabayashi, Kagura, and Sawabe—the latter of whom had herself first learned about American lesbian feminists through participation in Ribu Shinjuku Center translation activities—set to work to produce a Japanese version of the slide show.[47] While they were unsuccessful in creating the show due to concerns about privacy, these women ended up founding a new *minikomi*, *Regumi Communications* (*Regumi tsūshin*, 1985–); a new group, Regumi no Gomame; and, in 1987, a new lesbian space, Regumi Studio Tokyo.[48] The group would eventually come to be known simply as Regumi Studio or just Regumi. And, in contrast with the erasure of lesbians in feminist translation projects in the 1970s,

Regumi was introduced in the late 1980s Japanese translation of the 1984 version of *Our Bodies, Ourselves* as a part of a two-page supplement on Japan to the volume's updated lesbian chapter, which was at last translated in full.[49]

For her part, Sawabe would go on to spearhead a new pair of surveys of and about lesbians in 1986. These surveys were inspired by American lesbian-feminist writing, by the experience of attending an international lesbian conference in Switzerland, and by the responses that came in from around the country to an article she wrote about the conference for the mainstream women's magazine *Fujin kōron* (Women's forum).[50] The results formed half of *Stories of Women Who Love Women* (*Onna o ai suru onnatachi no monogatari*).[51] Published in May 1987 as part of the popular Bessatsu Takarajima series, *Stories* was the first commercially published book created by—and, more or less, for—lesbians. This volume, available at bookstores around the country, has long been described as a "bible" for a generation of lesbians and bisexual (*baisekushuaru*) women, for whom it was often the first positive representation they saw of lesbian life.[52] Many women say that reading this book was the first time they were aware of the extent of the *rezubian* community—and for some, its very existence.[53]

Overlapping with these developments in the 1980s, an "English-speaking lesbian community" came together in Japan, centered around Tokyo.[54] This was initially facilitated by International Feminists of Japan (IFJ), founded in 1979 by Anne Blasing, "to provide a support network among feminists in Japan's international community and to provide a bridge between this feminist community and the many Japanese feminist organizations."[55] In 1985, a lesbian session was included in the program of an international feminist conference jointly hosted by IFJ and a Japanese feminist group. The enthusiasm at that session led those in attendance to plan an overnight gathering in November, which was the first of what would often be called simply "Weekends" (*Uīkuendo*). Around fifty women attended the initial retreat, but for a while over a hundred women were regularly coming to the Weekends.[56] While the Weekends have generally been dominated by the English language and English speakers, the events are in principle bilingual. About the lesbians from Japan involved in the English-speaking community, decades-long Japan resident Linda Peterson recalls, "All the Japanese dykes who showed up" in the 1980s and 1990s, when Peterson was most actively involved, "were definitely political. Either lesbian political or feminist political . . . or groovy green political."[57]

Conclusion

In the same breath in which Hara criticized the fear of lesbians among some feminists that I noted at the opening of this chapter, she also reflected on the progress of the community, noting that, "It has become easier for women to love women" in Japan "because self-identified lesbians and bisexual women have emerged to work on lesbian issues."[58] More recently, Sawabe has described the years from 1971 to 1980 as "the seeds," from 1981 to 1990 as "the sprouts," from 1991 to 2000 as "the flowering," and from 2001 onward as "the fruit" of lesbian activism.[59] To be sure, the 1990s also saw developments in the lesbian and gay communities that owe some debt to the early 1990s "gay boom" in the popular media.[60] While focused almost entirely on men, this surge in media attention in the early 1990s helped provide popular forums for lesbian discourse as well, no doubt attracting the attention of women who otherwise might have been unaware of the community, and made the production of commercial lesbian magazines and books seem viable to publishers. By the turn of the twenty-first century, the lesbian community in Japan had come to resemble counterparts in other industrialized countries in Europe, North America, and the Asia-Pacific in terms of its social activities, lifestyle publications, and nightlife. This is in no small part a function of transnational networking and exchange facilitated by increasingly interconnected queer communities. However, it may also be understood as a product of *ribu* and especially of the lesbian feminist activism of the 1970s and 1980s that I have outlined above.

Even now, in the middle of the second decade of the twenty-first century, we can continue to see the fruits of the lesbian feminism whose roots can be traced back to the *ūman ribu* movement. Regumi and its lesbian feminist activism carry on, with Wakabayashi still playing a prominent role. Although *Regumi Communications* ceased publication in print following issue number 294 (February 2013), it has transitioned to an online forum. The Weekends are also still being held several times a year in various parts of the country, continuing to provide a venue for networking among lesbian activists, as well as a space for simple socializing. To the extent that the lesbian and broader LGBT communities in Japan are at least superficially quite similar to their counterparts in other cultures, however, it should be unsurprising that activism of any sort, including lesbian feminist activism, remains marginal. It is also safe to say that issues of direct concern to lesbians in Japan are not a priority within mainstream Japanese feminism either—although resistance to lesbian issues within mainstream feminism is no longer as overt. Nevertheless, as I have briefly illustrated here, even in the face of marginalization and sometimes ostracism, both within society at large and within already marginal spheres including mainstream and radical feminism, since the 1970s some women in Japan have come together under the banner of lesbian feminism and engaged in activism that has had tangible effects on their own lives and on the lives of others.

Notes

1 This comes from an interview with Sharon Chalmers in Chalmers' *Emerging Lesbian Voices from Japan* (London: RoutledgeCurzon, 2002), 34. The women I refer to as lesbians or "*rezubian*" in this chapter have directly identified themselves with the terms. *Ūman ribu* is also discussed by Setsu Shigematsu in her chapter in this volume.

2 See Hara Minako, "Lesbians and Sexual Self-Determination," in *Voices from the Japanese Women's Movement*, ed. AMPO, *Japan Asia Quarterly Review* (Armonk, NY: M. E. Sharpe, 1996), 131. Hara now uses the masculine forename Minata in their activism and daily life.

3 In this chapter, I use "*ūman ribu*" rather than "women's lib(eration)" to distinguish between the movement in Japan and radical feminist movements that emerged around the same time in the United States and elsewhere.

4 For a discussion of the philosophy of the liberation of eros (*erosu no kaihō*) within the *ribu* sphere, particularly that articulated by its most visible proponent, Tanaka Mitsu, see Setsu Shigematsu, *Scream from the Shadows: The Women's Liberation Movement in Japan* (Minneapolis: University of Minnesota Press, 2012).

5 Within *ribu* were, for instance, a few prominent groups that experimented with raising children collectively, including Tokyo Komu'unu, whose name combines "*ko umu*" [birth a child] with "*komyūn*" [commune]. See Saeki Yōko, "Tōkyō Komu'unu," in *Shiryō Nihon ūman ribu shi*, vol. 2, ed. Mizoguchi Akiyo, Saeki Yōko, and Miki Sōko (Kyoto: Shōkadō Shoten, 1994).

6   For further discussion of the status of lesbians within *ribu*, see Sugiura
    Ikuko, "Nihon ni okeru rezubian feminizumu no katsudō: 1970-nendai no
    reimeiki ni okeru," *Jendā kenkyū* [Tōkai jendā kenkyūsho] 11 (December
    2008): 150–154.

7   Asakawa Mari, "Ribusen de deatta 'subarashī onnatachi,'" oral history
    taken by Sugiura Ikuko, in Sugiura Ikuko, *Nihon no rezubian komyuniti:
    Kōjutsu no undō shi* (Tokyo: privately printed, 2009), 1–6 passim. Lesbian
    activist Izumo Marou also recalls *rezubian* within *ribu* taking issue with
    Tanaka, perhaps including Asakawa. See Izumo Marou et al., "Nihon no
    rezubian mūvumento," *Gendai shisō* 25, no. 6 (May 1997): 59–60.

8   Amano Michimi, interview, April 2, 2009; Amano Michimi, pers. comm.,
    May–June 2010. See also Amano Michimi, "Women in Japan: Lucy Leu
    Interviews Michimi," *The Second Wave* 3, no. 4 (Winter 1974).

9   Boston Women's Health Book Collective (hereafter BWHBC), "*Rezu to
    yobarete*" ("In Amerika They Call Us Dykes," by Boston Gay Collective),
    2 parts, trans. Amano Michimi, *Onna erosu*, no. 2 (April 1974); no. 3
    (September 1974).

10 Sookie Stambler, compiler, *Women's Liberation: Blueprint for the Future*
    (New York: Ace Books, 1970) and its translation, Kate Millett et al., *Ūman
    ribu: Josei wa nani o kangae, nani o motomeru ka*, trans. Takano Fumi
    et al. (Tokyo: Hayakawa Shobō, 1971); BWHBC, *Our Bodies, Ourselves:
    A Book by and for Women* (New York: Simon & Schuster, 1973) and its
    translation, *Onna no karada: Sei to ai no shinjitsu*, trans. Akiyama Yōko,
    Kuwahara Kazuyo, and Yamada Mitsuko (Tokyo: Gōdō Shuppan, 1974).

11 During this same period, translation of a third highly influential
    collection of radical feminist writing from the United States, Shulamith
    Firestone and Anne Koedt, eds., *Notes from the Second Year: Women's
    Liberation; Major Writings of the Radical Feminists* (New York: Radical
    Feminism, 1970), was published in 1971 as Shulamith Firestone and
    Anne Koedt, eds., *Onna kara onnatachi e: Amerika josei kaihō undō
    repōto*, translation and commentary by Urufu no Kai (Tokyo: Gōdō
    Shuppan, 1971), but it cannot be critiqued in the same way for erasing
    the representation of lesbianism. Unlike *Women's Liberation* and *Our
    Bodies, Ourselves*, this volume does not have a chapter focused on lesbian
    experience. While lesbians and lesbian experiences are not mentioned in
    the editorial content contributed by the translators, the translation does
    maintain the brief references to lesbian sexuality in Koedt's influential
    "The Myth of the Vaginal Orgasm." See Firestone and Koedt, *Notes from
    the Second Year*, 41, and its translation, Firestone and Koedt, *Onna kara
    onnatachi e*, 129–130.

12 James Welker, "The Revolution Cannot Be Translated: Transfiguring Discourses of Women's Liberation in 1970s–1980s Japan," in *Multiple Translation Communities in Contemporary Japan*, ed. Beverley Curran, Nana Sato-Rossberg, and Kikuko Tanabe (New York: Routledge, 2015), 63–64.

13 Ibid.

14 In BWHBC, *Our Bodies, Ourselves*, 56–73.

15 Akiyama Yōko, Kuwahara Kazuyo, and Yamada Mitsuko, "Yakusha atogaki," in BWHBC, *Onna no karada*, 345. See also Akiyama Yōko, *Ribu shishi nōto: Onnatachi no jidai kara* (Tōkyō: Inpakuto Shuppan Kai, 1993), 158–159.

16 BWHBC, *Onna no karada*, 101–106; BWHBC, *Our Bodies, Ourselves*, 23–41.

17 Akiyama, Kuwahara, and Yamada, "Yakusha atogaki," 345.

18 Akiyama Yōko, interview, March 4, 2009.

19 Amano, interview.

20 BWHBC, *Our Bodies, Ourselves*, 56.

21 Ibid.

22 At the time she ran across the translation, Kagura was looking at an issue of *Onna erosu* at a neighbor's home. As she recalls, "one look at the word 'lesbian' gave me a start, and I slammed the magazine shut." See Hisada Megumi, "Genki jirushi no rezubian: 'Regumi no Gomame' tōjō!" in *Bessatsu Takarajima*, no. 64, *Onna o ai suru onnatachi no monogatari* (Tokyo: JICC Shuppankyoku, 1987), 123.

23 In reviewing *Onna erosu* for a special reflection on "20 years of *ribu*" in 1992, Kakefuda praises the magazine for the centrality of the individual "I"/*watashi* speaking from "my"/*watashi no* own experience—something she finds lacking in women's studies and more contemporary feminism. Yet she bemoans the fact that there are so few references to lesbian existence in its pages. See Kakefuda Hiroko, "*Onna erosu*," *Inpakushon* 73 (February 1992), 137.

24 I treat *Ribu News* as representative of *ribu* discourse at the time both based on its prominence within the *ribu* sphere and based on comparison with the many other *minikomi* I have examined. The complete run was republished, with minor changes to protect the privacy of individuals involved, as Ribu Shinjuku Sentā Shiryō Hozon Kai, ed. (hereafter, RSSSHK), *Kono michi hitosuji: Ribu Shinjuku Sentā shiryō shūsei* (Tokyo: Inpakuto Shuppankai, 2008).

25 *Ribu nyūsu: Kono michi hitosuji*, "Rosunzerusu ūmansentā no 2-nen," no. 1 (September 30, 1972); reprinted in RSSSHK, *Kono michi hitosuji*.

26 Yoshihiro Kiyoko, "Za Shikago uimenzu ribarēshon yunion: America no undō," *Ribu nyūsu: Kono michi hitosuji*, no. 5 (October 10, 1973), 11; reprinted in RSSSHK, *Kono michi hitosuji*, 79.

27 Nancy (New People's Center), and Kathy (National Lawyers' Guild), "Netsuretsu apīru: Onnatachi o kaihō shi, jibun jishin o kaihō shiyō!" translated by Ishida Tama, *Ribu nyūsu: Kono michi hitosuji*, no. 10 (April 20, 1974); reprinted in RSSSHK, *Kono michi hitosuji*.

28 Su and Bi, "Resubian: Onna to onna ga dakiau toki," *Ribu nyūsu: Kono michi hitosuji*, no. 14 (November 23, 1974), 7; reprinted in RSSSHK, *Kono michi hitosuji*.

29 Those from Ribu Shinjuku Center who left for Mexico City and elsewhere were Tanaka Mitsu, Wakabayashi Naeko, and Takeda Miyuki. Wakabayashi is discussed below; Takeda was involved in Tokyo Komu'unu, a group using the center. See Endō et al., "Ribusen o taguri yosete miru," in *Zenkyōtō kara Ribu e*, ed. Onnatachi no Ima o Tō Kai (Tokyo: Inpakuto Shuppankai, 1996), 209. They were not the only *ribu* women to head to Mexico City, however.

30 Asakawa, "Ribusen de deatta 'subarashī onnatachi,'" 8–9.

31 *Subarashī onnatachi*, "Zasshi no hakkan ni atatte," no. 1 (November 1976), and "Zadankai 'rezubian ōi ni kataru,'" no. 1 (November 1976): 6. The *minikomi* may have sold as many as 1,000 copies. See Anne Blasing, "The Lavender Kimono," *Connexions*, no. 3 (Winter 1982).

32 This description of Wakabayashi's experience is summarized from Wakabayashi Naeko, "Onna no nettowāku no naka de ikiru," oral history taken by Sugiura Ikuko, in Sugiura, *Nihon no rezubian komyuniti*, 17–25; and *Anīsu*, "Komyuniti no rekishi, 1971–2001: Nenpyō to intabyū de furikaeru," (Summer 2001): 38–41; and [Wakabayashi] Naeko, "Lesbian = Woman," in *Queer Japan: Personal Stories of Japanese Lesbians, Gays, Bisexuals, and Transsexuals*, ed. Barbara Summerhawk, Cheiron McMahill, and Darren McDonald (Norwich, VT: New Victoria Publishers, 1998). When asked in a 1996 roundtable why she went to the United States, she could not remember her initial reason, but Yonezu Tomoko, another roundtable participant, recalled that Wakabayashi talked about needing a change of scenery. See Endō et al., "Ribusen o taguri yosete miru," 209.

33 Wakabayashi, "Onna no nettowāku," 24.

34 Ibid., 24–25.

35 Wakabayashi, "Onna no nettowāku," 25. The article she translated is probably Barbara Lee Barbara, "Rezubian, kono onnatachi wa nani mono da?" trans. Hazama Natsu [pseud. Wakabayashi Naeko?], *Subarashī onnatachi*, no. 1 (November 1976).

36 Wakabayashi, "Onna no nettowāku no naka de ikiru," 31.

37 Izumo Marou, pers. comm., July 9, 2009.

38 Sugiura, "Nihon ni okeru rezubian feminizumu no katsudō," 162–163.

39 Izumo, pers. comm.

40 The group's Japanese name involves layered word play. The English word "dyke," when transliterated into Japanese, is homophonous with the Japanese word for carpenter (*daiku*). It is this English meaning that is used in the group's name, which is a twist on the expression "Sunday carpenter" (*nichiyō daiku*), meaning "do-it-yourselfer."

41 See Mainichi Daiku, "'Mainichi daiku' no hōshin," *Za daiku*, no. 2 (June 1978).

42 Sugiura, "Nihon ni okeru rezubian feminizumu no katsudō," 162–163; Izumo et al., "Nihon no rezubian mūvumento," 58–62; Sawabe Hitomi, "The Symbolic Tree of Lesbianism in Japan: An Overview of Lesbian Activist History and Literary Works," trans. Kimberly Hughes, in *Sparkling Rain and Other Fiction from Japan of Women Who Love Women*, ed. Barbara Summerhawk and Kimberly Hughes (Chicago: New Victoria Publishers, 2008), 8–9.

43 See *Za daiku*, "Hikari guruma sōkan-gō," no. 2 (June 1978). A lengthier history of 1970s *rezubian feminizumu*, including an analysis of *The Dyke* and *Shining Wheel*, can be found in Sugiura, "Nihon ni okeru rezubian feminizumu no katsudō."

44 Sugiura, "Nihon ni okeru rezubian feminizumu no katsudō," 163.

45 Vera Mackie, "Kantō Women's Groups," *Feminist International* [Japan], no. 2 (June 1980): 108.

46 Blasing, "The Lavender Kimono"; Sawabe, "The Symbolic Tree of Lesbianism," 9; Mackie, "Kantō Women's Groups," 107–108.

47 Sawabe Hitomi, "*Onna o ai suru onnatachi* o meguru hyōgen katsudō," oral history taken by Sugiura Ikuko, in Sugiura, *Nihon no rezubian komyuniti*, 39–40; Hisada, "Genki jirushi no rezubian," 122–123; Wakabayashi, "Onna no nettowāku," 27–28. A transcript of the slideshow narration is reproduced in Sugiura, *Nihon no rezubian komyuniti*, 85–97.

48 The group's original name, Regumi no Gomame, combines an abbreviation for "lesbian group"—Regumi (*rezubian* + *gumi* [group])—with an oblique reference to the idea that working together is powerful. See Hisada, "Genki jirushi no rezubian," 122.

49 BWHBC, *Karada, watashitachi jishin* (The New Our Bodies, Ourselves: A Book by and for Women), trans. *Karada, Watashitachi Jishin* Nihongo-ban Hon'yaku Gurūpu, ed. *Karada, Watashitachi Jishin* Nihongo-ban Henshū Gurūpu (Kyoto: Shōkadō Shoten, 1988), 146–148.

50 Hirosawa Yumi [Sawabe Hitomi], "Sekai rezubian kaigi ni sanka

shite," *Fujin kōron* 71, no. 7 (June 1986). The conference was the eighth International Lesbian Information Service Conference, held in March 1986. See Sawabe, "*Onna o ai suru onnatachi no monogatari*," 52–54.

51 Bessatsu Takarajima, no. 64, *Onna o ai suru onnatachi no monogatari*. Sawabe was using the pseudonym Hirosawa Yumi at the time. A majority of the articles appearing under other names in this volume were also penned by Sawabe, who was encouraged by the publisher to make the volume appear to be more of a collective project (pers. comm., October 2004).

52 Tenshin Ranran, "Media ga nakatta koro no baiburu," in *Kuia sutadīzu '96*, ed. Kuia Sutadīzu Henshū Īnkai (Tokyo: Nanatsumori Shokan, 1996); Yamaga Saya, "Rezubian no 'baiburu,'" in *Niji-iro no hondana: LGBT bukkugaido*, ed. Hara Minata and Dohi Itsuki (Tokyo: San-ichi Shobō, 2016).

53 One woman recollects that, after moving from Okinawa to Tokyo she happened to find *Stories*, through which she contacted Regumi Studio; her subsequent involvement in the community helped her accept herself as a *rezubian*. See Wim Lunsing, *Beyond Common Sense: Sexuality and Gender in Contemporary Japan* (London: Kegan Paul, 2001), 232–233. I heard similar experiences from several of the women I interviewed for my research on the lesbian community and the *ūman ribu* movement in the 1970s and 1980s.

54 I borrow the expression "English-speaking lesbian community" from Linda Peterson, "English Language Journal in Japan," *Lesbian News and Views* [Japan; also called *The DD*], no. 1 (May 1986). Peterson's label is more accurate than two other terms sometimes used: "foreign lesbian community," which fails to incorporate the women from Japan who played (and play) a vital role in the community, and "international lesbian community," which fails to make clear that the community is largely limited to those who speak English.

55 Anne Blasing, "International Feminists of Japan," *Feminist International* [Japan], no. 2 (June 1980): 109; Audrey Lockwood, pers. comm., April 2009; Linda M. Peterson, "Rezubian in Tokyo," in *Finding the Lesbians: Personal Accounts from Around the World*, ed. Julia Penelope and Sarah Valentine (Freedom, CA: Crossing Press, 1990), 129–130; Blasing, "The Lavender Kimono."

56 *Anīsu*, "Komyuniti no rekishi," 40; Linda M. Peterson, interview, April 26, 2009; Izumo et al., "Nihon no rezubian mūvumento," 63.

57 Peterson, interview.

58 Hara, "Lesbians and Sexual Self-Determination," 129.

59 Sawabe, "The Symbolic Tree," 6, 10, 17, 25.

60 For a discussion of the gay boom, see Wim Lunsing, "Gay Boom in Japan: Changing Views of Homosexuality?" *Thamyris* 4, no. 2 (1997). A broader discussion of life for gay men in Japan in the 1990s, with some attention to the gay boom, can be found in Mark J. McLelland, *Male Homosexuality in Modern Japan: Cultural Myths and Social Realities* (Richmond, England: Curzon, 2000).

~

CHAPTER 4

The Mainstreaming of Feminism and the Politics of Backlash in Twenty-First-Century Japan

TOMOMI YAMAGUCHI

I N 1999, the Basic Law for a Gender-Equal Society (Danjo kyōdō sankaku shakai kihon-hō; hereafter, the Basic Law) and subsequent Basic Plan for a Gender-Equal Society (Danjo kyōdō sankaku shakai kihon keikaku) were enacted.[1] The Basic Law defines "gender-equal society" as "an affluent and dynamic society in which the human rights of both men and women are respected and that can respond to changes in socioeconomic situations." It also lays out basic principles for the achievement of a "gender-equal society."[2] Municipal governments across Japan, starting with Tokyo and Saitama, followed suit by making their own gender equality promotion ordinances (danjo kyōdō sankaku suishin jōrei). The new buzzword used in the new law and ordinances, "danjo kyōdō sankaku," literally means "co-participation and planning of men and women," for which the official government translation in English is "gender equality." As Ayako Kano points out, the use of the vague and unfamiliar expression "danjo kyōdō sankaku" was a way to avoid a more commonly used Japanese term with a much clearer meaning, "byōdō" (equality).[3] Around the same time, funded by large sums of tax money, many new municipal gender equality centers (danjo kyōdō sankaku sentā) were built in non-urban areas.[4] The centers had meeting rooms and libraries, offered counseling services, and housed many educational projects for citizens. This mainstreaming of gender equality policies, however, sparked a conservative backlash that peaked between 2002 and 2006.

The backlash occurred as a reaction to the perceived "invasion" of feminism into the local political arena as a result of the passage of municipal gender equality ordinances and the building of the centers. The conservative attacks against *danjo kyōdō sankaku* began around 2000, starting in newsletters and pamphlets produced by conservative organizations, and then spreading into the conservative mass media and the Internet. These criticisms influenced the direction of local policy making, the content of some municipal gender equality ordinances, and the content of the Second Basic Plan for Gender Equality, which was approved by the cabinet in December 2005. Conservative politicians, journalists, critics, and activists also harshly criticized seminar programs and the library holdings of municipal gender equality centers, gender equality education and sex education in public schools, and feminist writing and talks.

My discussion here is based on long-term field research that I conducted from 2004 to 2011 on the struggles between feminists and those whom feminists have labeled "the backlash faction," a conflict that started in the early 2000s. As part of this research, with my co-researchers based in Japan, Saitō Masami and Ogiue Chiki, I conducted in-depth interviews and participant observation related to the debate between feminists and anti-feminist conservatives in local communities, especially in the rural periphery. We visited people considered to be part of the backlash faction, who issued harsh criticisms against feminism, and listened to stories about their backgrounds and the motivation behind their actions. We also met with local citizens and feminists who acted in response to, or against, the backlash, and heard about their experiences and thoughts as well. We also conducted archival research entailing print media, websites, blogs, message boards, and social media sites, and participated in such discussions as feminist bloggers writing in Japanese. In 2012, we published the results of this research as a book in Japanese, entitled *Social Movements at a Crossroads: Feminism's "Lost Years" vs. Grassroots Conservatism (Shakai undō no tomadoi: Feminizumu no "ushinawareta jidai" to kusa no ne hoshu undō).*[5]

In this chapter, I will explain who the anti-feminist conservatives are and why and how they attacked feminism, using two case studies from the above-mentioned book, detailing struggles over the passage of gender equality ordinances in Ube City in Yamaguchi Prefecture, and Miyakonojō City in Miyazaki Prefecture. These concrete cases from local communities highlight power relations and tensions between the center (national/urban) and the periphery (local/rural), and the problems facing *danjo kyōdō sankaku* policies in local areas and national politics in Japan in the early 2000s. In addition to the case studies from the book, I will follow up on the recent state of feminism, especially under the ultra-conservative administration of Prime Minister Abe Shinzō, in power since 2012. In particular, I will discuss his problematic slogan of building a "society in which women shine" (*josei ga kagayaku shakai*), and his promotion since 2015 of a "society in which all 100 million people can be active" (*ichioku sō katsuyaku shakai*).

Backlash against *Danjo Kyōdō Sankaku*

The controversy over *danjo kyōdō sankaku* was ignited by the use of words such as "gender free" (*jendā furī*), another newly created buzzword coined by non-feminist scholars in Japan in 1995, to vaguely refer to freedom from compulsory gender roles. The term had spread quickly via many governmental projects, and thus became a core target of attacks by conservatives, and a potent symbol of the backlash against feminism.[6] The meanings of both of the newly created terms "gender free" and *danjo kyōdō sankaku* were unclear for the general public, enabling conservatives to utilize this vagueness to interpret them in an intentionally skewed fashion, for instance by defining them as "the complete erasure of the biological difference between the sexes" and "an extreme Communist plot," and then attacking them extensively. Around 2005, a planned lecture in Kokubunji City by feminist scholar Ueno Chizuko, sponsored by the Tokyo Metropolitan Government, was canceled because it was thought that Ueno might use the term "gender free." Starting with this incident, feminist scholars came to be involved more visibly in the fight against the backlash.[7] They began referring to conservative attacks against feminism as "gender-bashing," suggesting that the concept of "gender" itself, not simply the term "gender free," was the main target of the criticism.[8] Ueno, for example, states that she used to misunderstand the target of conservative attacks to be the idea of "gender free," but came to conclude that the real target of backlash was in fact the concept of "gender," which is an established academic term that conservatives confused with "gender free."[9]

This illustrates how some feminists have often not sought to grasp with any sort of precision the kinds of people who criticize them. Hence, the "backlash faction" has been imagined to consist of "ordinary people,"[10] "middle-aged and old conservatives and young men,"[11] or "housewives,"[12] or to constitute a "nationwide organized movement."[13] Feminists have also posited the existence of a central leader who was mobilizing people using large sums of money.[14] However, the actual strategies of the conservatives were never investigated, which is unfortunate because this might have enabled feminists to better strategize their actions against the backlash.

Many of the conservatives who were actively involved in the anti-feminist movement were a part of the so-called "grassroots conservative" (*kusa no ne hoshu*) movement. The most visible of these were Nippon Kaigi (Japan Conference), Japan's largest conservative alliance organization, established in 1997; traditional right-wing organizations such as the Japan War-Bereaved Families' Association (Nippon Izokukai); and conservative religious organizations affiliated with it, such as the Association of Shinto Shrines (Jinja Honchō).[15] While the large-scale media (such as the conservative newspaper and magazine publisher Sankei), famous politicians and intellectuals, and active online message boards (e.g., *2 channel* and the "Message Board to Watch the Femi-Nazis" [*Femi nachi o kanshi suru keijiban*]) may have been attracting most of the attention, the backlash was in fact sustained by the hidden work of people in religious organizations that may or may not have been affiliated with the Japan Conference. In particular, these included Shinsei Bukkyō ("Newborn" Buddhism) and its paper, *Nihon jiji hyōron* (Japan current review), based in rural Yamaguchi Prefecture in southwestern Japan; and Tōitsu Kyōkai (the Unification Church, more colloquially called "the Moonies" in the United States) and its paper *Sekai nippō* (The world times), headquartered in Tokyo. The results of this coverage, along with the activism of local conservatives—groundwork laid by those grassroots conservatives—then spread to the larger-scale Japan Conference, to the conservative mass media, and eventually to the many nameless and seemingly unaffiliated individuals on the Internet.

Now I will turn to specific cases of backlash in which the journalists of *Nihon jiji hyōron* and *Sekai nippō* were involved in activities in local communities in rural Yamaguchi and Miyazaki prefectures.

Nihon Jiji Hyōron's Critique of the "Model Ordinance"

As already noted, after the passage of the Basic Law in 1999, municipal governments started to enact gender equality ordinances. A number of my interviewees, many of whom are part of the religious right and are conservative local politicians, described the prefectural and city ordinances as based on the "model ordinance" passed in the Tokyo metropolitan area. They believed that this was subsequently imposed on other prefectures, which made them furious about the direction of *danjo kyōdō sankaku* politics. Consequently, in June 2002 conservatives successfully passed a conservative-friendly gender equality ordinance in Ube City, Yamaguchi Prefecture. By that point, municipal gender equality ordinances generally followed the content of the Basic Law, which clearly rejects the traditional gendered division of labor. The Ube City ordinance, however, included phrases such as "we must not unilaterally dismiss the idea that there is innate masculinity and innate femininity" and "we must not dismiss the role of the full-time housewife." Feminists considered this wording to be directly contrary to the aims of the Basic Law, and for this reason, the passage of this ordinance shocked them. The following year, the Chiba Prefectural Assembly, under feminist governor Dōmoto Akiko, failed to pass the gender equality ordinance bill that she had brought to the assembly; it was the first time that a bill proposed by a governor had failed to pass in the history of the Assembly. While the conservatives became energized as a result of the Ube ordinance, the cases in Ube and Chiba were tremendous shocks for feminist scholars and activists, and they started to become more vocal on the issue of the backlash.

Nihon jiji hyōron led the anti-feminist ordinance movement in Ube City, and later in Chiba Prefecture. Nihon Jiji Hyōron, Inc., the publisher of *Nihon jiji hyōron*, initiated the campaign against feminism and led the movement to pass a "sensible" (*ryōshiki-teki na*) gender equality ordinance by disseminating information about it.[16] *Nihon jiji hyōron* is an opinion paper with an official circulation of 30,000, and is put out by the relatively small religious organization Shinsei Bukkyō, which has about 10,000 followers. The religion considers vertical family lines and ancestor worship as crucial in its beliefs, and its followers join the religion not as individuals but as families.[17] Many conservative local politicians I met as part of this research said they received *Nihon jiji hyōron* for free. Since 2002, Nihon Jiji Hyōron, Inc. has also published *Yūsen* (Rising spring), an occasional series of booklets generally composed of past articles from the paper, and its first two volumes were thematic issues that addressed *danjo kyōdō sankaku*.

The paper started to pay attention to the concept of "gender free" and, as part of their efforts to undermine it, began to criticize the growing practice of mixing female and male names during roll calls at public schools starting in 1998, earlier than any other publications that I could find. It began extensive criticism of *danjo kyōdō sankaku* starting around 2000, and functioned to set the agenda for other larger-scale conservative media, the mass media, and the Internet, such as message boards, blogs, and Wikipedia. The paper and its booklets were extremely powerful tools for organizing conservatives by making local politicians aware of the *danjo kyōdō sankaku* "problem" and providing various kinds of information to conservative intellectuals.

In order to examine the background of the passage of the Ube ordinance, it was necessary that I visit Yamaguchi Prefecture, and meet people involved in the production and distribution of *Nihon jiji hyōron*. Among them, I met its editor-in-chief and the leader of the movement, Yamaguchi Toshiaki, six times in Yamaguchi Prefecture and Tokyo since 2005, while keeping in touch with him by email as well. Yamaguchi and another reporter on the paper, both in their late forties then, also took me to some sightseeing spots near Yamaguchi City, and introduced me to some conservative activists involved in the drafting and passage of the Ube ordinance, as well as a conservative city council member, Hiroshige Ichirō. I was invited to the house of the *Nihon jiji hyōron* employee, and attended barbeques with the followers of Shinsei Bukkyō in three consecutive summers. Yamaguchi also took me to the Shinsei Bukkyō headquarters, and we talked extensively over meals and coffee. After my co-authored book in Japanese was published, I followed up with further meetings with Yamaguchi and Hiroshige, as well as female conservative activists involved in the Ube and Chiba cases.[18]

As a result of my attempts to listen to their religious views, everyday lives, and thoughts on feminism and *danjo kyōdō sankaku*, it became clear to me that the backlash was in fact a very strategic move, carefully planned and organized in great detail by the conservatives. Yamaguchi was a major force behind the Ube ordinance. He successfully organized local politicians and other religious organizations, and assumed the leadership of the conservative movement against feminism in Ube and, later, nationally through the paper and behind-the-scenes organizing. Being a modest person, Yamaguchi never openly claimed the ordinance as his achievement, but it was indisputably clear that he singlehandedly led much of the campaign behind the scenes.

Local politicians started to create networks across Japan as their cities gradually worked on the ordinances. For this purpose, Yamaguchi told me, it was necessary to intentionally write overly sensationalistic stories on feminism in the *Nihon jiji hyōron* and other conservative media, as these media clearly recognized their role as agenda setters. Making conservative people—especially politicians—aware of the importance of the local ordinances was the key goal. They struggled to get fellow conservatives interested in the issues surrounding family and gender, rather than in such issues as national defense and politics. Based on my interaction with the people of *Nihon jiji hyōron*, I also learned that the conservatives' practices might not necessarily be the same as what they profess in their writings. For example, while they have argued for the importance of protecting professional housewives, I actually found that conservative women and the wives and mothers of male conservatives whom I met were mostly working women, in part- or full-time jobs.

Even though Yamaguchi does not like the principles of the Basic Law, with his belief in the significance of parliamentary democracy, he felt that he had no choice but to accept the unanimous passage of the Basic Law in the Diet. Thus, he adopted the strategy of using the law to create ordinances that could nullify the feminist intent of the law and turn the law on its head for the benefit of the conservatives. At the core of Yamaguchi's criticism against feminism and *danjo kyōdō sankaku* was the resistance against the "model ordinance" idea promoted by feminist scholars, specifically, the idea that the gender equality promotion ordinances from urban prefectures could become the model for all of Japan and could be enacted with only minor changes.[19] He was against the idea that the ordinance should come from urban centers, written by bureaucrats and scholars. Rather, he emphasized the necessity for local politicians to become much more aware of the power of such ordinances, and be directly involved in their making. In organizing the movement, the conservatives also emphasized concepts such as local citizens' (especially women's) voices and grassroots movements, which had been much more connected to leftist movements.[20] When I met him in 2013 Yamaguchi also told me that, as a conservative nationalist, everything he did was also for the national interest, or *kokueki*. Further, he emphasized that to work on both local and national levels at the same time was the key strategy of his activism.

The process followed by conservatives in organizing their movement was not necessarily the top-down process from the national center that feminists, myself included, imagined them to employ. Leadership came from small-scale organizations with deeply committed members that may not previously have been central to the conservative hierarchy. While new leaders like Yamaguchi used the already existing conservative networks to revise the way history is presented in school textbooks, and created new ties and networks, they also strengthened their connections with mainstream conservative organizations and media, such as Nippon Kaigi and its affiliates, and Sankei. With the combination of both local activities led by small-scale organizations and local politicians, and large-scale dissemination of information via national conservative networks, the conservatives effectively spread the movement against feminism.

Sekai Nippō and "Sexual Orientation"

I interviewed many feminists who pointed out that *Sekai nippō* was the most influential conservative voice against feminism, and the leader of the backlash against it. In the mid-2000s, the paper stood out among other papers for its skilled use of its website to spread its claims. The paper's supporters actively used blogs and message boards to disseminate their voices. *Sekai nippō* is closely connected to the Unification Church, although it is not defined as an official organ of the church. Originally established in South Korea by Reverend Sun Myung Moon in 1954, the Unification Church has a long history of being involved in conservative and anti-communist activism in postwar Japan.[21] The religion considers marriage via mass wedding ceremonies, with a partner designated by the church, to be a necessary step in the creation of the "ideal family," which is the starting point of a holy world and heaven. Married couples are encouraged to have as many children as possible. The Unification Church and *Sekai nippō* also have a strong stance against premarital sex, abortion, and homosexuality, and promote abstinence-only sex education, as well as the idea of intelligent design.

Since June 2009, I have met with people associated with *Sekai nippō* multiple times, and particularly with two of its reporters, Kamono

Mamoru and Yamamoto Akira, both in their mid-fifties, who were covering the *danjo kyōdō sankaku* issue extensively. When I first met Yamamoto at the paper's office in Shibuya in 2009, I learned from him that it was the "extremely radical" content of the gender equality ordinance of Miyakonojō City, Miyazaki Prefecture, that made him wary about the direction of *danjo kyōdō sankaku* ordinances and policies in general. In 2004, this ordinance passed by just one vote. Miyakonojō is a rural city whose main industry is livestock farming. The residents said repeatedly that this area has a tradition of male chauvinism often associated with the Tokugawa-era (1603–1868) Satsuma Domain, to which Miyakonojō once belonged. And yet it also passed a highly controversial gender equality ordinance bill with a clause protecting the rights of individuals regardless of their sex/gender and sexual orientation. The ordinance was the first in Japan that clearly referred to the rights of gay, lesbian, bisexual, and transgender people and other sexual minorities.

In addition to the content, the process of drafting the Miyakonojō ordinance was unique; rather than using ordinances from other prefectures and municipalities as models, an ordinance committee composed of Miyakonojō citizens conducted surveys, interviews, and other research to uncover the problems that residents faced. A local organization working on issues related to LGBT people also participated in this process actively, and formed a coalition with local politicians. Furthermore, these groups did not include feminist scholars and intellectuals from outside of the Miyakonojō area. Thus, the process of making and passing the 2004 ordinance was much more grassroots-based than in many other cities, and included lots of discussion of the content of the ordinance and the concept of *danjo kyōdō sankaku* by citizens. The conservative mayor, Iwahashi Tatsuya, proposed the bill, and the Japan Communist Party and Social Democratic Party supported it, while the Liberal Democratic Party (LDP) representatives were divided. This political situation of a conservative mayor working with the Communist Party has been rare in Japanese politics.

In 2006, however, Mayor Iwahashi lost his bid at reelection, and the new conservative mayor, Nagamine Makoto, backed by the people who opposed the gender equality ordinance, proposed a revision of the ordinance. The new ordinance they eventually implemented merely states that all people's human rights should be protected, without use of the term "sexual orientation."

Sekai nippō, in collaboration with local politicians and local Unification Church followers, was heavily involved in the struggle over the Miyakonojō ordinance, including the replacement of the mayor with someone amenable to the ordinance's revision. The paper led the revision movement both in 2004, when the original ordinance passed, and 2006, when the ordinance was modified to delete the term "sexual orientation." Yamamoto Akira, a reporter from the paper, visited the city multiple times from Tokyo and published many articles on the issue in *Sekai nippō*.

Clearly, the core concern for *Sekai nippō* was not "gender" in general, but the inclusion of the term "sexual orientation" in the ordinance.[22] This is in contrast to the concerns of *Nihon jiji hyōron*, which primarily regarded gender roles and traditional family values as highly significant. Yamamoto writes that including clauses on the rights of sexual minorities was a sign of the "extremist gender free" part of feminists' agenda to promote "homosexuality" among citizens with the feminist aim of creating a "free-sex commune."[23] When I met with people of *Sekai nippō*, they often said things such as "homosexuality is a disease, so it can and should be cured."

As noted above, academic feminists considered the backlash to be an attack against the concept of "gender." The examples from Ube and Miyakonojō, however, demonstrate that the concept of "gender" might not be the primary target of conservative attacks after all. Rather, as I have just illustrated, *Nihon jiji hyōron* questioned the way that gender equality ordinances were introduced, discussed, and imposed from the center to the periphery, and the major concern for *Sekai nippō* was sexuality—in particular, sexual orientation and sex education—rather than gender.

Reexamining *Danjo Kyōdō Sankaku*

Feminists, particularly feminist scholars, did not pay much attention to the conservatives' strategies in their writing and academic presentations, and feminist scholars and other academics whom I interviewed for this study also saw the conservatives' actions as top-down moves directed by national-level large organizations, such as Nippon Kaigi. However, the conservatives were much more grassroots than feminists imagined. Feminists also grossly underestimated the role that religion played in organizing the movement, as well as in reaching out to rural, working-class people who may have felt alienated by gender equality centers and feminist organizations. The anti-feminists whom I met were friendly and humble people who had no trouble talking to and gaining the trust of other citizens in local communities. They were not ignorant people lacking an understanding of feminism, nor did they make outrageous claims in their everyday lives. Rather, the conservatives' kind and modest personalities, their ability to explain issues in readily understandable language, and their skill at developing grassroots networks contributed to their success. These assets combined with other resources and strategies—including ties to mainstream conservative organizations, media, and politicians, as well as active use of the Internet—to make them successful at challenging and undermining feminist efforts to promote gender equality ordinances and other *danjo kyōdō sankaku* projects in local communities.

Nihon jiji hyōron editor-in-chief Yamaguchi posed a question to me at a family restaurant while we were having coffee: "What has been the result of the past ten years, since the Basic Law for a Gender Equal Society was enacted?" He said that the problem of *danjo kyōdō sankaku* might be that even ten years after the passage of the Basic Law, the intent of the policies remains unclear. Yamaguchi asked me, how did such laws change the actual lives of people in local communities? Yamaguchi's criticism of such feminist-inspired policies as ineffective in changing the everyday lives of struggling people suggests that *danjo kyōdō sankaku* policies may pose problems from a feminist perspective as well. That is, particularly in rural areas, *danjo kyōdō sankaku* policies and practices—which are concentrated mostly on educational projects and seemingly irrelevant cultural activities in which many of the participants are retired, middle-class, and elderly citizens—have not brought about many concrete changes in the lives of women. For example, Saitō Masami shows that the events and workshops held at local gender equality centers in some cities in Toyama Prefecture ranged from cooking classes for men, to skits with the theme of being kind to the elderly while protecting traditional values (including the extended family ideal), to providing dating opportunities for young women and men, and even to holding arranged marriage workshops for the parents of sons and daughters in search of marriage partners.[24] Ironically, some conservatives whom my co-researchers and I interviewed have been using the systems introduced by feminists under *danjo kyōdō sankaku*, such as the grievance system, much more actively than feminists. Hence, the lack of clarity of the *danjo kyōdō sankaku* concept, combined with conservative backlash and subsequent self-restraint of the local and national governments, suggests that *danjo kyōdō sankaku* now seems to be perceived by conservatives as nonthreatening, and as a result many of the backlashers have lost interest in criticizing it. Instead, they have begun to mobilize this framework in support of their own interests.

Anti-feminist conservatives whom I interviewed also mentioned how much privilege feminists gained by building and operating the centers, given that they were provided a budget for *danjo kyōdō sankaku* seminars, for buying feminist books, and employing many feminists, all with tax money. Conservatives lacked interest in the realities of the labor conditions of the workers at the centers, and the limited amount of monetary resources that actually supported feminist groups there. Privileged, elite feminist leaders, such as feminist scholars who give lectures at the centers and become members of governmental committees on *danjo kyōdō sankaku*, seem to be the only visible figures for the conservatives and, likely, for many others too.[25] Yet in reality, women workers at gender equality centers that are supposed to promote women's rights and independence are unable to fully support themselves given their positions as temporary workers with low wages who cannot renew their contracts beyond three years.[26] The workers are far from being elite, and they are living lives that run counter to what a gender-equal society should help foster—that is, labor conditions in which both women and men have stable jobs and earn decent wages. This demonstrates the painful reality that *danjo kyōdō sankaku* policies lacked concrete measures to fight against gender-based discrimination, and that its resources have gone toward goals that have little to do with creating a gender-equal society.

In December 2012, the conservative Liberal Democratic Party regained control of the government, with the ultra-conservative Abe Shinzō becoming prime minister. This significantly added to the already unclear and troubling direction of *danjo kyōdō sankaku*. The Abe administration now avoids using *danjo kyōdō sankaku*, and instead refers to "*josei no katsuyaku*," or "women's active roles (in society)." Claiming "womenomics" (*ūmanomikkusu*) as one of his core economic policies, Abe and his administration also tout support for building "*josei ga kagayaku shakai*," namely a "society in which women shine." And yet, in this neoliberal vision of Japan that appears to resonate with certain strands of liberal feminist discourse, the "society in which women shine" in their "active roles" is one in which the "shining" is limited to a small number of elite women. In this vision of society, a majority of women are still expected to be "active" as laborers who are part of a cheap labor force working to strengthen Japan's faltering economy, as mothers increasing Japan's troublingly low birthrate, and as caregivers taking care of Japan's rapidly increasing elderly population, but not as individuals actually benefiting from gender equality and women's rights.[27] Even worse, the most heavily promoted policy by the minister in charge of women's empowerment, Arimura Haruko, in 2015 was the "Japan Toilet Challenge," the idea that quality of life for women starts with pleasant toilets. This seemingly trivial policy was the most heavily promoted by the government. Then, in September 2015, Prime Minister Abe unveiled the slogan "all hundred million [Japanese citizens] taking an active part" (ichi oku sō katsuyaku), which goes beyond "women's active roles." Abe then appointed a new male minister for promoting dynamic engagement of all citizens, Katō Katsunobu, who is also in charge of women's empowerment and gender equality. With "all hundred million taking an active part" policies, even "women's active roles" are becoming quickly forgotten.[28]

Under these conditions, it is even more important to reflect critically on the policies and practices, past and present, under the rubric of *danjo kyōdō sankaku*. With the current (as of early 2017) relatively high approval rating of Prime Minister Abe, a strong push for the revision of the postwar Constitution—including not only a revision of Article 9, renouncing war and the maintenance of a military force, but also of Article 24, stipulating equality between the sexes within marriage—is in the foreseeable future.[29] The revision of the latter article might be seen as part of a move toward the mobilization of women to shore up traditional family values and, consequently, a conservative vision of the Japanese nation, similar to that embodied in the Meiji Constitution.[30] At this juncture, it would seem impossible to resist these conservative moves to weaken women's social status by employing liberal language that has already been co-opted by conservatives. As this chapter has demonstrated, feminists and feminist scholars should not adopt the rhetoric of "women's active participation in society" without adequate critical reflection on what has happened with the language of "gender free" and "*danjo kyōdō sankaku*" over the last twenty years.

Notes

The author would like to thank the editors of this volume, Julia Bullock, Ayako Kano, and James Welker, as well as Norma Field, Bethany Grenald, Saitō Masami, and Setsu Shigematsu for their valuable comments and editorial help. Funding to support this research was provided by a Suntory Foundation Grant for the Humanities and the Social Sciences, a Scholarship and Creativity Grant from Montana State University, and the Japan Committee at the University of Chicago's Center for East Asian Studies.

1   While it cannot be denied that feminist activism against gender discrimination played a role in the passage of this law, there are two other major factors behind its passage. First, the discussions and action plans suggested by the United Nations, such as those proposed at the International Women's Conference in Beijing held in 1995, impacted the Japanese government. Secondly, Japanese society, which was experiencing extreme economic and social change, was in need of new labor power due to the low birthrate, rapid aging of society, and long-term recession. In other words, there was a definite political and bureaucratic interest behind the passage of this law. See Patricia Boling, "State Feminism in Japan?" *U.S.–Japan Women's Journal*, no. 34 (2008): 69–71; Tomomi Yamaguchi, "'Gender Free' Feminism in Japan: A Story of Mainstreaming and Backlash," *Feminist Studies* 40, no. 3 (Fall 2014): 543–546; and Yamaguchi Tomomi, Saitō Masami, and Ogiue Chiki, *Shakai undō no tomadoi: Feminizumu no "ushinawareta jidai" to kusa no ne hoshu undō* (Tokyo: Keisō Shobō, 2012), 12–13.

2   Gender Equality Bureau Cabinet Office, "Basic Law for a Gender Equal Society," http://www.gender.go.jp/english_contents/about_danjo/lbp /laws/pdf/laws_01.pdf, last accessed January 31, 2016.

3   For more detailed discussion of the term "*danjo kyōdō sankaku*" and the contention among feminists over the term "*byōdō*," see Ayako Kano, "Backlash, Fight Back, and Back-Pedaling: Responses to State Feminism in Contemporary Japan," *International Journal of Asian Studies* 8, no. 1 (2011): 43–45.

4   For more information on municipal women's centers, see chapter 3, "Feminism and Bureaucracy—Women's Centres," in Laura Dales, *Feminist Movements in Contemporary Japan* (London: Routledge, 2009), 66–82.

5   Yamaguchi, Saitō, and Ogiue, *Shakai undō no tomadoi*.

6   On the concept of "gender free," see Tomomi Yamaguchi, "'Gender Free' Feminism in Japan," 541–572.

7 Feminists organized discussions at academic conferences and activist symposiums, issued a Q&A document on the backlash, published books and articles on the theme, developed a new listserv, and created websites proclaiming that they were fighting against the backlash.

8 For example, the symposium that feminist scholars and activists held in the fall of 2005, organized after the Kokubunji City incident, was entitled "Symposium to Discuss the Concept of Gender." The proceedings of the symposium may be found in Wakakuwa Midori, Minagawa Masumi, Katō Shūichi, and Akaishi Chieko, eds., *Jendā no kiki o koeru: Tettei tōron bakkurasshu* (Tokyo: Seikyūsha, 2006).

9 Ueno Chizuko, "Bakkurasshu-ha no kōgeki no honmaru wa jendā da! Fukui tosho tekkyo to Kokubunji jiken no tenmatsu," *Tsukuru* (November 2006).

10 Satō Fumika, "Femizumu ni iradatsu 'anata' e: Ikari wa doko e mukau beki na no ka," *Ronza* (April 2006): 215–216; Kanai Yoshiko, *Kotonatte irareru shakai o: Joseigaku jendā kenkyū no shiza* (Tokyo: Akashi Shoten, 2008), 225.

11 Satō, "Feminizumu ni iradatsu 'anata' e," 215, 216.

12 Kanai, *Kotonatte irareru shakai o*, 225.

13 Mitsui Mariko and Asakura Mutsuko, eds., *Bakkurasshu no ikenie: Feminisuto kanchō kaiko jiken* (Tokyo: Shunpōsha, 2012).

14 For a review of feminist characterization of "backlashers," see Yamaguchi, Saitō, and Ogiue, *Shakai undō no tomadoi*, 38–44.

15 On Nippon Kaigi, see David McNeill, "Nippon Kaigi and the Radical Conservative Project to Take Back Japan," *Asia-Pacific Journal* 13, issue 48, no. 4 (December 14, 2015), http://apjjf.org/-David-McNeill/4409; and Sato Kei, Hayashi Keita, and Sasagase Yuji, "Japan's Largest Rightwing Organization: An Introduction to Nippon Kaigi," trans. Victor Koschmann, *Asia-Pacific Journal* 13, issue 47, no. 5 (December 14, 2015), http://apjjf.org/-Mine-Masahiro/4410.

16 "Sensible" (*ryōshiki-teki na*) was the term frequently used in the coverage of the movement in *Nihon jiji hyōron*, by which supporters mean an ordinance to protect traditional gender roles and conservative family values. The original postwar conservative movement to use the language of bringing back "good sense" (*ryōshiki*) was in fact the anti-Marxist, anti-communist movement first promoted by Shinsei Bukkyō in the 1960s, and the idea has been emphasized frequently by the religion since then.

17 The Ube City Gender Equality Promotion Ordinance is posted at http://www.city.ube.yamaguchi.jp/kurashi/shiminjinken/danjokyoudou/jourei/index.html.

18 The conservatives whom I interviewed were aware of my stance as a
feminist who does not agree with their position on issues related to gender
and sexuality. They likely cooperated with my research request, at least
to a certain extent, due to its timing. After 2008 when I did most of my
research on this theme, the conservatives considered the struggles over
danjo kyōdō sankaku to be settled, having concluded with the passage of
the Second Basic Plan for Gender Equality enacted in December 2005.

19 Yamashita Yasuko, Hashimoto Hiroko, and Saitō Makoto, *Danjo kyōdō
sankaku suishin jōrei no tsukurikata* (Tokyo: Gyōsei, 2001), 2–3.

20 A local feminist activist and scholar in Ube, as well as the city's Japan
Communist Party representatives, also indicated to me in my interviews
that one of the major factors that caused the eventual passage of the
conservative-friendly ordinance was the top-down, "model ordinance"
approach taken by Ube City and committee members, without much
discussion of its contents by the committee and local citizens.

21 The Unification Church and its political organization Kokusai Shōkyō
Rengō (International Federation for Victory over Communism), founded
in 1968, have been involved in anti-communist activism in Japan since the
1960s and maintain ties with conservative politicians. In 2015, the Japan
branch of the organization officially changed its name to Sekai Heiwa
Tōitsu Katei Rengō (Family Federation for World Peace and Unification).

22 The reference to gender identity disorder could be seen in some other
ordinances, such as that of Koganei City in Tokyo. Ordinances including
the concept of "sexual orientation" were also introduced in Kotoura-chō,
Tottori Prefecture; Nishihara-chō, Okinawa Prefecture; and Sen'nan City,
Osaka Prefecture. See Saitō Masami, "Seiteki shikō o meibunka shita jōrei
ga seitei sareteita!" *Jendā to media burogu*, January 5, 2013, http://d
.hatena.ne.jp/discour/20130105.

23 Yamamoto Akira, "Dōseiai kaihōku ni mukau Miyakonojō-shi (ge),"
Sekai nippō, August 31, 2003.

24 Yamaguchi, Saitō, and Ogiue, *Shakai undō no tomadoi*, 211–212, 218–219.

25 In addition to the labor issue visible in the local government and the
public gender equality centers, there is an additional issue: within
feminist organizations themselves, the exploitation of women's labor is
also a problem related to the economic struggles of women workers in
general, but it frequently remains unaddressed, and several organizations
have faced labor disputes with former workers. The lack of critical
discussion on working conditions within feminist organizations could
be a factor that contributes to the further spread of the discourse about
"privileged feminists." See Yamaguchi, Saitō, and Ogiue, *Shakai undō no
tomadoi*, 318.

26 See Sawai Hidekazu, "Josei no jiritsu karamawari: Kakuchi no danjo kyōdō sankaku sentā," *Chūnichi shinbun*, March 29, 2013, on the labor condition of women workers at gender equality centers.

27 In August 2015, a new law to promote "women's active roles" was passed by the Diet. In September 2015, the Worker Dispatch Law was revised to allow companies to hire temporary workers as long as they want on the condition that they replace the workers every three years. With the revised Worker Dispatch Law, it became even clearer that the "society in which women shine" is limited to elite women, while the dispatched, temporary, and part-time workers become much more easily fired in three years, and their chances for becoming full-time workers are now much slimmer. Thus, only a very limited number of women will actually flourish under Abe's "womenomics," while it is likely that the wage gap among women will increase further. See Tomomi Yamaguchi, "Will Women Shine if Toilets Shine? The Abe Government's Convoluted 'Womenomics,'" *CGS Newsletter*, September 2015, http://web.icu.ac.jp /cgs_e/2015/09/will-women-shine-if-toilets-shine-the-abe-governments -convoluted-womenomics.html.

28 Tomomi Yamaguchi, "Ichioku sō katsuyaku to kenpō 24-jō no kaiaku e no ugoki," *Onnatachi no 21-seiki*, no. 84 (December 2015): 46–47.

29 Japanese conservative parties and citizens' movements, such as the Liberal Democratic Party and the Japan Conference, have been engaging in an effort to revise the postwar Constitution. The LDP, for example, came up with their own proposed revised version, with many parts they sought to delete or edit from, or to supplement, the current Constitution. See Colin P. A. Jones, "The LDP Constitution, Article by Article: A Preview of Things to Come?" *Japan Times*, July 2, 2013. Since 2004 I have been attending various study meetings and symposiums by conservative groups and reading their newsletters. Based on these sources, it is clear that there are three points that the conservative groups consider as priorities in their quest to revise the postwar Constitution: 1) the addition of a clause on emergencies that would give the prime minister the power to declare a state of emergency (and thereby limit fundamental human rights); 2) the addition of a phrase on traditional family values, and the revision of Article 24, which currently declares equality between women and men to be the basis of marriage and the family; and 3) the revision of the second paragraph of Article 9, which states, "land, sea, and air forces, as well as other war potential, will never be maintained," so that Japan would be able to build and maintain a military with the potential to engage in war. Having attended many conservative gatherings and study meetings in 2015 on constitutional reform, I am convinced that, among these three

proposed changes, the revision of Article 24 is the highest priority among conservatives, and it is said to be the ultimate goal for Prime Minister Abe in his efforts to revise the Constitution.

30 On December 16, 2015, the Supreme Court upheld a law that requires married couples to have the same surname. This issue has been a major issue for the conservatives, particularly Nippon Kaigi, which has argued since its establishment in 1997 that having the same surname is critical to maintaining traditional family values in Japan. For news coverage of the issue, see Jonathan Soble, "Japan's Top Court Upholds Law Requiring Spouses to Share Surname," *New York Times*, December 16, 2015, http:// www.nytimes.com/2015/12/17/world/asia/japan-court-ruling-women -surnames.html.

PART II

Rethinking Education
and Employment

THE CHAPTERS IN THIS SECTION all rethink conventional assumptions regarding women's education and labor from a feminist perspective, meaning that they seek to disrupt ideologies of gender that assume binary distinctions between women's labor that is necessarily performed in "private" space, and men's labor that is presumed to belong to the "public" sphere. In the process, they also rethink conventional assumptions about Japanese feminism, arguing for a more complex and sophisticated understanding of the periodization and methodological approaches currently brought to bear on the topics of women's education and labor in modern Japan.

This part begins with Julia Bullock's chapter on the feminist thought of Koizumi Ikuko (1892–1964), a prewar educator and feminist activist whose arguments about gender difference and the purpose of women's education contrasted markedly with contemporary ideologies that expected women to embody the "good wife, wise mother" ideal. Bullock's discussion of Koizumi's thought illustrates the complexity of an era that is typically characterized solely in terms of maternalist feminist discourse in the support of state projects like imperialism. Nancy Stalker and Chris McMorran likewise challenge postwar assumptions of a gendered division of labor that understands women's work as unpaid and confined to the domestic sphere, in contrast to a male breadwinner who performs labor in the public sphere for financial remuneration. Stalker's chapter explores the way that women appropriated the traditional art of ikebana, once a predominantly male preserve, as a form of gendered labor in the domestic sphere that could nevertheless be repurposed toward the goal of financial self-support, thus creating a new category of female breadwinner that disrupts facile distinctions between public and private space. McMorran's chapter likewise complicates this binary by portraying ostensibly domestic labor that allows some women to earn their own living without relying on male financial support. These *nakai*, or female workers in traditional Japanese inns, thus violate presumptions of feminine nurturing behavior as a selfless form of other-directed care, while simultaneously operating within those very stereotypes. In directing attention to female protagonists whose stories are typically left out of mainstream feminist scholarship, all three chapters fulfill this volume's purpose to "rethink" Japanese feminisms as a plural category.

—JCB

CHAPTER 5

~

Coeducation in the Age of "Good Wife, Wise Mother"

Koizumi Ikuko's Quest for "Equality of Opportunity"

JULIA C. BULLOCK

IN THE YEARS SINCE WORLD WAR II, Japanese women have increasingly taken advantage of the many Occupation-era legal reforms that were intended to promote gender equality. One of the most important of these reforms, the Fundamental Law of Education of 1947, formally "recognized" coeducation for the first time in Japanese history, thus officially encouraging schools from elementary to university levels to offer women the same educational opportunities as men. As a result of this new policy, women in the postwar period have completed increasingly higher levels of education in increasing numbers, which in turn has encouraged many women to envision life paths outside of the conventional roles of housewife and mother.[1]

While coeducation has frequently been portrayed by conservatives as a reform that was forced on the Japanese as a product of foreign intervention, more recent research has demonstrated that progressive Japanese educators played pivotal roles in the promotion and eventual adoption of coeducation as a goal of postwar educational reform. One such educator was Koizumi Ikuko (1892–1964), a graduate of the prestigious Tokyo Women's Upper Normal School (Tokyo Joshi Kōtō Shihan Gakkō) who went on to study in the United States, receiving a bachelor's degree in divinity from Oberlin College in 1927 and a master's degree in education from the University of Michigan in 1928 before enrolling in a PhD program at that institution in educational psychology. (Both schools were coeducational at the time of Koizumi's enrollment.) She returned to her native country in 1930 to collect data for her dissertation, and became involved with a group of progressive educators who were advocating for coeducation.[2] This was in the early 1930s, when the liberal era of "Taishō democracy" was rapidly giving way to the strident militarism and cultural conservatism that followed the Manchurian Incident of 1931, setting Japan on the road to total war. While the publication of Koizumi's 1931 treatise *Danjo kyōgakuron* (On coeducation) was thus badly timed,[3] the text found new life in the years immediately following World War II, and its arguments and presumptions are strikingly consistent with the language of subsequent Occupation-era directives on educational reform and gender equality.

Koizumi's work is important not just because her arguments for equality of educational opportunity were ahead of their time, but also because she couched those arguments in terms of the inherent equality of men and women. She argued for the potential of women to contribute to society on an equal footing with men, at a time when the Japanese educational system was structured around the assumption that women should be trained as "good wives and wise mothers" (*ryōsai kenbo*), whose contributions to society were best kept confined to the domestic realm. Though many women did in fact work outside the home at this time, such wage-earning labor was more often than not seen as a temporary prelude to marriage and motherhood, which was understood to be the natural and primary duty of Japanese women. *Danjo kyōgakuron* is thus both an argument for educational reform and a statement of feminist philosophy that challenged constructions of conventional gender roles, anticipating later works of liberal feminist theory such as Simone de Beauvoir's *The Second Sex*.

This chapter will examine four fundamental aspects of Koizumi's thinking about gender and education that highlight her contributions to prewar Japanese feminist thought. These four categories of analysis are: 1) her views on gender difference, 2) the relationship between femininity and motherhood, 3) the purpose of women's education, and 4) her understanding of the term "equality of opportunity." I will give particular attention to points of intersection and departure with other contemporary feminists and progressive educators. In the following discussion, I will demonstrate that while Koizumi's advocacy of coeducation for

Japan in the 1930s was by no means unprecedented, her understanding of the nature and importance of coeducation was underwritten by a presumption of "equality" between the sexes that was radical for its time, and remarkable for its anticipation of Occupation-era debates on gender and education that transformed the postwar discursive landscape. Understanding Koizumi's theories about sexual equality thus helps us to rethink histories of Japanese women during the 1930s that characterize them as compliant with the contemporary "good wife and wise mother" ideology of women's roles.

Gender Difference

In the preface to *Danjo kyōgakuron*, Koizumi lists four principles upon which her views on gender, as well as educational policy, are based: 1) the absolute equality of men and women as individuals; 2) the importance of distinguishing between men and women on the basis of physical and psychological difference; 3) the notion of equality between men and women as based on physical and psychological similarities; and 4) the importance of distinguishing between individual personalities (*kosei*) on the basis of individual (*kojinteki*) differences.[4] Careful examination of these four principles shows that they echo the same tension between "equality"- and "difference"-based arguments that underlie many modern feminist debates. Should feminists argue for equality on the basis of the similarities they share with men as human beings, or should they instead insist on a "separate but equal" status based on the understanding that men and women can be fundamentally different from one another and yet nevertheless equal?

Koizumi's answer to this dilemma is to privilege the value of the individual above and beyond the problem of difference or equality between the sexes. In other words, she argues that differences between individual members of the human species are far more salient than differences between men and women, in terms of their potential for intellectual growth and their ability to contribute meaningfully to society. In doing so, she effectively has to combat the presumption that individualism is fundamentally un-Japanese and anathema to the ideal of social harmony that was traditionally prized by Confucian cultures, including Japan, and more recently harnessed by the Japanese authorities for the project of modern nation-building.

She manages this tightrope act by situating her arguments within, not in opposition to, this logic of social harmony. She argues that although many Japanese might assume the principles of individualism and social harmony would naturally conflict with one another, this is not necessarily the case:

> To emphasize and display one's individuality does not mean to stubbornly insist on antisocial or socially deviant behavior. It is not to emphasize development of an evidently deranged character that is far removed from the realm of everyday society. It is said that unusual genius is in some ways identical to madness. [It is true that] scholars and artists of extraordinary talent often deviate from the commonly accepted rules of behavior. However, that does not mean that conversely, genius is equivalent to perverse and deranged behavior. Also, this kind of deranged genius is exceedingly rare. Therefore, the aim of today's education ultimately must be to create individuals with balanced characters who are able to cooperate with their fellow citizens. As it is often said, we live in an age that is based on the principles of social coexistence and harmony.[5]

What she offers, then, is the possibility of individualism harnessed in the service of society. According to Koizumi, the individual and society are not separable from one another but rather two sides of the same coin, such that development of one naturally entails the progress of the other.[6]

This focus on individual difference over gender difference not only contrasted with the contemporary societal focus on conformity and self-sacrifice for national goals, but also directly contradicted the underlying logic of education for women at that time, which was based on an assumption of fundamental difference between the sexes. As E. Patricia Tsurumi notes, "As early as 1877 . . . [Ministry of Education official] Nishimura Shigeki criticized [the notion of] identical primary school education for boys and girls. He argued that because the future work of men and women was different, after their earliest years at primary school, male and female pupils should be taught different subjects."[7] From 1879, the Japanese government began promoting gender-specific educational policies that by the end of the century would be articulated in terms of producing "good wives and wise mothers."[8] Furthermore, these policies

were promoted not only by government bureaucrats, but also by prominent female educators, who seized upon this ideology of conventional
femininity as a means of legitimizing and ennobling women's potential
to contribute in gender-specific ways to nationalist goals.[9]

Femininity and Motherhood

While Koizumi is careful in *Danjo kyōgakuron* not to mount a wholesale
attack on the prevailing ideology of "good wife, wise mother,"[10] she nevertheless insists that, while this model of femininity may offer some women
an important means of contributing to society, it should not be imposed
on all women in a categorical fashion. She decries attempts by conservatives who would try to contain women within women's space, whereby
"intoning that women's interests are in feminine things—the realm of
the private, the maternal, the kitchen—they would stamp women's fore-
heads with the fateful brand of 'mother.'"[11] Furthermore, she argues that
"confining women's activities to a sphere circumscribed by the maternal
is tantamount to treating human women like female animals" and creates an "obstacle to human progress."[12] Finally, in a rather amusing play
on the term *"ryōsai kenbo"* (good wife, wise mother), she acerbically notes
that although contemporary education for women repeatedly insists on
the importance of women's responsibilities as wives and mothers, nothing is said to men about the need to behave as *"ryōfu kenfu"* (good husband, wise father).[13] Her theoretical arguments against gender typing
thus stress the values of equality and fairness, as well as the illogical prop-
osition of reducing all women to a feminine stereotype rather than treating them as individuals.

While many prewar intellectuals, both male and female, wrote in
support of the notion of "equality of the sexes," most still ultimately
assumed the appropriateness of conventionally gendered roles for men
and women, based on Confucian assumptions of absolute difference
between the sexes and the contemporary emphasis placed on motherhood as a defining aspect of femininity. When male writers during the
Meiji period (1868–1912) discussed "equality," for example, they were
mainly concerned with relationships between husbands and wives within
domestic space, not in the public sphere, and their own treatment of
women in their private lives often failed to match their public pronounce-
ments.[14] Even progressive intellectuals like Ueki Emori, who argued for

equality of the sexes on the basis of natural rights, nevertheless based his discussion of women's rights on the value of their contributions to society as wives and mothers.[15] Furthermore, many prewar feminists also presumed motherhood to be a defining characteristic of feminine experience. For example, Hiratsuka Raichō, who challenged conventional stereotypes of femininity in many ways, nevertheless argued that women with children should be prohibited from working until their child turned five years of age, and that the state should protect women as mothers because of their contributions to the state as nurturers of future generations.[16] Thus, Koizumi's challenge to this logic of conventional femininity placed her in a distinct minority of opinion.

The Purpose of Education for Women

Gender-specific education prior to 1945 was of course intended to produce gender-specific outcomes, and here too Koizumi bucked "commonsense" notions of femininity by arguing that women should be afforded opportunities for personal and professional development beyond the conventional role of "good wives and wise mothers." The problem with education for girls today, Koizumi says, is that it merely reinforces traditional notions of women's roles, rather than nurturing girls' dreams for the future or cultivating their interests.[17] Present differences in professional outcomes for men and women are simply a reflection of the way they have been educated. She sees a future where women will make great strides into all sorts of professional activities; in her opinion, the day is near when "almost all" women will be both housewives and have occupations outside the home. Naturally this will require either an improvement in the conditions of household labor or the professionalization of it, but she "believes without a doubt" that in the future all types of housework will be professionalized and each individual will be able to choose their profession based on their own abilities and interests.[18]

Koizumi further argues for the practical utility of preparing women to support themselves financially, concluding that women must have financial independence in order to attain equality with men.[19] She notes that the "good wife, wise mother" lifestyle is not possible for the vast numbers of women who must work to help support their families.[20] She highlights the fact that the industrialized economy itself encourages women to enter the workplace, with new factory jobs deliberately marketed to women because they can be paid less than men for doing the same work.[21] Women's current low status and lack of ability to support themselves is the direct result of the poor education that they have received to date, and this is why they are willing to engage in paid labor even for low wages if it offers them the opportunity for freedom, equal rights, and internal satisfaction.[22] In making such arguments, she implies that the contemporary gendered division of labor is both unjust and impractical, and that providing women with equal opportunity in education and employment would benefit society as a whole, not merely individual women.

While Koizumi's argument that education for women should prepare them for more than housework and motherhood was not entirely unprecedented, few had argued so forcefully that women should be offered professional opportunities on par with men. Even as women in the prewar period took strides toward financial self-sufficiency, most preferred to do so in occupations that were considered compatible with gendered expectations of women's roles, as illustrated by the ikebana teachers discussed in Nancy Stalker's chapter in this volume, as well as the seamstresses and sewing instructors profiled in the research of Andrew Gordon.[23] By contrast, Koizumi argued that women should be given access to any occupation that matched their abilities and inclinations, including those positions conventionally assumed to be "masculine."

Like socialist feminist Yamakawa Kikue,[24] discussed in chapters by Elyssa Faison and Sarah Frederick in this volume, Koizumi made extensive use of social scientific evidence and theoretical argumentation to buttress her claims for gender equality. Koizumi's doctoral training in educational psychology allowed her to counter the objections of opponents of coeducation by employing the kind of scientific language that at the time was monopolized primarily by male intellectuals. She employed a wealth of statistical data on employment and education, references to the latest Western scientific research on biological sex difference and childhood development, and social scientific research on educational theory and pedagogical practice to support her claims that not only were women as intellectually capable as men, but also that educating boys and girls together on equal terms had demonstrably beneficial effects on society.[25]

Equality of Opportunity

The purpose of education, then, according to Koizumi, is to provide equality of opportunity so that each individual can develop their talents to their fullest potential. This does not mean educating all students with the same curriculum, but rather tailoring the curriculum to the individual desires and abilities of each student, regardless of gender. She thus defines coeducation as "assembling male and female students in the same facility, dividing them appropriately on the basis of subject matter and individual character (*kosei*), and employing educational methods appropriate to their individual needs and the demands of society."[26] While she does not deny the need to "discriminate" between students, she advocates doing so on the basis of ability and inclination rather than gender.[27]

She also stresses the social benefits of this type of equality of opportunity, not merely because it would enable each individual to maximize their contribution to social progress, but also because it would promote "harmony" and "cooperation" between the sexes that is currently lacking. She insists that instructing students in social adaptation and cooperation must become an important objective of education. In her view, this necessarily entails educating men and women together so that they can develop mutual understanding based on actual experience of one another, rather than the kind of idealized notions of the opposite sex that inevitably result from isolating them from one another during their formative years.[28]

> Unless all people are able to stand as resolute selves on the basis of equal status relative to one another as independent individuals, we cannot expect a properly harmonious society. . . . Men and women must be absolutely independent individuals in this sense. However, in our country the relative social status of men and women is far from this ideal. [Contemporary] education divides people into classes, and reinforces the boundaries between men and women. In particular, education for women subordinates them to men, rendering them inferior and incapable of attaining independence. Women have been raised to be weak, obedient, parasitic, and dependent playthings, and to see these qualities as virtuous. One important mission of today's education is to cultivate men and women as future members of society by training

them as sound and healthy individuals based on a foundation of equality. I am proclaiming the necessity of coeducation as a means of fundamentally revolutionizing our conventional educational system, which is crippled and imperfect.[29]

The strident tone of Koizumi's attack on women's status as "weak" and "parasitic" creatures underscores not only the passion with which she defended coeducation as a moral good, but also the fact that her understanding of "equality of opportunity" necessarily included gender equality.

However, this definition of "equality of opportunity" set Koizumi's arguments apart from those of other progressive educators of the time, many of whom were more concerned with addressing problems of class difference than gender discrimination. In 1937, Prime Minister Konoe Fumimaro established an Education Council (Kyōiku Shingikai) to make recommendations to the government for educational reform. While this council recommended establishing higher schools (*kōtō gakkō*) for women that would parallel existing schools for men, as a way of preparing more women to compete successfully for entrance to universities, most of those advocating this step nevertheless seem to have assumed that such higher school curricula would include substantial amounts of coursework in home economics. Debates concerning whether to establish universities for women similarly presumed their purpose to be gender-specific training in conventionally feminine subjects. Although some committee members took a different view, arguing that women should be offered the full range of educational opportunities extended to men, these voices did not carry the day, and the government declined to act on any of the proposed gender-equality measures.[30] Koizumi's claim that "equality of educational opportunity" must necessarily include gender parity was thus somewhat radical for its time, even within the context of progressive educational circles.

Conclusion

On the strength of publication of *Danjo kyōgakuron*, Koizumi helped to form the Coeducation Research Society (Danjo Kyōgaku Mondai Kenkyūkai), in cooperation with progressive educators like Noguchi Entarō, Ichikawa Genzō, Harada Minoru, Yasui Tetsuko, Kōra Tomiko, and Fukushima Shirō. The group first met on April 13, 1932, and continued meeting periodically over the next several years. By the fourth meeting, on March 15, 1933, they were making plans to petition the Diet to consider coeducational reforms. The actual text of the petition was based on a document drafted by Koizumi, entitled "A Statement in Favor of Coeducation" (*Danjo kyōgaku e no shuchō*). While the petition was adopted by the lower house on March 25, 1933, it failed in the more conservative upper house. Subsequent attempts to persuade the Ministry of Education of the wisdom of coeducation were similarly unsuccessful.[31]

However, the specific changes to the law requested in the petition bear striking similarity to the coeducational reform initiatives promoted by Occupation staff during the negotiations leading up to the Fundamental Law of Education of 1947. Koizumi and her colleagues specifically advocated for repeal of the sections of the law governing elementary school education that mandated separate education of girls and boys. Additionally, they requested removal of other legal barriers to coeducation, including language from the Middle School Law (Chūgakkō rei) and Higher School Law (Kōtō gakkō rei) stipulating that these schools were designed for boys, so as to allow girls to enroll as well.[32] They also advocated that the Girl's Higher School Law (Kōtō jogakkō rei), which provided for separate education of girls beyond elementary school, be eliminated entirely, effectively creating one unified system of secondary education that would be open to both boys and girls. The petition also requested amendment of the requirements for admission to technical colleges (*senmon gakkō*), to allow women to enroll alongside men at this level.

Thus, the streamlined and coeducational system proposed by the Coeducation Research Society anticipated the wholesale overhaul of the Japanese educational system during the Occupation period in many respects. This suggests a need to rethink narratives of Occupation-era reform that characterize coeducation as a reform that was forced on the Japanese, and by implication alien to the values and expectations of Japanese society. It is clear that some progressive Japanese educational reformers advocated this system well in advance of Occupation-era reforms. This research also suggests that we rethink the history of prewar Japanese feminism to include voices like Koizumi, whose vision of sexual equality was not qualified by efforts to work within the prevailing discourse of "good wife and wise mother."

According to some Japanese sources, shortly after the end of World War II Koizumi was called into the office of the Civil Information and Education section of Occupation headquarters by a female staff member.[33] Upon arrival, she was confronted with an English-language translation of *Danjo kyōgakuron*, and asked if she was the author of the text. When she said yes, she was informed that the translation had been circulated among CI&E staff, who had concluded that coeducation should be promoted in Japan. Koizumi was thereupon offered a position as education advisor, which she turned down in order to focus on her duties as head of Obirin, the school that she and her husband were in the process of founding.

Although it is perhaps premature to conclude that Koizumi's influence on Occupation policy was decisive, it is clear that Koizumi and the American Occupation authorities were in pursuit of similar goals for similar reasons. U.S. policy documents from the pre-surrender and early Occupation period consistently stress the values of equality, individuality, and freedom of thought and expression that underline Koizumi's arguments for coeducation in *Danjo kyōgakuron*. While this may not be surprising given that Koizumi was herself educated partly in the United States, it is important to note that the bold future of equality of opportunity that Koizumi envisioned went well beyond what was available to American women at the time when she studied there. It is also important to note that while Koizumi's arguments for coeducation likewise went further than the proposals of other prewar progressives, she was not alone in advocating "equality of educational opportunity" at that time. Rather, Koizumi was part of a wave of liberal intellectuals whose calls for educational reform were unable to penetrate the cordon of militaristic propaganda that surrounded them in the 1930s. Such progressives would have to wait for the opportunity provided them by defeat and Occupation to see their reform agenda enacted.

Notes

1 According to Kimi Hara, "The percentage of girls within the appropriate age group entering upper secondary school (tenth through twelfth grade) doubled within a mere twenty-five-year period, from 47.4 percent in 1955 to 95 percent in 1979. Within the same period the percentage of young women studying at junior colleges increased eightfold and those in

four-year universities grew sixfold" (p. 104). See her chapter "Challenges to Education for Girls and Women," in *Japanese Women: New Feminist Perspectives on the Past, Present, and Future*, ed. Kumiko Fujimura-Fanselow and Atsuko Kameda (New York: The Feminist Press, 1995).

2   For a thorough biographical study of Koizumi, see Kurematsu Kaoru, *Koizumi Ikuko no kenkyū: Obirin Daigaku Kokusaigaku Kenkyūjo kenkyū shirīzu* 4 (Tokyo: Gakubunsha, 2000).

3   The publication information at the back of *Danjo kyōgakuron* says it was printed on October 1 and issued on October 5, 1931. The Manchurian Incident took place September 18, 1931. As Tomoko Akami notes, the national discourse quickly deteriorated after this point into "jingoism" and militaristic rhetoric. The subsequent election of Prime Minister Inukai Tsuyoshi in February 1932 by an "electorate [that] supported aggression in China provid[ed] a mandate that encouraged Japan to embark on fullscale war in China in 1937 and the Pacific War against the United States and the Allied forces subsequently." Akami further notes that Inukai's assassination on May 15, 1932 "mark[ed] the beginning of the end of parliamentary democracy in pre-war Japan." See Tomoko Akami, "When Democracy Is Not Enough: Japan's Information Policy and Mass Politics in Diplomatic and Economic Crisis in the 1930s," *Asia–Pacific Journal* 11, issue 15, no. 1 (April 15, 2013), http://japanfocus .org/-Tomoko-AKAMI/3926.

4   Koizumi Ikuko, *Danjo kyōgakuron* (Tokyo: Nihon Tosho Sentā, 1984), 12. All translations from this text are my own.

5   Ibid., 75.

6   Ibid., 76.

7   E. Patricia Tsurumi, "The State, Education, and Two Generations of Women in Meiji Japan, 1868–1912," *U.S.–Japan Women's Journal*, no. 18 (2000), 18.

8   Hashimoto Noriko, *Danjo kyōgakusei no shiteki kenkyū* (Tokyo: Ōtsuki Shoten, 1992), 33–34.

9   Sally A. Hastings profiles three such female educators in her article "Women Educators of the Meiji Era and the Making of Modern Japan," *The International Journal of Social Education: Official Journal of the Indiana Council for the Social Studies* 6, no. 1 (Spring 1991). See also Margaret Mehl, "Women Educators and the Confucian Tradition in Meiji Japan (1868–1912): Miwada Masako and Atomi Kakei," *Women's History Review* 10, no. 4 (2001). Even prominent institutions of higher education for women during the prewar period, such as Tsuda English Academy and Japan Women's University, were known for policing their students' behavior to ensure conformity with conservative notions of femininity.

See for example Barbara Rose, *Tsuda Umeko and Women's Education in Japan* (New Haven: Yale University Press, 1992); and Ann M. Harrington, "Women and Higher Education in the Japanese Empire (1895–1945)," *Journal of Asian History* 21, no. 2 (1987).

10 Koizumi, *Danjo kyōgakuron*, 62.

11 Ibid., 61.

12 Ibid.

13 Ibid., 75.

14 Hashimoto, *Danjo kyōgakusei no shiteki kenkyū*, 44–48. See also chapter 2 in Sharon L. Sievers, *Flowers in Salt: The Beginnings of Feminist Consciousness in Modern Japan* (Stanford, CA: Stanford University Press, 1983). For example, in spite of Mori Arinori's famed signing of a "marriage contract" that bound both parties to "equality in marriage," he bristled at the notion of legal equality for both sexes, clarifying his views in this way: "I indeed said that wives and husbands should be honored without distinction because they are on the same level. I absolutely did not touch on equal rights, however" (quoted in ibid., 21).

15 Julia Adeney Thomas quotes Ueki as arguing for the value of women's education as an instrument of nationalism: "Women are responsible for educating the household. If these women do not have patriotism, and do not think about politics, then they cannot awaken appropriate national sentiments in their children. . . . If mothers can raise their children in the national spirit it will bring great justice and benefits to all" (p. 155). See chapter 6 of her book *Reconfiguring Modernity: Concepts of Nature in Japanese Political Ideology* (Berkeley: University of California Press, 2001).

16 Hashimoto, *Danjo kyōgakusei no shiteki kenkyū*, 108. For a concise discussion in English of the debates surrounding "protection of motherhood" in the Taishō period, see Laurel Rasplica Rodd, "Yosano Akiko and the Taishō Debate over the 'New Woman,'" in *Recreating Japanese Women, 1600–1945*, ed. Gail Lee Bernstein (Berkeley: University of California Press, 1991).

17 Koizumi, *Danjo kyōgakuron*, 66.

18 Ibid., 67.

19 Ibid.

20 Ibid., 62–63.

21 Ibid., 65.

22 Ibid., 66.

23 See Andrew Gordon, *Fabricating Consumers: The Sewing Machine in Modern Japan* (Berkeley: University of California Press, 2012).

24 See E. Patricia Tsurumi, "Visions of Women and the New Society in Conflict: Yamakawa Kikue versus Takamure Itsue," in *Japan's Competing*

Modernities: Issues in Culture and Democracy, 1900–1930, ed. Sharon A. Minichiello (Honolulu: University of Hawai'i Press, 1998), 347–348.

25 References to Western scientific and educational theories permeate *Danjo kyōgakuron*. To offer just one example, in the course of a discussion of evolutionary theory in chapter 2 ("Kyōgaku kisoron"), Koizumi veers deeply into a rather technical analysis of genetic variation, including a sustained examination of eugenicist and statistician Karl Pearson's employment of the "correlation coefficient" to analyze the degree of dependence between two variables (p. 55).

26 Koizumi, *Danjo kyōgakuron*, 14.

27 Ibid., 13.

28 Ibid., 74.

29 Ibid., 77.

30 Hans Martin Kramer, "The Prewar Roots of 'Equality of Opportunity': Japanese Educational Ideals in the Twentieth Century," *Monumenta Nipponica* 61, no. 1 (Winter 2006). See pp. 538–539 for a discussion of attitudes toward college preparation for women.

31 Hashimoto, *Danjo kyōgakusei no shiteki kenkyū*, 221–222.

32 According to SCAP records, these same legal barriers to coeducation were specifically targeted by Occupation staff for elimination. See "Coeducation," Folder 12 ["Co-Education—Staff Studies"], Box no. 5391, GHQ/SCAP Records (RG 331), National Archives and Records Service.

33 See Hashimoto, *Danjo kyōgakusei no shiteki kenkyū*, 276; and Kurematsu, *Koizumi Ikuko no kenkyū*, 164–165. Both are relying on accounts of the incident by Shimizu Yasuzō, Koizumi's husband. Hashimoto cites his memoir, *Obirin monogatari*, while Kurematsu relies on essays by Shimizu in *Fukkatsu no Oka*, the university magazine published by Obirin Daigaku (vols. 71 and 120).

CHAPTER 6

~

Flower Empowerment

*Rethinking Japan's Traditional
Arts as Women's Labor*

NANCY STALKER

T HE 1950S AND 1960S IN JAPAN are sometimes referred to as the
Shōwa Genroku, as this era resembled the late eighteenth century in
terms of the marked increase in popular participation in the arts, particularly among women who flocked into studying traditional dance, tea
ceremony (*chanoyu*), and especially ikebana, the art of Japanese flower
arrangement.[1] The population of those studying ikebana swamped that
of all other arts at its peak in the 1960s. Nishiyama Matsunosuke, the
leading authority on Japan's traditional arts at that time, estimated a population of ten million ikebana practitioners in 1965, roughly 10 percent of
the population.[2] By the late 1960s, the top three ikebana schools, Ikenobo,
Sogetsu, and Ohara, had over a million students each, and a dozen or so
second-tier schools had up to 200,000 pupils each.[3] Schools themselves
multiplied at an incredible rate in the postwar period. In 1930, there were
500 schools. By the late 1960s there were over 3,000.[4]

Prior to World War II, ikebana was viewed as a necessary skill for
future brides and homemakers. Few female students aspired to become
teachers. Postwar ikebana, however, was reconceived as modern and
artistic while retaining firm roots in Japanese tradition; this potent combination was one factor in the massive wave of interest. Another factor
propelling Japanese women into ikebana was its popularity among foreign women during the Occupation, because following defeat by the
United States, many Japanese adopted and idealized all things American.

One author estimated that 95 percent of foreign women in Japan tried ikebana during this era; many became avid students and over 10,000 became licensed teachers themselves.[5] In the 1960s, the largest ikebana schools established branches in the United States and Europe to facilitate foreign interest. Such attention by Western women raised ikebana's status and profile in the eyes of Japanese women.

Hundreds of thousands of Japanese women became licensed ikebana teachers in postwar Japan, when women from all walks of life sought new avenues of employment in a devastated economy. War widows needed respectable and feasible sources of support; other women sought to supplement family income or make an independent living. Teaching ikebana or other traditional arts provided women with unprecedented professional opportunities but did not threaten normative gender roles. In this way it was similar to "home work" (naishoku) jobs described by Andrew Gordon—including sewing, embroidering, and crafts—that were commonplace among middle-class women after World War I and also did not challenge ideals of women as mothers and household managers.[6] Unlike the understanding of gender roles as unnecessarily restrictive of women's employment options espoused by Koizumi Ikuko, discussed by Julia Bullock in this volume, ikebana teachers utilized traditional gender roles to forge new employment opportunities. They engaged in domestic tasks gendered feminine, but did so for financial remuneration, disrupting received divisions between "public" and "private" labor.

Yet teachers of ikebana and other traditional arts have been missing from studies of women's labor in Japan, which have largely focused on the so-called blue-collar, pink-collar, and black-panty trades (i.e., factory work, office ladies, and sex industry workers). The 2013 edited volume, *Modern Girls on the Go: Gender, Mobility, and Labor in Japan*, added women in service industries like shop girls, stewardesses, and bus tour guides, seemingly minor jobs that "bring to light unexpected ways women have supported, even challenged the corporate structures underpinning the Japanese economy."[7] The focus of the volume is "modern girls," a category that, in the 1920s and 1930s in Japan, evoked immodesty, consumerism, and foreign influence. Like these girls, female ikebana teachers co-opted jobs once reserved for men and were culturally and economically significant, acting as the underpinning of the massive, multinational ikebana industry. Yet they were not stigmatized in the same way as "modern girls," but were instead highly respected and associated with traditional femininity. Perhaps feminist scholars of Japan have not addressed the realm of traditional arts because practices like ikebana and the tea ceremony demand conformity to gendered stereotypes of the female body as demure and servile. Nevertheless, while cloaked in tradition, ikebana offered women opportunities to become respected professionals and business owners in a manner unmatched by any other Japanese industry.

In this chapter, I trace the trajectory of women's opportunities in ikebana, beginning with early twentieth-century educational reforms that made ikebana an essential element of the curriculum for girls. Postwar educational reforms also facilitated the training of ikebana teachers in junior colleges. I examine the practical concerns of teachers and the increasing professionalization of the teacher workforce in the postwar period, the use of ikebana in other workplaces, and the ways in which women challenged the patriarchal *iemoto* (headmaster) system. I argue that adding ikebana and traditional arts to studies of women's labor helps us rethink Japan's modern economic development, especially postwar recovery and growth, in new ways that give greater consideration to women's hidden labor and social contributions.

Meiji Educational Reforms

In the Edo period (1603–1868), traditional arts were overwhelmingly male. Nishiyama estimates that only 1 percent of students in an average eighteenth-century tea school was female.[8] Ikenobo, the largest and oldest of all ikebana schools, accepted only males of the elite classes, refusing to teach not only women but also commoners. Male dominance in ikebana scarcely changed in the early Meiji period (1868–1912), although traditional arts overall went into steep decline following modernizing reforms. Meiji-era changes in women's compulsory education, however, led to a complete reversal of the gender ratio in ikebana in a few short decades. In 1899, the Ministry of Education mandated etiquette as a subject for higher girls' schools, a category that subsumed sewing and knitting, home economics, and deportment, among other topics. With the rise of official "good wife, wise mother" (*ryōsai kenbo*) ideology came the idea that women must create a pleasant home environment to help nurture the family and protect the nation.[9] To achieve equality with the West, Japanese gender relations would be based on a nuclear family system with separate spheres for men and women, the latter rooted in notions of mid-dle-class Victorian womanhood.

The patronage of high school girls and graduates was the most decid-ing factor behind the prewar growth of ikebana schools.[10] Always cog-nizant of the Western gaze, the Ministry of Education realized that pastimes like flower arranging and tea parties were viewed as feminine pursuits in the United States and Europe. In 1903, spurred by Imperial Prince Komatsu Akihito's "order for revival/renaissance of *kadō* (the way of flowers),"[11] the Ministry added ikebana and *chanoyu* to higher girls' school curriculums, noting that it might be taught outside of regu-lar school hours.[12] This is likely because most schoolteachers were nei-ther licensed nor qualified in these subjects at the time. In the Taishō period (1912–1926), as tea and ikebana were increasingly normalized as school subjects, many schools constructed special facilities for teaching these subjects on campus. By the 1920s and early 1930s, the tea ceremony and ikebana were universally accepted as significant aspects of the girls' school curriculum.[13] After graduation many students continued their study with the same teachers.

By that time, ikebana was no longer considered a male pursuit, nor a pastime limited to upper-middle-class women, but a domestic skill that all would-be brides should possess. In 1928, popular bridal manu-als (*hanayome bunko*) urged brides to use ikebana to give their homes an air of upper-class cultivation.[14] By 1942, these manuals claimed that proficiency in ikebana was expected regardless of the social class of the student, and it was even "shameful" for women not to count ikebana among their accomplishments.[15] It was not just higher school students and potential brides who were urged to take up ikebana, but also young working women subject to domestic training from paternalistic factory managers who assumed these women would become wives and mothers, in keeping with state ideals. Beginning in the 1920s, large factories such as Kanebō offered a variety of educational and cultural courses to help recruit young women, including a three-year program that matched girls' higher schools in offering the domestic and etiquette skills necessary for finding a desirable marriage partner.[16]

Despite the fact that female ikebana students greatly outnumbered male students by the first decade of the 1900s, the *iemoto* and the vast majority of senior teachers continued to be male. Before the Russo–Japanese War in 1904, few female students aimed at becoming teachers.

Given ikebana's new role in the girls' school curriculum, some widows who lost their husbands in the war began to pursue licenses as the means to a respectable self-sufficiency. During and after World War I, when many men left the profession of teaching ikebana for more lucrative jobs in industry, the number of middle-class women entering teaching as a career increased notably. Ohara estimates this population to have comprised around 10 percent of their students during this period.[17] In response to the rising cost of daily necessities, from rice to rent, newly educated middle-class daughters entered the job market as teachers to help support their families before marriage.[18] Other single, widowed, or divorced women sought to make an independent living.

Ohara, one of the three largest schools, attributes much of its success in this period to the efforts of Taira Ichiyō, a war widow who became one of their first female teachers.[19] The school was established in 1912, based on Ohara Unshin's new form of arrangement called *moribana*, a horizontal style that uses low basins and can incorporate Western flowers, in contrast with the existing, classical schools that featured upright styles and were limited to traditional materials. Ohara was able to expand rapidly because the other well-established schools allowed their licensed teachers to study *moribana*, at odds with the usual norms of the *iemoto–* disciple relationship, which limited students to practicing only the styles associated with the particular school to which they belonged.

Ichiyō had studied tea and ikebana since childhood. After her husband Shigeharu's death in the Russo-Japanese War, she was left to provide for seven children and thus obtained licenses to teach tea and ikebana at age thirty-four. In 1913, seeing an example of Ohara Unshin's new style in the magazine *Jogakusei gahō* (Female students' pictorial), she immediately became a disciple. She taught *moribana* to elite women and to many teachers from other ikebana schools. In 1920 Ichiyō's reputation as one of Ohara's leading authorities was cemented with her solo exhibition in Tokyo. She traveled from Hokkaido to Kyushu giving lectures on *moribana*, a fresh, new approach that appealed to emerging mass consumers tired of the static forms of classical ikebana.

Ichiyō was instrumental in creating cooperative regional teacher associations—a first among ikebana schools—which significantly strengthened Ohara's foundations for growth. As she traveled the nation, she convinced teachers from other ikebana schools to obtain *moribana* licenses. Realizing that such "outsider" teachers' primary loyalties were with their original schools, cooperative associations would provide a mechanism for teachers from disparate schools to meet, to learn, and practice Ohara styles and thus to maintain ties to Ohara headquarters. Ichiyō convinced the second *iemoto*, Kōun, to approve the new associations, even though they posed the danger of school secrets being co-opted by other schools. Kōun recognized that these outsider teachers were Ohara's most valuable resource for proselytization and decided to discard the long-standing norm of "secret" techniques by disseminating clear principles based on proportions and positions of flowers.[20]

While new schools increased in number throughout the prewar period, many of which incorporated modernist aesthetics adopted from Western art, ikebana did not reach mass proportions in terms of either the number of schools or students until the postwar period. The real boom in ikebana, from the Occupation forward, can be attributed to a number of factors, including Japan's national mission to become a "country of culture" (*bunka kokka*); the evolution of avant-garde styles that suited the more open postwar atmosphere that encouraged creativity and democratic participation; charismatic headmasters who competed fiercely amongst themselves; and the deep interest of Western women, who made ikebana appear glamorous and cosmopolitan. Another key factor was postwar educational reform and the establishment of women's junior colleges by leading ikebana schools.

Postwar Educational Reforms

In 1947, the U.S. Occupation, seeking an end to rigid centralized control over education, mandated an American-style school system, with nine years of compulsory schooling, three years of high school, and four years of college.[21] Only twelve four-year universities received official approval, and thus the demand to attend college outstripped supply immediately. To widen the door to college education, the Private School Law of 1949 allowed for the creation of junior colleges that would provide technical training in a shorter time frame than regular universities. Furthermore, the law limited the degree of interference the Ministry of Education could impose on these schools, prohibiting state control over issues such as tuition, fees, and enrollment limits.[22] Private junior colleges founded after 1950 varied in scale and quality; many provided short-term education for women in home economics or nursing, strongly resembling the prewar gender-segregated curriculum. By the early 1960s there were 321 junior colleges, comprising 70 percent of Japan's total number of institutions of higher education. Among the female students, 38.7 percent majored in domestic sciences.[23]

These developments in education opened the door for large ikebana schools to participate in the private education business. Ikenobo first established an accredited women's junior college in 1952, and its educational enterprises grew rapidly throughout the next decade. In June 1966, when interest in ikebana was peaking, it built Ikenobo Gakuen in central Kyoto at the cost of 350 million yen (nearly $1 million), aggressively raising the funds from Ikenobo members and assessing students special facilities' fees to help pay for construction loans.[24] The eight-floor Venetian-style building encompassed over 4,500 square meters and housed Ikenobo headquarters, galleries, studios, and classrooms for 700 students. In October of the same year, Ikenobo opened Ochanomizu Gakuin in Tokyo, the nation's largest ikebana facility, at a cost of 500 million yen. This facility accommodated 5,000 students and included a 1,500-person lecture hall, as well as lodging and restaurant facilities.[25] Ikenobo was not alone in its educational enterprises. According to Nishiyama, there were ten legally established junior colleges tied to sponsorship by ikebana schools.

Teacher Recruitment

From 1946 to 1956, a steep spike in demand for lessons required the largest schools to compete fiercely for qualified instructors in order to quickly absorb the new masses.[26] Ikenobo's junior colleges provided a ready pool of new teachers. Schools of ikebana without their own junior college could recruit teachers from amongst those seeking new avenues of employment, such as war widows and other women seeking self-support or supplemental family income. It was a general rule of thumb that a teacher with forty students could earn a living comparable to a salaryman. Teachers with an adequate student base even became *iemoto* in order to improve their earnings potential, often parting amicably from the original school. For a large fee, some classical schools agreed to allow spinoffs to include the name of the original within the name of the new school, providing instant credibility by association for budding headmasters. In this way, dozens of schools included terms like Ikenobo, Saga, etc., within their names. The majority of these new postwar *iemoto* were female, giving women unprecedented opportunities to become the leaders of small commercial enterprises.

Practically minded women who wished to be teachers carefully considered the opportunities offered by different schools. They were interested in factors like the ease, duration, and expense of teacher certification, the availability of curricular materials, and the reputation of the school. In the late 1950s, schools had elaborate systems for ranking pupils and teachers but most did not have a unified curriculum, although a few, including Ohara, had already developed textbooks in the prewar period. Sogetsu, which experienced the most rapid postwar growth, required teachers to attend classes at the headquarters several times each year but there were no textbooks or standards of instruction for beginning students. Instead, beginners were given a list of fifty principles, called *Sogetsu Ikebana Notes* (*Sogetsu ikebana nōto*), that offered pithy, ambiguous aphorisms to inspire student creativity, such as "All flowers are beautiful but not all ikebana is necessarily beautiful," and "Correct ikebana is not isolated from its era and contemporary lifestyles."[27] In order to compete effectively, however, by the mid-1960s, all large schools had created standard curricula designed for organized group classes. Furthermore, they rationalized their promotion systems, providing clear guidelines for teacher advancement based on units completed and qualifications demonstrated.

The time and tuition fees required to obtain a license were important concerns for would-be teachers. During the prewar period, the Adachi school grew dramatically when it shortened the time required to earn a teaching license to three years, in contrast with seven to ten for most schools. Adachi declined in the postwar period because of the *iemoto*'s refusal to embrace popular new avant-garde styles. In the late 1960s, Adachi Chōka tried to re-invigorate the school, building a seven-story facility in Shibuya and creating a new licensing system that took only a single year. Promotional materials claimed that one Adachi lesson was equivalent to a month of practice with other schools and emphasized the potential income opportunities for teachers.[28]

Other major schools also attempted to make the certification process as rapid and automatic as possible. In short, during the postwar boom, anyone could become a teacher if they invested the time and necessary fees, irrespective of ability. It was rumored that certain schools with pressing needs would instantly license anyone who paid the required fees.[29] Ikenobo, notorious for its long, laborious licensing process, cut its accreditations from thirty-three stages, requiring thirty years to obtain the highest qualifications, to eighteen stages.[30]

Ikenobo remained the most rigorous school, heavily focused on classical styles that allowed only traditional plant materials. In order to make Ikenobo more attractive to young women, its junior colleges began to issue a quick and easy special license called *sanshu ike* (three-variety ikebana) that used classical principles as a framework but focused more on color and allowed flexibility in selecting materials. It enabled Ikenobo to offer updated aesthetics more in tune with modern lifestyles and allow for individual creativity and freedom of choice.[31] The new system drew many young women to study at Ikenobo's colleges but became a source of confusion, as teachers from outside the junior college system, however senior, were not permitted to teach or exhibit *sanshu ike* styles, and junior college licensees were not allowed to automatically progress to higher levels of Ikenobo. The separate teaching tracks created controversy and tension between the junior colleges, teachers, and Ikenobo administration.

Ohara initiated some of the most substantive and innovative measures for teacher recruitment and retention, including its pension plan, a legally incorporated nonprofit retirement fund. It remains the only school with such a system. Under the initial plan, teachers were paid one thousand yen per month, receiving a lump sum at age sixty-five and a small monthly income until age eighty. The system demonstrated that Ohara had begun considering its teachers from a larger, "human resources" perspective, simultaneously allowing teachers, for the first time, to plan for a degree of independence and financial self-sufficiency in return for their professional service. In contrast with the public retirement system, which one had to enter by age twenty-five, Ohara's members could enter as late as age seventy.[32] The system was very progressive; in the mid-1960s, retirement plans were still relatively unknown among the public and many large Japanese corporations had yet to offer retirement benefits. Kikyōkai, an Ohara teachers' association formed in 1963, initiated and campaigned for the idea after discovering that many teachers were impoverished, even destitute. Ohara's pension plan required a large and growing membership to support the arrangement. It initially enrolled over 24,000 teachers, helping to secure their loyalty to Ohara, as few were willing to take financial losses resulting from switching schools or becoming independent. The system gave teachers a stake in the over-all success of the school, and they in turn worked hard to recruit and retain students.

Another facet of women's agency and empowerment via ikebana was arts education, providing teachers and student members with broader knowledge of art history and trends so they could be more confident in arranging and teaching, thereby creating a better informed and better educated professional workforce. In the 1950s, Ohara, Sogetsu, and Ikenobo all used their monthly journals to provide teachers and mem-bers with primers on art historical topics. In the prewar period, journals had focused on news of exhibitions or erudite essays on ikebana phi-losophy by senior teachers. The few "educational" articles centered on botany, detailing the characteristics of plants and flowers used. By 1951, Ohara's journal *Sōka* (Flower arrangement) offered a series of articles on Egyptian and Grecian statuary and on modern masters like Picasso, Matisse, Gauguin, and Renoir. In later years, they covered ancient and contemporary pottery, Surrealism, photography, and primitive art. *Sogetsu* tended to focus more on contemporary, abstract art and pro-vided a monthly dictionary for explaining art forms like reliefs, collages, and lithography and movements like *informel* (a European parallel to American abstract expressionism) and academism (painting and sculp-ture produced under the influence of European academies). Ikenobo, the last to embrace modernist trends, transformed its journal in response to the competition, offering articles on impressionism, Western architec-ture, and avant-garde art. Ikenobo, too, included a dictionary so its stu-dents could negotiate words like *mochīfu* (motif), *purasuchikku* (plastic), and *konpojishon* (composition).

In sum, with new associations, benefits, and training programs, the largest ikebana schools professionalized their workforce and imple-mented human resource policies more in keeping with the major corpo-rations of their day than with traditional feudalistic patterns of *iemoto* authority. While most of the headmasters of the oldest and largest schools remained men, there was not a single school without senior female execu-tives and a predominantly female teaching corps, a situation unfathom-able for other Japanese industries.

Ikebana in the Workplace

In the postwar boom, it was not only teachers who were empowered by ikebana through new career opportunities. Working women in other industries, possessing their own economic means, were a large component of the postwar student body, and ikebana provided them with a skill they could bring to their places of employment. In the prewar period, ikebana was considered a domestic skill, but in the 1950s and 1960s, it became something that signified women's special contributions to the workplace.

In 1952, publishing company Shufu no Tomo's bridal manual series (*Katei kōza*) began to include a section entitled "Ikebana for a Bright, Fun Workplace."[33] The manuals thus tacitly acknowledged that some of their readership were not "good wives and wise mothers" confined full time to the household. Here, it was proclaimed that, just as in the home, flowers in the workplace expressed fondness for others within women's everyday lives. The manual provided "Ten Tips for Flowers in the Workplace," including ensuring adequate water for weekends and keeping extra materials on hand to quickly replace withered stems. Wilted flowers were said to express stagnant business prospects, while lively, well-kept arrangements demonstrated a company's active good fortune. The tips were followed by images of sample arrangements for reception desks, conference rooms, cafeterias, bathrooms, and even the elevator. Enthusiastic "office ladies" could indulge in their hobby while contributing to a mood of corporate prosperity, helping to motivate and attract their salaryman colleagues. Realizing these benefits, many major corporations began to sponsor subsidized programs of ikebana study for their employees held at corporate facilities, sometimes even offering a selection of different schools of ikebana.

Other working women who practiced ikebana at home and in the workplace, including blue-collar workers and small business owners, were celebrated in the journals of the top schools.[34] These included female bus conductors, who placed miniature arrangements on fare boxes to create a cheerful environment for the driver and passengers, school cafeteria workers, beauticians, and small business owners who similarly beautified their workspaces to please themselves and their clients.

Challenging Patriarchy

Women's incorporation of ikebana into male-dominated work environments can be viewed as either a form of empowerment or, from another perspective, as evidence that working women were expected to provide the same type of nurturing atmosphere in the office that they were exhorted to create at home, as an extension and perpetuation of patriarchy. Nevertheless, some women directly challenged the patriarchy inherent within ikebana's *iemoto* system. In the 1960s, women gained increasingly public profiles as senior instructors and even *iemoto*. Daughters of several famous headmasters, including Teshigahara Kasumi, Ohara Wakako, and Adachi Tōko, were glamorous, talented artists in their own right, sometimes the object of more media attention than their fathers. As they obtained their own followers, they sometimes defied the authority of their fathers and the *iemoto* system. For example, Kasumi, the designated heir of Teshigahara Sōfū of the Sogetsu school, had her own group of seven hundred disciples and, along with her father, was one of Japan's wealthiest individuals. Nevertheless, she publicly vowed to change the system to inhibit excessive profits, thus critiquing the hierarchical and absolutist structure of the system that provided the most benefit to the patriarch.

Perhaps the most well known of the dissident daughters was Adachi Tōko, who issued a public "Declaration of Independence" from her father in April 1968, just before the completion of lavish new school facilities she was slated to direct. Tōko harbored doubts about hereditary *iemoto* succession; she wished to earn a reputation based on her own talents without being tied to ikebana forms and practices initiated by her father. After her Declaration, she opened her own school and became a celebrity, appearing frequently on TV and writing regular magazine columns. Known as a playgirl, she further denied patriarchy by claiming it "absurd to think someone should get married just because they're a woman." Her goal in life was "not marriage, but ikebana."[35]

Female students in college ikebana clubs also publicly challenged the hierarchy and absolutism mandated by headmasters. In December 1968, the Waseda University ikebana club held an exhibit at Shinjuku station that included a large panel declaring:

> Creative ikebana is produced when unrestrained free originality can be exhibited. . . . To create something is to struggle with one's self. There should be no additional externally imposed restraints

or limitations. For example, the work of someone in a given school should not be criticized just because it doesn't suit that school's style. . . . [W]e must transcend the individual school.[36]

The declaration pointedly indicated the contradictions between artistic consciousness and the goal of commercial profits underlying the current system, in which *iemoto* claimed to support artistic originality but imposed limitations that shackled creativity and encouraged conformity to keep students within the bounds of the school. The students complained that they were only supposed to copy the works of the *iemoto*; such a practice meant ikebana could not actually be called art.

The established ikebana world dismissed this rhetoric as naive student activism, in keeping with the air of widespread protest in 1968, but the girls had actually touched a sore spot. Ikebana clubs at prestigious universities like Waseda, Keiō, Aoyama Gakuin, and Gakushūin rejected affiliation with a single school, holding independent exhibitions and study camps. Although instructors from a given school might be hired to teach necessary technical skills to clubs, the student members refused affiliation or certifications because they did not want to support the *iemoto* system. Student clubs openly discussed and debated subjects that were taboo among the schools, such as whether the commercialization of ikebana was positive and whether disciples rather than family members should succeed as headmasters.

Conclusion

Today, many young Japanese women consider ikebana an old-fashioned practice for overachieving housewives. Examining ikebana history, however, demonstrates that it only became associated with women in the twentieth century. Since the postwar period, ikebana has provided women with professional opportunities inconceivable in other Japanese industries, while simultaneously supporting official ideological stances on gender and national cultural identity.

The metanarrative of Japan's postwar recovery describes an "economic miracle" from the 1950s to the 1970s, attributable to factors that include the close relationship between business and the state, and the export of high-quality consumer products such as cars, electronics, and household appliances. This is largely a masculine narrative focused on the salaryman as corporate warrior, relegating women to the role of private consumers. On the other hand, an emerging counternarrative about the 1960s focuses on countercultural movements that were critical of mainstream society and values, including student and political protests and avant-garde art, film, and literature. Both narratives ignore the economic and social effects of Japan's traditional cultural activities. During this period the Agency for Cultural Affairs wielded a large budget and sponsored numerous programs to develop Japan as a "country of culture" and to promote this image abroad, in order to erase its wartime image as imperialist aggressor and ameliorate its emerging image as ruthless economic competitor. Japan's modern national reputation as feminized purveyor of cherry blossoms and geisha, ikebana and tea ceremony, is not simply the product of the Orientalizing West, but a brand image that was promoted by the state itself and deeply internalized by both domestic and international audiences.

The ikebana boom of the 1950s and 1960s helps us rethink not only women's labor, but also Japan's postwar recovery in new ways. Ikebana's economic situation reflected that of corporate Japan, with high-speed growth and three large, multinational schools diversifying and dominating the market. Despite its reputation as a polite parlor art, ikebana generated diverse and copious economic activity in fields ranging from education and publishing to retail activity and construction. Yet in contrast with the economic pride engendered by the successes of Toyota or Panasonic, which brought equity with the West, ikebana engendered cultural pride and nationalism based on difference and on an understanding that Japan was aesthetically superior to the West. Analyzing ikebana and other traditional arts in historical terms helps us better understand the nature, force, and tenacity of Japanese cultural nationalism. It further helps us rethink Japanese feminisms, which have tended to emphasize how traditional gender roles limited women's options, by revealing how some women were able to capitalize on gender norms embedded in traditional arts to empower themselves and forge independent lives while contributing to Japan's national projects of economic and cultural recovery.

Notes

1   Shōwa denotes an era of modern Japanese history encompassing the years 1926–1989. The Genroku period, an early modern historical era from

1688–1704, was considered a "golden age" because of the flourishing of popular arts during that time.

2 Nishiyama Matsunosuke, *Gendai no iemoto* (Tokyo: Kōbundō, 1962), 36.

3 Nishiyama Matsunosuke, "Geijutsu to iemotosei no kōyō: Sogetsukai Nihon no kyodai soshiki," *Asahi jānaru* 7 (1965): 35–40.

4 Nishiyama, *Gendai no iemoto*, 146.

5 Haneda Sei, *Ikebana hiketsushū: Hana no kokoro o ikasu 112 no chie* (Tokyo: Sanpō, 1972), 90.

6 Andrew Gordon, *Fabricating Consumers: The Sewing Machine in Modern Japan* (Berkeley: University of California Press, 2012), 72–78.

7 Alisa Freedman, Laura Miller, and Christine Yano, eds., *Modern Girls on the Go: Gender, Mobility, and Labor in Japan* (Stanford, CA: Stanford University Press, 2013), 2.

8 Nishiyama, *Gendai no iemoto*, 77.

9 This phrase was coined in the Meiji period to represent an ideal for women who, for the sake of the nation, should strive to both master domestic skills such as cooking and cleaning to create a smoothly running household, and develop moral and intellectual skills to raise and guide their children.

10 There are no comparable numbers available for ikebana but, for example, the number of students in the Urasenke summer seminar grew from one-third to one-half the total between 1912 and 1920. Kobayashi Yoshiho, *"Hana" no seiritsu to tenkai* (Osaka: Izumi Shoin, 2007), 175–180.

11 Kudō Masanobu, *Nihon Ikebana Bunka shi*, vol. 3: *Kindai ikebana no kakuritsu* (Kyoto: Dōhōsha Shuppan, 1993), 99.

12 Kobayashi, *"Hana" no seiritsu*, 178.

13 Hiramoto Ryōsaku, "Jogakkō to ikebana," *Kadō* (February 1932).

14 Shufu no Tomo, *Jitsuyō hyakkai sōsho*, vol. 12: *Moribana to nageire no ikekata* (Tokyo: Shufu no Tomo, 1928), 2.

15 Shufu no tomo, *Hanayome kōza*, vol. 2: *Ikebana to chanoyu* (Tokyo: Shufu no Tomo, 1942), 1.

16 Elyssa Faison, *Managing Women: Disciplining Labor in Modern Japan* (Berkeley: University of California Press, 2007), 2–17. While not mentioned explicitly, ikebana was undoubtedly a component of this program.

17 Ohararyū Henshūkai, *Ohararyū no rekishi* (Tokyo: Kōbunsha, 2000), 102.

18 Margit Nagy, "Middle-Class Working Women," in *Recreating Japanese Women, 1600–1945*, ed. Gail Lee Bernstein (Berkeley: University of California Press, 1991), 203–207.

19 Ohararyū Henshūkai, *Ohararyū no rekishi*, 102–107.

20 Un'no Hiroshi, *Hana ni ikiru: Ohara Hōun den* (Tokyo: Heibonsha, 2010),

40–45. Secret teachings (*hiden*) were the norm for Japanese schools of all traditional arts, a practice derived from esoteric Buddhism. Usually, to advance within the school, students would purchase scrolls containing the school's secret techniques from the *iemoto*. See Maki Morinaga, *Secrecy in Japanese Arts* (New York: Palgrave Macmillan, 2006).

21 See Nakata Yoshifumi and Carl Mosk, "The Demand for College Education in Postwar Japan," *Journal of Human Resources* 22, no. 3 (Summer 1987): 386–387; and John E. Blewett, *Higher Education in Postwar Japan: The Ministry of Education's 1964 White Paper* (Tokyo: Sophia University Press, 1965), 1–9.

22 Nakata and Mosk, "The Demand for College Education in Postwar Japan," 386.

23 Blewett, *Higher Education*, 81–82.

24 Haneda, *Ikebana Hiketsushū*, 180–184.

25 Ibid.

26 Kudō Masanobu, *Nihon ikebana bunkashi*, vol. 4: *Zen'ei ikebana to sengo bunka* (Kyoto: Dōhōsha Shuppan), 128–130.

27 Originally thirty principles called *Sogetsuryū dokushū jōtatsuhō sanjū kajō* published in Teshigahara Sōfū, *Sogetsu ikebana no ikekata* (Tokyo: Shufu no Tomo, 1943).

28 Haneda, *Ikebana Hiketsushū*, 109–114.

29 Ibid.

30 *Shūkan bunshū*, "Ikenobo tai sogetsu ohararyū," November 18, 1974, 123.

31 Yamamoto Tadao, *Gendai ikebana sanshu-ike: Shugihen* (Tokyo: Bunka Jitsugyōsha, 1965), 15–20.

32 Ohararyū Henshūkai, *Ohararyū no rekishi*, 239–242.

33 Shufu no Tomo, *Katei kōza*, vol. 2: *Ikebana to chanoyu* (Tokyo: Shufu no Tomo, 1952), 303–332.

34 In 1958, Ohara's *Sōka* magazine profiled a variety of working women from different classes and occupations, including a school cafeteria worker, beautician, alpinist, and art gallery owner, who practiced ikebana at work in a brief series called "Lifestyles of Certain Women" (Aru josei no seikatsu).

35 Haneda, *Ikebana Hiketsushū*, 210–213.

36 Ibid., 230–237.

CHAPTER 7

~

Liberating Work in the Tourist Industry

CHRIS McMORRAN

W HAT IS THE IDEAL MAN? The question arose out of nowhere on a cold, rainy day in March 2007, deep in the mountainous interior of Kyūshū. The topic came up as I headed to a café in the hot springs resort of Kurokawa Onsen with Shimada-san (62) and Nishihara-san (48), two women who worked with me at a nearby *ryokan*, or Japanese inn. For Shimada-san, the ideal man was simple: "He would be wealthy, but stuck in the hospital." Nishihara-san erupted with laughter as Shimada-san continued, "I would only need to stop in every day to check on him. Otherwise I could shop all day and spend time with friends."

Nishihara-san agreed, "That's a great idea! Yes, the only useful man is a rich one who leaves you alone." Feigning disappointment that I was not rich (and that I was married), my coworkers lamented the absence of any man to fit their narrow criteria.[1] However, they expressed gratitude that their jobs meant they actually "did not need a man" (*otoko wa iranai*). For these women, both of whom are divorced, the *ryokan* provides a necessary livelihood, including a daily wage, a uniform, three meals a day, and a dormitory room. Because of this, for Shimada-san and Nishihara-san and tens of thousands of women in similar circumstances around Japan, *ryokan* work provides liberation (*kaihō*) from the institution of marriage and its associated reliance on a man.

This chapter explores the *ryokan* as a site of women's liberation. Here, I do not mean the women's lib (*ūman ribu*) movement associated with early 1970s feminism (discussed in chapters by James Welker and Setsu

Shigematsu in this volume). Instead, I mean a private sense of social and geographical liberation from the limitations (and occasional dangers) women feel elsewhere. At first glance, the *ryokan* may seem an unlikely space of liberation. Typically translated as "traditional Japanese inn," *ryokan* cater to both domestic and international tourists longing to experience "traditional" Japan, imagined as a time and space vanishing since the arrival of Perry's "Black Ships" in the 1850s.[2] A major feature of the *ryokan*'s presentation of traditional Japan is its incorporation of a model of gender that fits conventional ideas of femininity and a woman's "place" in Japanese society. Specifically, *ryokan* typically feature *nakai*, women like Shimada-san and Nishihara-san who welcome guests, escort them to their rooms, serve them tea and meals, and clean their rooms following departure.

In this chapter I show that while this work seems to recreate gender ideologies that define women's work and spatially fix it in the home, it also provides *nakai* an opportunity to upset those ideologies and find a personal sense of liberation. This chapter highlights women typically overlooked in Japan, both in general and in feminist scholarship: the tens of thousands of divorced, separated, and single female employees in the country's inns and hotels whose limited education, lack of recognized job skills, and decision to leave their homes convince them they have "no place to go" (*ibasho ga nai, iku tokoro ga nai*) besides the *ryokan*. I show that through their work, *nakai* disrupt the ideologies they seem to reproduce—specifically that of the nurturing woman in domestic space and the supporting member of an extended corporate family in commercial space. I explore the agency of *nakai* through their labor, recognizing not only the limitations but also the possibilities of conceptualizing *nakai* work as feminist praxis in contemporary Japan. In doing so, I echo the insights of Nancy Stalker in this volume by showing how women use conventional femininity as a tool to create spaces for individual freedom and enrichment despite gender inequalities that remain in Japanese society.

This chapter stems from a research project about the emotional and physical labor necessary to create the tourist refuge of the *ryokan*.[3] The study also found that the *ryokan* is a refuge for some employees: a refuge from abusive spouses, unhappy marriages, and financial reliance on a man. The research is based on twelve months of "working" participant observation in a dozen inns in and around Kurokawa Onsen starting in 2006, as well as follow-up interviews with inn workers and owners almost annually through 2015. As a *ryokan* employee I washed dishes, carried luggage, scrubbed baths, laid out bedding, parked cars, vacuumed *tatami* mats, prepared dinner trays, cleaned toilets, and did countless other tasks that put me in direct contact with both guests and the people who create a place of refuge for tens of thousands of guests each year.

Locating Women in *Ryokan*

Ryokan are found throughout Japan, from large cities to small villages. However, most are in tourist destinations like hot springs resorts. There are over 50,000 *ryokan* around the country, averaging 15 rooms each.[4] *Ryokan* are typically owned and operated by a husband-and-wife team, similar to a bed and breakfast. While this couple's labor may suffice in small inns, larger and busier ones require a staff of full- or part-time employees, which may include one or more chefs, front desk staff, drivers, gardeners, and *nakai*.

The title *nakai* is always gendered female and identifies maids or servers in Japanese-style inns or restaurants. Consisting of the *kanji* characters *naka* (relationship, 仲) and *i* (to reside or exist, 居), *nakai* suggests a spatial in-betweenness, someone who shuttles food and drink between the kitchen and the guestroom or dining room. The *nakai* also serves as an intermediary between the owner of an establishment and the guests. This position and responsibility of "in-betweenness" is taken very seriously in the *ryokan* industry, where family-owned inns are said to reflect the personalities of their owners, particularly the *okami*, or proprietress.[5] The *nakai*'s job is to absorb as much of the *okami*'s personality (often described as her *aji*, or flavor) as possible and share it with guests through her emotional and embodied labor. In other words, she must attempt to faithfully recreate the hospitality that would be offered by her boss.

A *nakai*'s workday begins with serving breakfast at 7:00 a.m. and ends at 8:30 p.m. or later, when she has retrieved the last dirty dish from the guestrooms, where dinner is often served. A short afternoon break interrupts an otherwise nonstop cycle of caring for the needs of others that lasts ten to twelve hours a day. Students of Japanese society should recognize a resemblance between *nakai* labor and the caring, embodied labor expected of Japanese women, both in the domestic sphere and the workplace. Most of the country's emotional labor, both at home and work, still rests on the shoulders of women. In this way, *nakai* labor neatly recreates and perpetuates conventional gender stereotypes associated with women's place and role in contemporary Japanese society.

Interestingly, however, the *nakai* work schedule and location prevent many women from accepting this position: those who must prepare morning and evening meals for family members; those who must be available to collect an ill child from school at a moment's notice; those who must contribute time and energy to a neighborhood organization or PTA; those who must care for the disabled or elderly. In other words, although a *nakai* appears to recreate conventional ideologies of women's work, a *nakai* must "be there" for guests and no one else in her life. She must remain rooted in or near the *ryokan*, yet be completely mobile to meet the needs of guests. As I show later, while their personal circumstances mean constant economic uncertainty for many *nakai*, the daily lack of responsibility to family members and the absence of an anchor of home provide many *nakai* with a sense of liberation rare among Japanese women today.

The geographical location of women has long been an implicit concern of scholars of Japan, with women's place often revolving around or being defined with respect to the home.[6] This is evident in Vera Mackie's work on early feminists banned from attending political events in public; Miriam Silverberg's scholarship on "modern girls" who caused moral outrage by freely moving about 1920s Tokyo; research by Joy Hendry and Robin LeBlanc on "professional housewives" who center their social and political worlds on the home; and work by Karen Kelsky on unmarried women who challenge society's expectations that "place" them in the home by refusing to marry or by moving overseas.[7] Even women who work full or part time after marriage often continue to feel spatially and temporally bound to the home in some way, by accepting work that will not interfere with (or will complement) duties like housework and "being there" for family members.[8]

Location with reference to the home also matters to *nakai*, only for very different reasons. Take Suzuki-san (58). A victim of domestic violence, she fled from her husband to the open arms of the *ryokan* industry decades ago and has been working around Japan ever since. At her first job, in a resort near Tokyo, she worked with over fifty women from all over Japan who had also turned to *ryokan* to escape violence and other troubles at home. According to Suzuki-san, "Some had escaped terrible things." For such women, "The *ryokan* is a refuge for women (*kakekomidera*).[9] You can go there and immediately have meals and a place to live. You don't have to worry about anything."

Most of the women I met and worked with turned their backs on the home, and many purposefully tried to move as far away from it as possible. Some reared children and cared for husbands for years or decades, before eventually leaving. Whether to escape physical abuse, an unfulfilling relationship, or financial troubles, or to achieve a sense of self-reliance previously missing in their lives, they all relocated outside the home and away from a man. Unfortunately, they often lack academic credentials, and those who retired from paid employment upon marriage typically have few job skills valued by employers. For these and other reasons many *nakai* claim they have no place to go besides the *ryokan*. This makes them pliant employees, but it also means they may quit in the middle of the night, never to be seen again. In many ways, these women live a complex "in-betweenness" neatly encapsulated by their job title and constitute one of the most mobile groups in Japanese society.[10]

Liberating Work

Despite the precariousness of the position, I never heard a *nakai* regret trading the home for the *ryokan* industry. Instead, most *nakai* acknowledged the difficulties that led them to *ryokan* work and expressed intense satisfaction at being able to survive without a man. No one expressed this more strongly than Nishihara-san (48), who earlier joked about the ideal man. She had her first child at the age of twenty. "It was a mistake," she admits, "but I finally married the father three years later. He was the second son in his family, but because his older brother lived and worked elsewhere, we had to move in with his parents." The living situation was especially difficult because her mother-in-law doubted the child was really her son's offspring. Eventually, they had a second child, but the relationship soon fell apart. Following the divorce, "He kept our second son, eventually marrying another woman and incorporating the child into his household."

With no money or job, Nishihara-san moved into her parents' home with her son, who was six at the time. "Because I had married so young, I didn't have any career or training. I didn't even have a driver's license." She needed a job without any special requirements, with on-site housing, and with the potential to save money to study for a different career. "That was the only way I would be able to live independently." For Nishihara-san location was important: far enough from home to become self-reliant, yet close enough to visit her eldest son, who lived with her parents. Eventually she found work in a *ryokan*. Within two years she earned her driver's license and saved enough money to train to become a nurse.

Unfortunately, despite her nursing qualifications, permanent full-time employment has eluded Nishihara-san. Most care work is temporary or part time, and it features irregular schedules and backbreaking labor. Her employment history is a patchwork of one- or two-year positions in elderly care facilities, offices, and five different *ryokan* and hotels around Kyūshū. Because she has no permanent home, she accepts positions with the kind of security associated with marriage, like subsidized food and housing. When referring to her dormitory room, she admits that it is tiny, "but it's mine." She proudly adds, "This job has a dorm and three meals, so I no longer need a man. That is very liberating." (*Kono shigoto dewa, sanshoku, ryō mo atte, otoko wa hitsuyō ga nai. Hijō ni kaihō desu.*)

Ryokan as Site of Feminist Praxis

The *ryokan* industry provides what many *nakai* consider to be the only viable alternative to a home life defined by patriarchy and repression, and in some cases, violence. However, the assertion of the *ryokan* as a solution to so many social, economic, and political problems affecting women might appear hollow. After all, working in a *ryokan* will not change the conditions that lead women to the industry in the first place. Moreover, their job provides no outlet for political self-expression. Most women are guarded about their pasts, and many have a fatalistic attitude about changing their own circumstances, let alone the gender ideologies that continue to keep women "in their place" in Japan. Similar to women who have "raced for the exits" by leaving paid employment before challenging its restrictions on career mobility and family lives, the *nakai* I worked with left the institutions of marriage and the household (*ie*) before trying to improve those institutions for others.[11] They have little job security and find it best to keep their heads down and slowly work their way up the social hierarchy of a particular inn. Therefore, one might ask how their labor can be understood in feminist terms.

Certainly, this is not feminism as a public, political project. It does not involve consciousness-raising or assertiveness training.[12] And given its position outside the home, it is not "housewife feminism."[13] At its most extreme it rejects the institutions of marriage and the *ie* through the physical act of running away. For Nishihara-san this is "liberation" (*kaihō*), wherein she no longer needs a man. In the *ryokan*, then, one may understand feminism not as part of a public social movement, but in terms of a private pride for one's risky and radical decision to leave the socially accepted institution and space of the home. If feminism is about resistance to or liberation from the oppression or exploitation of women, then the *ryokan* may qualify as a feminist space.

Of course, *nakai* often trade one form of exploitation for another. They may feel personally liberated by leaving a violent or useless spouse, but they enter into a relationship with capital that tends to exploit their vulnerabilities, including their need for steady income, a lack of a permanent residence, and for some, limited mobility due to a lack of transportation. Plus, their job is to play the hostess, thus recreating and reinforcing societal expectations that *place* women in the home and devalue their labor. Indeed, *nakai* continually say their work is natural, that what they do is "women's work" and that as women they are naturally suited to hospitality. Through their caring labor, therefore, *nakai* seem to reproduce the very naturalized categories that limit their vocational choices and place them in such a vulnerable position.

However, I suggest that through their work, *nakai* both reinforce and resist commonly held beliefs about domestic labor and the appropriate place of women. By being paid to use conventional femininity to create a retreat for tourists outside domestic space, *nakai* help undermine the ideology that connects femininity and the home. As I explain below, understanding *nakai* labor as a performance enables one to appreciate their embodied and emotional activities as more than simply recreating the conditions of their exploitation, and instead opens up the possibility that their practices might reconfigure ideas about domestic labor in Japan and elsewhere.

Let's return to the "typical" *nakai*. She either is, or has been married, but lives apart from her husband and desires work that provides accommodations. She also may lack work experience after years as a housewife. On the surface, she may seem a pitiable figure. However, before we feel sorry for the *nakai*, we must question outdated, even nostalgic ideas about both the home and group-centered Japanese society that lead to this judgment. If we only view the *nakai* through a narrow normative idea of home, then we see her as deviant and vulnerable: rootless, homeless, and reliant on the economic success of another family. Such a perspective fails to recognize the radical potential of *nakai* work to actually undermine the normative notion of home and the ideologies that tie women to domestic space and labor.

The *nakai* proves that home need not be central to Japanese women's identities, by living and working independently of the home. The *nakai*'s lifestyle deviates from the norm, but it offers social and economic rewards, including a decent wage, to perform the emotional and physical labor previously unremunerated, and underappreciated, in the home. Moreover, the *nakai* undermines beliefs about the centrality of the home to Japanese femininity precisely through her performance of conventional gender roles for the benefit of tourists. The *nakai* faithfully reproduces the role of the helpful and subservient female. She cares for and caters to guests, and whether she is having a wonderful day or seething inside, she cannot refuse to play the part of the hospitable hostess without the risk of losing her job.

In this faithful performance of the role of hostess, the *nakai* demonstrates a particularly powerful potential to undermine conventional femininity and its "natural" association with domestic space. Here, Judith Butler's insights on gender are instructive.[14] In her powerful critique of the assumed natural one-to-one relationship between biological sex and gender, Butler focuses on drag, cross-dressing, and other performances of gender. She argues that those who cross-dress often faithfully reproduce the gender-appropriate behaviors, and through this performance undermine the assumed naturalness of gender. This realization led Butler to conceive of gender not as natural but as "*a stylized repetition of acts*."[15] Similarly, one can see *nakai* labor as "a stylized repetition of acts" normally associated with Japanese women in domestic space. However, the repetition of these acts in nondomestic space, particularly by women who have shunned the normative home, enables these acts to be seen instead as a parody of the caring labor at the heart of conventional femininity. In this way, the *nakai* actually undermines the assumed "naturalness" of women's work, especially its connection to the home.

The *nakai* performs the role of the nurturing wife/mother, which is the model of appropriate female behavior in Japan. However, this is the very role that she has shunned by leaving her husband and turning to *ryokan* work. After all, she is obviously not the "good wife, wise mother" if she is working ten to twelve hours per day in some remote tourist village. In fact, she shows that the role can be turned on at the sliding of a door or the arrival of a guest to the inn's entrance. And she undermines the norm most when she plays it most earnestly, such as when she fawns over guests she finds annoying or pretends to be married in order to reject the advances of lecherous male guests. Playing the conventional feminine role provides the space for parody of what she has rejected and an avenue for expressing agency despite the limitations that come from her personal circumstances. Like the everyday forms of peasant resistance, or "weapons of the weak," highlighted by James Scott, a *nakai*'s performative acts may not lead to a violent upheaval and rearrangement of society, but they show that the women do not idly participate in reproducing their own inequality.[16] While always playing the ideal hostess and seemingly reproducing an unequal set of gender relations, *nakai* should be seen not as helpless victims of their employment situation, but as astute observers of others, able to satisfy guests' needs while achieving liberation for themselves.

Conclusion: Dis-placing Gender

Every day, *nakai* perform norms that help maintain several social hierarchies. For instance, as women performing domestic duties they satisfy the norm that women belong not in the world of work, but in the domestic sphere. As workers in their employers' *ie*, they fulfill a norm that places women as dependent upon the salary of a man, in this case the owner. They have no ownership of the means of production, besides their own bodies, and rely on the continued economic success of another family's *ie* for their housing, clothing, food, and daily wage. By working in a *ryokan*, then, *nakai* seem to legitimate the institution, the *ie*, from which they have escaped. Indeed, *ryokan* owners hope the company as *ie* can stand in for the household/family as *ie* for their employees, and thus inspire similar levels of commitment and self-sacrifice. The performativity of the *nakai*'s daily acts seems to show their acceptance of this arrangement. However, their words say otherwise. For the overwhelming majority of *nakai* I encountered, the *ryokan* is just a job, and their emotional connection to each day's guests is often stronger than their connection to their employers.

What implications, if any, does this resistance to the institution of the *ie* have for the women of this study, and for women everywhere? The concept of performativity can be used to argue that through an individual's acts, one can either reproduce society's norms of gender, race, sex, or nationality, or one can consciously act in ways that transgress these norms, and thus help create a resistant subjectivity. So, a new question must be raised: What of those people who perform acts that perpetuate society's norms, *but are paid to do so*?

I return one last time to Butler: "The task is not whether to repeat, but how to repeat or, indeed, to repeat and, *through a radical proliferation of gender*, to displace the very gender norms that enable repetition itself."[17] Butler speaks of displacing gender norms. However, reexamined with a geographer's twist, one may imagine dis-*placing* gender norms, or removing gender norms from their normal location. Although this is not Butler's intention, the prospect prompts several questions: Could the daily repetition of gender norms in the *ryokan* help to displace these norms from the home? Might the repetition of home-focused gender norms in tourist space take them out of the realm of daily practice and into the realm of the exotic other?

As Japanese women spend more hours working outside the home, society's expectations of women and domestic labor may be challenged. In the future, the domestic hostess may become a nostalgic icon, an unattainable ideal from yesteryear whose selfless labor made the home feel comfortable. Perhaps the performance of idealized gender norms in the *ryokan* will not lead to their reproduction throughout society. Perhaps instead they will become a quaint tradition to be experienced only in the *ryokan*, or even "played" in the home, as a bodily memory of what was seen while on vacation. This may be one way to disrupt existing ideologies of gender and space. In the meantime, for Shimada-san, Nishihara-san, Suzuki-san, and the many *nakai* in similar precarious circumstances, the *ryokan* provides a location for feminist praxis, a space in which women can actively undermine the centrality of the institutions of marriage and household to their own lives, and live lives of personal satisfaction and liberation that come from not relying on a man.

Notes

1 My positionality as a white, heterosexual male married to a Japanese woman with whom I resided during this research was known to my coworkers and was relevant. Additionally important to many coworkers was my status as a child of divorce, a fact that arose early in conversations with a few coworkers and soon became common knowledge.

2 On the rise of nostalgia-focused travel, see Jennifer Robertson, "Furusato Japan: The Culture and Politics of Nostalgia," *Politics, Culture, and Society* 1, no. 4 (1988); "It Takes a Village: Internationalization and Nostalgia in Postwar Japan," in *Mirror of Modernity: Invented Traditions of Modern Japan*, ed. Stephen Vlastos (Berkeley: University of California Press, 1998); and Marilyn Ivy, *Discourses of the Vanishing: Modernity, Phantasm, Japan* (Chicago: University of Chicago Press, 1995). On *ryokan*, see Sylvie Guichard-Anguis, "Japanese Inns (*Ryokan*) as Producers of Japanese Identity," in *Japanese Tourism and Travel Culture*, ed. Sylvie Guichard-Anguis and Okpyo Moon (London: Routledge, 2008).

3 Chris McMorran, "Practising Workplace Geographies: Embodied Labour as Method in Human Geography," *Area* 44, no. 4 (2012); "A Landscape of 'Undesigned Design' in Rural Japan," *Landscape Journal* 33, no. 1 (2014); "Mobilities Amid the Production of Fixities: Labor in a Japanese Inn," *Mobilities* 10, no. 1 (2015).

4 Doi Kyūtarō, *Yoku wakaru hoteru gyōkai* (Tokyo: Nihon Jitsugyō Shuppansha, 2009).

5 Proprietress is a term used by Fuji Jeanie, a US citizen who married into a multigeneration *ryokan* family and became its *okami*. In an interview, she claimed this term came closest to encompassing all of her (highly gendered) duties. She has also written about the experience of being *okami* and Japanese hospitality in general. See Jeanie Fuji, *Nipponjin wa, Nihon ga tarinai* (Tokyo: Nihon Bungeisha, 2003); and *Amerikajin ga mananda Nihon no omotenashi kokoroechō* (Tokyo: Gentōsha, 2004).

6 Beyond Japan, geographers in particular have analyzed the complex and problematic ways gender intersects with domestic space in politically, economically, and culturally significant ways. See especially Alison Blunt and Robyn M. Dowling, *Home* (New York: Routledge, 2006); and Linda McDowell, *Gender, Identity, and Place: Understanding Feminist Geographies* (Minneapolis: University of Minnesota Press, 1999).

7 Vera Mackie, *Feminism in Modern Japan: Citizenship, Embodiment and Sexuality* (Cambridge: Cambridge University Press, 2003); Miriam Silverberg, "The Modern Girl as Militant," in *Recreating Japanese Women, 1600–1945*, ed. Gail Lee Bernstein (Berkeley: University of California

Press, 1991); Robin M. LeBlanc, *Bicycle Citizens: The Political World of the Japanese Housewife* (Berkeley: University of California Press, 1999); Joy Hendry, "The Role of the Professional Housewife," in *Japanese Women Working*, ed. Janet Hunter (London: Routledge, 1993); Karen Kelsky, *Women on the Verge: Japanese Women, Western Dreams* (Durham, NC: Duke University Press, 2001).

8   Kaye Broadbent, *Women's Employment in Japan: The Experience of Part-Time Workers* (London: RoutledgeCurzon, 2003); Dorinne K. Kondo, *Crafting Selves: Power, Gender, and Discourses of Identity in a Japanese Workplace* (Chicago: University of Chicago Press, 1990); Sawa Kurotani, *Home Away from Home: Japanese Corporate Wives in the United States* (Durham, NC: Duke University Press, 2005); Nancy Ross Rosenberger, *Dilemmas of Adulthood: Japanese Women and the Nuances of Long-Term Resistance* (Honolulu: University of Hawai'i Press, 2013); but see also Glenda Susan Roberts, *Staying on the Line: Blue-Collar Women in Contemporary Japan* (Honolulu: University of Hawai'i Press, 1994).

9   *Kakekomidera* refers to temples that offered refuge for women during the Edo period (1603–1868). At the time, women were not allowed to initiate a divorce. However, they could seek shelter in some Buddhist temples, which would provide safety and help initiate a divorce for them. For Suzuki-san, the *ryokan* resembles the *kakekomidera* as a place of flight and eventual liberation from marriage. See Diana E. Wright, "Severing the Karmic Ties That Bind: The 'Divorce Temple' Mantokuji," *Monumenta Nipponica* 52, no. 3 (1997).

10   McMorran, "Mobilities."

11   Leonard J. Schoppa, *Race for the Exits: The Unraveling of Japan's System of Social Protection* (Ithaca, NY: Cornell University Press, 2006).

12   Mackie, *Feminism in Modern Japan*, 150.

13   Ibid., 151.

14   Judith Butler, *Gender Trouble: Feminism and the Subversion of Identity* (New York: Routledge, 1990).

15   Ibid., 140; emphasis in original.

16   James C. Scott, *Weapons of the Weak: Everyday Forms of Peasant Resistance* (New Haven: Yale University Press, 1985).

17   Butler, *Gender Trouble*, 148; emphasis added.

PART III

Rethinking Literature
and the Arts

E ACH OF THE CHAPTERS IN THIS SECTION takes up our invitation
to "rethink" feminism by exploring the diverse ways that literary
and artistic production may also be understood as forms of feminist
activism. Though these chapters explore a broad range of styles of creative expression, from the early twentieth to the early twenty-first centuries, there is also a remarkable degree of convergence between them,
in terms of the problems they address and the feminist methodologies
they employ. Common themes that cross boundaries of genre and time
period include women's responses to misogyny and male violence, critique of the conflation of feminine sexuality with reproductive function,
women's relationship to politics and the state, and the social uses of wom-
en's bodies. Together these chapters offer a rich and provocative exploration of the diversity of feminist expression over the course of modern
Japanese history.

The section begins with Leslie Winston's study of the visual art of
Takabatake Kashō (1888–1966), a Taishō-period (1912–1926) painter
and illustrator whose depiction of female bodies resisted the contemporary trend to reduce the feminine form to the status of sexual or maternal object. Winston's work demonstrates the utility of the visual arts to
challenge conventional binary thinking that socially positions women
according to gendered and sexualized stereotypes. Next we move to
the early post–World War II era, with Barbara Hartley's exploration
of the implications of work by two women writers of fiction who are

frequently overlooked in feminist literary analysis—Sono Ayako (b. 1931) and Ariyoshi Sawako (1931–1984). Considered conservative and even reactionary by many scholars, Sono's patriotism and allegiance to traditional values have rankled many feminists, whose postwar opposition to the state was the product of suspicion and self-reproach for the ways that feminist activism was subordinated to state goals during the age of prewar imperialism. The work of Ariyoshi, on the other hand, has been overlooked or underestimated as "traditionalist" even by feminist scholars intent upon reclaiming the voices of women lost to history. Hartley productively complicates these portrayals of Sono and Ariyoshi, demonstrating that both may be read as feminist authors.

Finally, Kathryn Hemmann brings us to the present day, with her analysis of the work of the blockbuster novelist Kirino Natsuo (b. 1951). Hemmann's reading of Kirino's work reveals this author's use of fiction to critique the scapegoating of women for contemporary social problems, such as the low birthrate and work-life (im)balance. Hemmann demonstrates that misogynist discourse, conventionally understood as a problem of male attitudes toward women, may also be internalized by women to have a corrosive impact on their self-image. Each of these scholars uncovers feminist discourse in an unexpected place—in "popular" culture, conventionally understood to be an apolitical form of entertainment, or else voiced in an unfamiliar cadence—effectively helping us to rethink the boundaries of "feminism" in postwar Japan.

—JCB

CHAPTER 8

~

Seeing Double

*The Feminism of Ambiguity in the
Art of Takabatake Kashō*

LESLIE WINSTON

P AINTER AND MAGAZINE ILLUSTRATOR Takabatake Kashō (1888–
1966) wielded great influence on those who followed him. He was
enormously popular in the Taishō (1912–1926) and early Shōwa (1926–
1989) periods and was pivotal in creating a vision of "Taishō chic." His
name, however, has long been forgotten, except by enthusiastic admirers.
One of them, Kano Takumi, opened an art museum dedicated to him in
1984 that flourishes today.[1]

Beyond personal correspondence, Kashō left behind no writings
regarding his influences or motivations. However, it is clear from his
cosmopolitan lifestyle and art that his interests lay in freer sexualities
than state or sexological discourses would allow. His work testifies to a
refusal to be locked into state-sanctioned, rigid definitions of "male" and
"female" and the roles prescribed for them.

Meiji and Taishō feminists, whether advocates of suffrage or not,
resisted women's exclusion from the public sphere and consignment to
domestic space. Kashō's female subjects generally reject those precepts
encouraging modesty and care of family, children, and the home. Often,
they are depicted in the public sphere or engaged in some physical activity. Stylish and sophisticated, they are of a class in possession of at least
some discretionary income, with the leisure to play tennis or engage
in other pastimes. Kashō's female subjects evoke the image of *moga*,

"modern girls." Yet in contrast to the stereotype of *moga* as sexualized or sexually available, they are not depicted as sexual objects. Rather, they own their sexuality; Kashō's young women are simultaneously demure, sexy, and self-assured. His aesthetic techniques were widely appealing, just as they were provocative in their renderings of the gendered body, challenging norms in a complicated way.

This essay will focus on two reasons why Kashō's work should be considered feminist. The first is that his female subjects, oftentimes modern girls, rebuff the norms of so-called traditional feminine behavior and also may have a mien of maleness about them. Male subjects, on the other hand, display femininity in gesture and appearance. Kashō's rendering of both types of subjects liberates them to engage in wider forms of behavior than those fixed by social conventions that presumed that sex determined gendered behavior, desire, and feelings. Through the hermaphroditic portrayal of his subjects, Kashō challenges this causal relation between gender and the body.

In this essay the term "hermaphrodite" refers to "subjects of anatomically double, doubtful, and/or mistaken sex."[2] Some consider the word offensive today.[3] However, Japanese words that would be translated as "hermaphrodite" at the time were used to refer to indeterminacy of sex. These include "*futanari*" (two shapes/appearances), "*han'nan'nyō*" (half man half woman), "*otoko-onna*"[4] (man-woman), and *ryōsei guyūsha* (person with genitalia of both sexes), among others. These terms may refer to individuals who are *ryōsei* (both sexes) or *chūsei* (neutral/in between), as Jennifer Robertson defines them. *Chūsei* "emphasizes the erasure or nullification of differences."[5] The gender markers, such as clothing, hairstyle, gestures, and so on, of the neutral (*chūsei*) body are inconsistent with the sex of the body, thereby contravening the belief that biological sex determines behavior.[6]

The second reason I consider Kashō's work feminist is that he depicts his female subjects as active, vibrant, and autonomous, in contrast to state ideology that defined women through their roles as daughters, wives, and mothers.[7] Kashō's art is not in the service of a heterosexual male gaze. His subjects suggest a world of fluid possibilities, as the body does not determine behavior, desire, or social roles.

I therefore argue that Kashō's collapsing of naturalized divisions between male and female and his female subjects' nonconforming behavior mark his work as feminist. I will further demonstrate that Kashō challenges other divisions as well—for instance, those between racial categories or between humans and animals. These efforts all have the effect of eradicating or problematizing restrictive categories of analysis.

An Artist for the Taishō Zeitgeist

Takabatake Kōkichi (Kashō) was born in 1888 and raised on the southwestern island of Shikoku, in an isolated area called Uwajima, in Ehime Prefecture. His merchant father Kazusaburō did not care for Kōkichi's "character and conduct" (*seikō*),[8] perhaps a euphemism for Kashō being "effeminate" (*memeshī*), another term he used to describe his son.[9]

Kashō went to study art first in Osaka and then in Kyoto. He was interested in Western-style painting (*yōga*), but persevered in exercises in Japanese-style painting first to please his mentors. Eventually he settled in Tokyo, where he kept a bevy of handsome male pupils (*deshi*) and painted in a variety of idioms, though he is best known for his Western, "Taishō chic" style, incorporating extensive knowledge of fashion.

Kashō's fans, male and female adolescents at the advent of modern-day graphic illustration, were extraordinarily ardent in their devotion to him, to the extent of forming Kashō clubs. His name even appears in the lyrics to a popular song from 1928 called "Ginza March" (*Ginza kōshin kyoku*): "*Kunisada egaku no otome mo yukeba, Kashō gonomi no kimi mo yuku*," that is, "Girls that Kunisada drew stroll [in Ginza], and you, who have the Kashō style, also go." A latent meaning of the lyric is that girls who *look like* the ones in the art of Utagawa Kunisada (1786–1864) stroll along Ginza streets. These refer to the "beauties" (*bijin*) and courtesans who were the frequent subjects of Kunisada's art. Kunisada, also known as Toyokuni III, was a woodblock print artist of the "floating world" (*ukiyo*)[10] who was extremely popular, prolific, and successful in his day, just as Kashō was in his. The lyric has the girls stroll in Ginza because this area of Tokyo was at the forefront of popular fashion during Kashō's day.

Kashō's name symbolized modernism.[11] The "you" (*kimi*) in the lyric refers to a "modern girl,"[12] the embodiment of modern female fashion and sensibilities at the time. The lyrics reflect how well known and appreciated he was. Furthermore, his popularity extended beyond the "modern girl" and "*mobo*" (modern boy) who might go "*ginbura*" (Ginza strolling), to encompass adults as well.[13]

Kashō's popularity began early when he was still studying to become an artist. In 1905 he started hand-painting picture postcards of modern young women to supplement his allowance. By the end of the Taishō period, he dominated the new profession of magazine illustration, unrivaled in demand for his work by magazine publishers such as Kōdansha. Kashō illustrated magazine stories, magazine covers, and frontispieces for dozens of magazines, such as *Shōjo kurabu* (Girls' club), *Shōnen kurabu* (Boys' club), *Fujin kurabu* (Ladies' club), *Gendai* (Modern times), *Kōdan kurabu* (Storytelling club), *Shōjo sekai* (Girls' world), *Nihon shōnen* (Japanese boys), *Fujin sekai* (Ladies' world), and *Fujokai* (Women's world), to name a few.

This period during which Kashō was at the top of his profession coincided with a time when sexology was holding sway in its strict bifurcation of the sexes, as well as when women were agitating for suffrage and becoming more involved in public life. Sexology was the study of human sexuality led by Austro-German doctors and other professionals from the mid-nineteenth century into the twentieth. Based on the premise that biological laws were the foundation of sexual behavior and could be understood scientifically, sexology presumed that it was the responsibility of the medical profession to regulate sexual behavior.[14] The knowledge about sex promoted by these sexologists ultimately became the hegemonic paradigm, but counter-discourses were myriad. For example, modern girls snubbed norms of so-called traditional feminine behavior, or at least ignored criticism for violations of such norms. Likewise, Kashō's representations of women flouted conventional gender roles as enshrined in the Meiji Civil Code,[15] yet were warmly embraced by his large following. Takabatake Asako, the great-granddaughter of Kametarō, Kashō's elder brother, notes that sexology informed the strict gender norms promoted by the Taishō-era government. "Kashō did not overtly protest the government, but he created art in which males weren't male and females weren't female."[16] This comment supports my argument that Kashō's art was liberating for both men and women. He maintains sexual possibilities in his art that the government had foreclosed, thereby releasing human behavior from its overdetermined link to the body.

This style in which females were not female and males were not male was not accidental. Manga artist Takemiya Keiko writes that Kashō's art was "characterized by the precision with which he drew the body three-dimensionally. His figures were so well defined that the viewer could sense the bones and around them the flesh. He distinguished the inner part of the feet from the outer part with great detail, and fingertips were particularly beautiful."[17] Therefore, this kind of skill allowed him to draw distinctly male and female figures if he had wanted to do so.

Regarding the androgyny of Kashō's subjects, Takemiya writes:

> I think the boys in Kashō's pictures are sexier than the girls because of the boys' expression of uncertainty. When it comes to his drawing skills, precisely because Kashō is someone who can clearly distinguish male figures from females, he depicts the masculinity in the females when drawing adolescent girls, and the femininity within adolescent males when drawing beautiful adolescent males. One may wonder if this is why Kashō's males appear to look sexier than females. . . . The figure of the beautiful boys that Kashō drew was feminine but the detail was masculine. . . . The attraction of Kashō's pictures is that while he distinguishes between male and female figures through differences in detail, the qualities of both sexes (*ryōsei*) in the subject spill over onto the canvas.[18]

Uno Akira concurs: "The boys, in fact, can be like girls, and the girls, in fact, can look like boys impersonating girls." No such sexual illusion or unorthodoxy exists in Takehisa Yumeji's (1884–1934) lyrical (*jojō*) artwork, by contrast.[19] Perhaps it is the very innocence of Yumeji's female subjects, or the fact that they more often conform to traditional roles and behavior that makes his images more iconic of the Taishō era. Today Yumeji's name is better known than Kashō's, though the work of both dominated prewar imagery of young women.

Artists familiar with Kashō, especially manga artists, take it for granted that Kashō's subjects contain pronounced elements of the "opposite sex." The figure of the hermaphrodite, literal and figurative, boldly emerges in one of the cornerstones of today's Japanese popular culture, manga. Fujimoto Yukari's statement that contemporary *shōjo* manga (girl comics) started with hermaphroditism, therefore, is hardly surprising. In her critique of *shōjo* manga, in a chapter entitled "Transgender: Female Hermaphrodites, Male Hermaphrodites," Fujimoto attributes the origins of *shōjo* manga to the Takarazuka Revue, the all-female theater troupe founded in 1913. She explains that Tezuka Osamu, celebrated manga artist and creator of the classic series *Princess Knight* (*Ribon no kishi*, 1953–1955), intended to reproduce in *shōjo* manga the world of the Takarazuka theater, in which both male and female parts are played by women.[20] Kashō's work emerged in this period of Takarazuka's growing popularity, when counter-discourses to dimorphic sex were numerous. One could say that Kashō offered a visual art version of the Takarazuka Revue.

Takemiya, one of the most popular *shōjo* manga artists of the 1970s and 1980s, who creates hermaphroditic characters herself, was impressed by Kashō's oeuvre from early on, writing that she had the sense that she had seen it a long time before she became even a novice artist.[21] It is worth noting here that while Yumeji's lyrical images (*jojōga*) were part of the shared imagination in Japan,[22] Kashō's androgynous images, too, imprinted themselves on the consciousness of many, just as the gender-crossing of Takarazuka had done on Tezuka.

Perhaps the sexual ambiguity of his subjects played a role in Kashō's strong influence on manga artists, just as it figured significantly in its appeal to Taishō-era youth. At the very least, a mien of sensuality emanates from his work. Takabatake Asako suggests that his avid young fans were excited by some sort of eroticism they sensed in his work. "For that very reason, his popularity derived not simply from the splendid fashion [of his subjects] or because they were pretty or stylish. . . . Rather, in technical terms it's called hermaphroditic (*ryōseiguyū*) . . . that sort of, that hermaphroditic, well, androgynous (*chūseiteki*) charm, I would say."[23] Perhaps it is this subliminal sexual appeal burgeoning at the right historical moment that accounts for Kashō's allure. Donald Roden writes in his frequently cited "Taishō Culture and the Problem of Gender Ambivalence"[24] that Japanese during the 1920s were enthralled by gender ambivalence. Furthermore, he observes that in addition to Tokyo, Berlin, Paris, New York, and London all witnessed this fascination in middlebrow and high cultures. A complex of factors, including the titillation of non-normative sex, energized perhaps by the growth of sexology, along with avant-garde art, contributed to this embrace of androgyny. In the following section, I explore how Kashō pushes the fascination with blurred lines of sex to other realms.

Collapsing Boundaries in Sexuality and in Race

Later in the same interview mentioned above, Takabatake Asako remarked, Kashō "chipped away at sexual difference and in the end, well, the subject is male and also female but is not [entirely] one or the other. Well, the subject is neither Japanese nor foreign. In that way, the categorization gradually disappears." By breaking down walls in categories of sex, race, and more, Kashō calls into question naturalized assumptions about these lenses through which people are seen.

Regarding sex, the blurring of boundaries can be alluring and mysterious. That Kashō obscured other lines of difference is also intriguing. "When Kashō wanted to draw a Westerner, he could certainly draw a very Western-looking person . . . but, consciously he did not draw that way." This comment, as well as "chipping away at sexual difference," reiterates Kashō's blurring of distinctions by drawing out the female in the male and the male in the female. This dismantling of categories gets to the heart of Kashō's art, which portrays subjects behaving in ways that do not adhere to the norms of their sex. With the categories obscured or removed, so too are the rules of conduct. Humans are freed to behave more in accordance with their inclinations.

His *Sea's Illusion* (*Umi no gensō*, 1926)[25] and *Young Sailor* (*Wakaki funabito*, 1926) (figure 8.1) provide other instances of this in-betweenness, in species and sex. *Sea's Illusion*, used as the frontispiece for an issue of *Shōjo gahō* (Girls' illustrated), is a fairly typical depiction of a mermaid, with the upper body that of a female and the lower body that of a large fish tail. Kashō drew *Young Sailor* not for a magazine but for use in writing paper. The fingers and hands of the sailor, and the way they are positioned, are the same as those of the mermaid, as well as those of many of Kashō's subjects. What is interesting here is the movement of the bodies in both works and the positioning of shoulders and backs. The sashaying of the sailor is apparent not only in the folds of the sailor suit (pullover and bell-bottomed trousers) but in the kick of the back foot, the flying flap of the pullover, and the dancing tally dangling from the flat white hat. The flow and dynamism of their bodies mitigate the stasis implicit in the rigidly polarized male and female bodies that the government implicitly promoted. The breaking waves, rushing water, the flying hair on the mermaid's head, and flapping tail accomplish this movement similarly in *Sea's Illusion*. In addition, the sailor maneuvers his shoulder to dip and arch his back, while the mermaid raises her shoulder and twists her torso. The sailor has the same face as the mermaid but is playful and flirtatious. The mermaid is overtly sexual and alluring. The sailor could easily be female; the mermaid seems quite human. The dynamism of these in-between bodies speaks to possibility born of the subversion of categorical absolutes that bind the subject to prescribed bodies, behaviors, and desires.

FIGURE 8.1 Takabatake Kashō, *Young Sailor* (*Wakaki funabito*, 1926). Copyright Yayoi Museum.

In addition to illustrating the permeability of borders of sex and species in the examples above, Kashō has diminished, if not subtly erased, analytical categories of race or culture in his portrayals of pairs of young women. In some cases, one is in Japanese clothing and the other in Western; in some cases they both wear Western dress. In a compelling article on Kashō's female subjects providing a model for female consumers, Barbara Hartley elaborates on the topic of Kashō's subjects embracing both Western and Japanese traditions in magazine illustrations from 1925 to 1937. Hartley invokes Miriam Silverberg's powerful reading of Japanese modern life in the 1920s not as the West replacing Japanese cultural ideals but as a "recod[ing] of Western institutions and practices for indigenous Japanese consumption."[26] Clearly, this "re-coding" and "assimilation" is deployed in Kashō's work, in which Hartley discerns Western images in Japanese contexts.

While maintaining Hartley's reading as a reasonable possibility, I, however, see a delicate operation in which, as Takabatake Asako says, Kashō renders the subject as neither Japanese nor foreign. Of course, the settings may contain clear markers of Japan and the West in hairstyle and clothing and more, but Kashō blurs the definitive identity of faces and body language. He collapses the boundaries into a hybridity of female and male, Japanese and Western, human and animal, and for that matter, *Nihonga* (Japanese-style painting) and *yōga* (Western-style painting) as well.

Deborah Shamoon writes that Kashō's great work *Changing Styles* (*Utsuriyuku sugata*, 1935)[27] "celebrates the mastery of the foreign by the Japanese female body."[28] Japanese, Chinese, and Western dress of various styles and fashions, uniforms, sports attire, and more, spanning periods and seasons, adorn the sixty figures in this giant opus. In contrast to a "mastery of the foreign," Silverberg (and Hartley) offer the more nuanced and incisive interpretation that Kashō actually *recodes* the non-Japanese dress. And as Silverberg effectively demonstrates, the Japanese "modern girl" could represent a variety of identities in the collective imagination— Japanese, European, cosmopolitan. Rather than a nationally and racially specific and embodied subject, the "modern girl" was a sketch, a reduction, a symbol upon which critics projected their fears and desires.[29] This is no less true of Kashō's modern girls. By effectively erasing borders, he creates subjects who defy categorical definitions.

In describing the zeitgeist in which Kashō began his career and in which it ascended, Takabatake Asako remarks, "In short, a new consciousness sprouted among the general populace. They wanted to accept new things, not passively but proactively, and also, selectively, without considering Western things different. And because there was this socio-psychological transformation, Kashō was supported with wild enthusiasm."[30] In other words, Kashō enjoyed popularity for the very reason that he embraced and expressed the spirit of the new age of Taishō (consumer) culture. In this new consciousness, the focus was not on material objects, let alone material bodies, as Western versus Japanese, certainly not in his images. Kashō's art represents this hybridity, transformation, and flux. Moreover, images of Japanese women in Western dress and short hair were not unusual in his work or in that of other artists.

We can view this hybridity from another angle by considering a French drawing and a Japanese one that emulated it. Appearing in the French magazine *Les feuillets d'arts* (The arts folio) in 1919, George Lepape's *Le miroir rouge* (Red mirror) is strikingly Orientalist in its extreme features of an Asian face that resembles a nō mask. It is a caricature of the quintessential Japanese face, as if one existed. Takehisa Yumeji turns this exoticized figure on its head by adapting it to a Japanese context for the cover of the October 1924 issue of *Fujin gurafu* (Ladies' graph), entitled *Autumn Makeup (Keshō no aki)*.[31] Yumeji's female subjects typically appear in mostly traditional clothing, in traditional settings, roles, and situations. Faces are wan; the expressions on them are innocent. In this picture, a rather Western-looking Japanese young lady peers into a mirror as she applies her makeup. The expression is simple and direct. The hand holding the mirror and the hand applying the powder are in the exact same positions as in Lepape's picture. However, Lepape's colors are saturated. His subject's lacquered nails are redder, her hair blacker. The tiny pupils of the Orientalized female's eyes can be seen just beneath slanting eyelids, while the relatively larger eyes of Yumeji's subject look blankly at the mirror. She evokes the bland, quotidian act of the toilet. Yumeji's subject here looks like most of his other "beauties" (*bijin*). The contrast of a hybrid Western/Japanese figure with Lepape's highly sexualized and Orientalized subject is stunning.

In two renderings of women peering into mirrors by Kashō, *Scarlet Camellia (Beni tsubaki, 1926)*[32] and *Gossamer (Keira, 1926)*,[33] the subjects have the same face as most others in his oeuvre, which is the same as his male faces. The field in each contains the woman from head to toe, holding a mirror out in front of her. In Lepape's and Yumeji's drawings, we see faces and mirrors fairly close up. Kashō chooses not to use close-ups in these images. Nonetheless, the viewer can see large eyes and lush eyelashes. The lips are pursed. In both cases the subjects each bend a leg and swivel their hips while fixing and admiring their hair in the mirror. Panache and sexiness emanate from the figures.

In comparing Lepape's and Yumeji's drawings to each other and then to Kashō's, I wish to emphasize two points. One is that an iconic image of Taishō chic features a delicate, sometimes wistful "beauty" in commonplace scenes by Yumeji. Sexuality plays no role here, let alone sexual ambiguity. In contrast, Kashō's female subjects are suffused with a dynamic energy and sometimes a sexual energy held in check, as they engage in somewhat uncommon activities, such as painting a picture, playing tennis, skiing, dancing, swimming, or speaking on a telephone. Secondly, while French and other Western artists relish *Japonisme* in sometimes racist articulations, Kashō and, at least in the case of *Autumn Makeup*, Yumeji as well, move beyond a Western–Japanese divide to a new sort of woman with a new consciousness that has already transcended a Japanese-versus-Western binary opposition.

Unfettered by the rigidity of tradition, Kashō created a new idiom that not simply combined different elements but allowed these elements to organically emerge in each other. The Western and Japanese amalgam is one example of this; representation of sex is another. It cannot go unremarked that Kashō began to develop this style in the same period that the famous writer Tanizaki Jun'ichirō wrote of the beauty of the protagonist's in-between sex in his stories "The Golden Death" ("*Konjiki no shi*," 1914) and in "Until Abandoned" ("*Suterareru made*," 1914),[34] with its female-in-male protagonist, to paraphrase Takemiya, above.[35] By that I suggest not an influence by Tanizaki but a spirit of the age.

Kashō's Sexual (In)Difference

The suggestion that Kashō's fans sensed something different, something sexual, in his art, coincides with notions of the spectacle, in which the subject in the artwork is separated from the viewer.[36] In most cases Kashō's hermaphroditic subjects are usually portrayed alone, such as in *Song of the Bandits* (*Bazoku no uta*, 1929) (figure 8.2), originally used as a frontispiece in *Nihon shōnen*; *Autumn in Kurama* (*Kurama no aki*, 1926),[37] another frontispiece from *Nihon shōnen*; *Young Sailor* (figure 8.1); and in the cover of an untitled stationery set (figure 8.3), discussed below. His oeuvre is rife with similar examples, but I mention these because the subjects are boldly conspicuous in their sexual ambiguity. In defying conventional norms of gender, thereby forcing the viewer to look more closely, the subjects prompt the viewer to reconsider those norms.

Kashō individuates and separates such subjects even beyond their sexual difference. An instance of Kashō's technique of directing the gaze in order to isolate the subject would be in *Atelier* (*Atorie*, 1926),[38] in which

FIGURE 8.2. Takabatake Kashō, *Song of the Bandits* (*Bazoku no uta*, 1929). Copyright Yayoi Museum.

a young woman paints another young woman, who has material draped over her nakedness. The viewer can see the two subjects, as well as the intervening picture that the artist is working on. This meta-view of art in the making, a *mise en abyme*, directs our attention to the model, since the artist in the picture is studying her, and the picture between them is a representation of her. At the same time, through its self-reflexivity, the artwork also implicates the viewer because we become aware that we are outside of the event, watching a process. The self-reflexivity highlights the process of art and the subject of art as constructed.

Kashō's subjects are often physically individuated but also distanced from the world of a binary sexual economy. Martin Jay's ideas on perspective are constructive here. He borrows Christian Metz's term "scopic regime" in identifying three visual subcultures, or "scopic regimes of modernity."[39] Two offer alternatives to the hegemony of the Cartesian tradition, which refers to a singular, eternal, scientific, and disembodied point of view. Kashō also offers an alternative to Cartesian perspectivalism in his visual order of sexual (in)difference. This economy is not in the service of a heterosexual male gaze or the dualism inherent in the Cartesian view. The subjects are outside of this economy in that they are both sexes and neither; consequently, the body that ought to determine gendered behavior, psychology, and emotion frustrates expectations. Kashō's scopic regime is fraught with possibility. It is flowing and sensual. Rich, deep colors resonate. The use of fabric is suggestive of the body beneath. His subjects, all with the same sexy eyes, murmur quietly to the viewer about a world of fluid sexualities.

The mise-en-scène focuses the gaze on the subject, in its entirety but also part by part. The movement of lines guides the gaze to the individuated parts of the body. For instance, in the cover of an untitled collection of stationery (figure 8.3) and in *Autumn in Kurama* (discussed above), the viewer focuses on feet, legs, arms, and the curve of the hip, one at a time. Conventionally feminine features, including tapered, slender fingers, small, red mouths, and soft, rosy flesh, surface in Kashō's *bishōnen* (beautiful young men). In this cover of an untitled collection of writing paper (figure 8.3), the subject lies on his side on a patch of grass, with his head propped up on one hand. A scarf covers most of his hair. One bird perches on his shoulder, another on his arm. His shorts and one sleeve are curiously torn. He gazes through large, heavy eyes beyond the frame

FIGURE 8.3. Takabatake Kashō, untitled image used as cover of stationery set, 1930. Copyright Yayoi Museum.

of the picture. The subject's double-sexed sensuality paired with the torn clothing disrupts the pastoral setting, leaving a highly charged impression of sexuality.

Other stationery covers, such as *White Bush Clover* (*Shirahagi*, 1926)[40] and *Young Sailor* (discussed above), replicate the beautiful young men with feminine hands and gestures. Such embellishments may be small or subtle, but they augment the sensuality of the image. Kashō's typically androgynous face induces the viewer to scrutinize the subject more closely. For example, the bowtie and short hair in an image in the *Kashō Lyrical Collection* (*Kashō jōjō gashū*, 1928) (figure 8.4) indicate maleness, but the subject could just as easily be a Takarazuka *otokoyaku* (female actor of men's roles). Or, in the case of *Modern Boy* (*Modan bōi*, 1928) (figure 8.5), the subject could be a "modern girl" dressed in a men's double-breasted suit (a ringlet of hair caresses the cheek of this "boy" instead of a sideburn). Little distinguishes male from female in these and myriad other drawings, save costuming and context.

Among body parts, the eyes are characteristic of Kashō's work and signify deeply in the total figure. Kashō usually draws eyes as *sanpaku*

FIGURE 8.4. Takabatake Kashō, untitled image, 1928.
Copyright Yayoi Museum.

gan (three-white eyes), in which the sclera (white of the eye) is visible in three areas around the iris: on both sides and below. *Sanpaku* eyes have a cultural association with sexiness or salaciousness that lends itself to Kashō's figures. Naturalist writer Ikuta Kizan uses the term *sanpaku gan* in his story "The City" ("*Tokai*," 1908), which was found to be "injurious to public morals" (*fūzoku kairan*) and banned.[41] In the work, *sanpaku gan* highlights the sexual appeal of the young wife, whom Jay Rubin describes as "voluptuous."[42] Kashō's rendering of the irises in his subjects' eyes in a non-normative fashion certainly contributes to the sexual mien

FIGURE 8.5. Takabatake Kashō, *Modern Boy* (*Modan bōi,*
1928). Copyright Yayoi Museum.

of the subjects, to which Takabatake Asako alludes. The sexiness of the
eyes enhances the prancing of the eponymous sailor in *Young Sailor,* or
the draped material covering the nakedness of a young woman posing for
another young woman painting her in *Atelier.* These gestures and attitudes (both disposition and posture) complete a picture of erotic sensibil-
ity. Yet, as mentioned earlier, these subjects own their sexuality, as they
manifest self-confidence. They appear comfortable, sophisticated, and
graceful, as well as sexy.

Representing Women Making Their Own Choices

In addition to the eroticism and sexual ambiguity that unchains the body from predetermined behavior and gender roles, young women in Kashō's works are portrayed outside of familial relationships and maternal roles. Most often they are at leisure, alone or with friends, perhaps engaged in a sport or pastime. The government ideology that dictated the gendered roles of imperial subjects of their class, for example, women at home taking care of family, is generally ignored. In fact, Meiji government pre-scriptions for gendered responsibilities were varied,[43] but I refer here to middle-class women, who are neither at home taking care of the family, nor in occupations newly accessible in the interwar years.[44]

Moreover, Kashō's female subjects are not only depicted outside of the domestic sphere, but they are active and sporty. The cover of an issue of *Shōjo gahō* from around 1928 shows a young lady bent over, fasten-ing her skis. She is poised and self-assured. In *Light* (*Hikari*, ca. 1927)[45] a young lady in a trendy sailor suit sits with one arm akimbo. In the background, in front of Ueno subway station[46] stands a large building with a clock on it that reads "subway" and "store." This self-confident, stylish woman has probably engaged in shopping and traveling around town today.

Many images of young female subjects are tinged with an awakening sexuality in settings of nature. The young female figure in *Shore* (*Nagisa*, 1927)[47] is uninhibited and at ease in her swimsuit with a frock draped over one shoulder. She gazes beyond the frame with the same large, heavy-lidded, sexy eyes characteristic of Kashō's work. The subject in *Autumn Leaves* (*Kōyō*),[48] the cover for the November 1929 issue of *Shōjo gahō*, looks directly at the viewer with her head slightly tilted, holding the stem of a leaf between her coy lips. Her large, heavy eyes seem slightly closed. The "butterfly" in *Dancing Butterfly* (*Maeru kochō*),[49] used as a cover illustration for the April 1926 issue of *Shōjo gahō*, is depicted as a young female figure with butterfly wings. In high spirits with blushed cheeks, she playfully revels in the pure joy of dance. All are unabashed and at ease in their bodies, whatever the pose or activity.

Numerous other images, including one called *Dance* (*Dansu*, 1930),[50] portray women in the society of each other, locking arms, holding hands, embracing, and touching in some way. They are intimate friends, representing the kind of female camaraderie and community found in girls' higher schools. Erotic expressions on their faces or mouths are alluring but not sexualized. The overall impression of these young ladies is self-determination and self-assurance. And when in a group, the bonds of solidarity among them are strong. Kashō's images of these female subjects contrast sharply with images of schoolgirls in prose fiction and print media from the 1890s into the early 1900s, when they were objects of criticism and derision.

The body has consistently been a contested site in feminism, from female subjection to male authority as head of household under the Meiji Civil Code, to reproductive rights. In Kashō's art, female bodies are liberated from government demands for reproduction and motherhood. They circulate in a world outside of male rule. Kashō imagines the body beyond binaries with their prescribed norms of behavior and expectations. Moreover, his subjects are masters of their sexuality. For their part, modern boys are given the freedom to assume sexualities also forbidden by state ideology and sexological discourse. Kashō assumes a feminist position by representing autonomous subjects, whose behavior and attitudes are freed from the bounds of the body, implicitly supporting equality among people of all sexes.

Notes

1   Information about Kano's Yayoi Museum can be found at "Museum Overview" (*Kan no gaiyō*), http://www.yayoi-yumeji-museum.jp/yayoi /outline.html, last accessed September 16, 2014.
2   Alice Domurat Dreger, *Hermaphrodites and the Medical Invention of Sex* (Cambridge, MA: Harvard University Press, 1998), 30.
3   Emi Koyama, "From 'Intersex' to 'DSD': Toward a Queer Disability Politics of Gender" (keynote speech delivered at the Translating Identity conference, University of Vermont, Burlington, February 2006); Alice Dreger et al., "Changing the Nomenclature/Taxonomy for Intersex: A Scientific and Clinical Rationale," *Journal of Pediatric Endocrinology & Metabolism* 18 (2005): 732.
4   Miyatake Gaikotsu, *Han'nan'nyokō* (1922), in *Miyatake Gaikotsu chosakushū*, vol. 5, ed. Tanizawa Eiichi and Yoshino Takao (Tokyo: Kawade shobō shinsha, 1986), 26.
5   Jennifer Robertson, *Takarazuka: Sexual Politics and Popular Culture in Modern Japan* (Berkeley: University of California Press, 1998), 50.

6 For more on confusion of terms, see Leslie Winston, "The Trope of the Hermaphrodite in Modern Japan," *Harvard Asia Quarterly* 16, no. 3 (2014).

7 The Meiji Civil Code, enacted in 1898, recreated the family system by rejecting female succession (*anekatoku*), by restricting married women from contracting loans or investing capital without permission of their husbands, and by other such provisions that manifested inequality between the sexes. See Kurt Steiner, "The Revision of the Civil Code of Japan: Provisions Affecting the Family," *The Far Eastern Quarterly* 9 (1950): 179–180. The expression that epitomized such delimitation of women was "*ryōsai kenbo*" (good wife, wise mother), a neologism coined by Nakamura Masanao during the first decade of the Meiji period, and disseminated by the Education Ministry in 1899. The ministry initiated policy in which women were to be educated in caregiving to children, husband, and parents. In her *Flowers in Salt: The Beginnings of Feminist Consciousness in Modern Japan* (Stanford, CA: Stanford University Press, 1983), Sharon L. Sievers notes that "The 'special qualities' women's education now assumed had more to do with making up any gap that might exist in the repressive socialization of Japanese women than with developing intellect" (pp. 112–113). Yet, women played an important role, averred the Home Ministry, through managing the home frugally, educating children, and supporting the entire family and thereby, the nation; see Sharon H. Nolte and Sally Ann Hastings, "The Meiji State's Policy Toward Women, 1890–1910," in *Recreating Japanese Women, 1600–1945*, ed. Gail Lee Bernstein (Berkeley: University of California Press, 1991). By the early 1920s, however, women's unrest, family disputes, and other factors threatened family-state ideology; see Miriam Silverberg, *Erotic Grotesque Nonsense: The Mass Culture of Japanese Modern Times* (Berkeley: University of California Press, 2006), 145–146.

8 Takabatake Kakō, *Gaka no shōzō: Takabatake Kashō no denki to sakuhin* (Tokyo: Kōdansha Shuppan, 1971), 24.

9 Takabatake Asako, *Kashō kara no tegami* (Matsuyama: Ehime-ken Bunka Shinkō Zaidan, 1997), 131.

10 *Ukiyo-e* are a genre of painting and prints that thrived from the seventeenth to the nineteenth century, depicting kabuki actors, beautiful women, landscapes, and more.

11 Takabatake, *Kashō kara no tegami*, 145.

12 Matsumoto Shinako, ed., *Takabatake Kashō: Taishō, Shōwa, retoro byūtī* (Tokyo: Kawade Shobō Shinsha, 2004), 8, 10.

13 Ozaki Hideki, "Takabatake Kashō no jojōga," in *Takabatake Kashō meiga taishū*, ed. Takabatake Kakō (Tokyo: Kōdansha, 1976), 152.

14 Gregory Pflugfelder, *Cartographies of Desire: Male-Male Sexuality in Japanese Discourse, 1600–1950* (Berkeley: University of California Press, 1999), 244.

15 Winston, "The Trope of the Hermaphrodite in Modern Japan."

16 Takabatake Asako, interview, October 27, 2008, Takabatake Kashō Taishō Roman Kan museum, Tōon, Ehime Prefecture, Japan.

17 Takemiya Keiko, "Danjo ryōmensei no miryoku," in *Takabatake Kashō: Bishōnen zukan*, ed. Korona Bukkusu Henshūbu (Tokyo: Heibonsha, 2001), 44.

18 Ibid., 46–47.

19 Uno Akira, "Watashi no Kashō," in *Takabatake Kashō meiga taishū*, ed. Takabatake Kakō (Tokyo: Kōdansha, 1976).

20 Tezuka Osamu, *Ribon no kishi* (1953–1955; Tokyo: Kōdansha Manga Bunko, 1999); Fujimoto Yukari, *Watashi no ibasho wa doko ni aru no? Shōjo manga ga utsusu kokoro no katachi* (Tokyo: Gakuyō Shobō, 1998), 132.

21 Takemiya, *Takabatake Kashō*, 44.

22 Uno, "Watashi no Kashō."

23 Takabatake, interview.

24 Donald Roden, "Taishō Culture and the Problem of Gender Ambivalence," in *Culture and Identity: Japanese Intellectuals during the Interwar Years*, ed. Thomas Rimer (Princeton, NJ: Princeton University Press, 1990).

25 This image is reproduced in Takabatake Kashō Taishō Roman Kan, ed., *Takabatake Kashō Taishō Roman Kan zuroku* (Shigenobu-chō, Japan: Taishō Roman Kan, 2004), 105.

26 Quoted in Barbara Hartley, "Performing the Nation: Magazine Images of Women and Girls in the Illustrations of Takabatake Kashō, 1925–1937," *Intersections: Gender and Sexuality in Asia and the Pacific* 16 (2008), http://intersections.anu.edu.au/issue16/hartley.htm.

27 Reproduced in Takabatake Kashō, *Takabatake Kashō meisaku gashū* (Tokyo: Kōdansha, 1967), 10–13.

28 Deborah Shamoon, *Passionate Friendship: The Aesthetics of Girls' Culture in Japan* (Honolulu: University of Hawai'i Press, 2012), 68. Shamoon mistakenly dates *Utsuriyuku sugata* to 1921.

29 Silverberg also finds one critic who claimed that the modern girl was anti-motherhood. *Erotic Grotesque Nonsense*, 57.

30 Takabatake Asako, *Kashō kara no tegami*, 83.

31 These two images are juxtaposed in the exhibition catalog Tōkyō-to Teien Bijutsukan, ed., *1930-nendai Tōkyō: Āru deko no yakata (Asakanomiya-tei) ga umareta jidai/Tokyo in the 1930s and the Birth of Prince Asaka's Art*

Deco Residence (Tokyo: Tōkyō-to Rekishi Bunka Zaidan and Tōkyō-to Teien Bijutsukan, 2008), 90.

32 Reproduced in Takabatake Kashō Taishō Roman Kan, *Takabatake Kashō Taishō Roman Kan zuroku*, 114.

33 Reproduced in Takabatake Kashō Taishō Roman Kan, *Takabatake Kashō Taishō Roman Kan zuroku*, 118.

34 Tanizaki Jun'ichirō, "Suterareru made," in his *Tanizaki Jun'ichirō zenshū*, vol. 2 (Tokyo: Chūō Kōron Sha, 1981), and "Konjiki no shi," in ibid.

35 I am referring here to Takemiya's depiction, cited above, of "femininity within adolescent males," as well as to Tanizaki's stories in which males are described in such terms.

36 Hal Foster, *The Return of the Real: The Avant-Garde at the End of the Century* (Cambridge, MA: The MIT Press, 1996), 220.

37 Reproduced in Takabatake Kashō Taishō Roman Kan, *Takabatake Kashō Taishō Roman Kan zuroku*, 96.

38 Reproduced in Takabatake Kashō Taishō Roman Kan, *Takabatake Kashō Taishō Roman Kan zuroku*, 112.

39 Martin Jay, "Scopic Regimes of Modernity," in *Vision and Visuality*, ed. Hal Foster (Seattle: Bay Press, 1988).

40 Reproduced in Takabatake Kashō Taishō Roman Kan, *Takabatake Kashō Taishō Roman Kan zuroku*, 111.

41 Jay Rubin discusses the famous trial of Ikuta and Ishibashi Shian, the editor and publisher of *Bungei kurabu*, in which the story was first published in February 1908. See Jay Rubin, *Injurious to Public Morals: Writers and the Meiji State* (Seattle: University of Washington Press, 1984), 83–89.

42 Ibid., 87.

43 Nolte and Hastings, "The Meiji State's Policy Toward Women."

44 Elise K. Tipton, "Moving Up and Out: The 'Shop Girl' in Interwar Japan," in *Modern Girls on the Go: Gender, Mobility, and Labor in Japan* (Stanford, CA: Stanford University Press, 2013).

45 Reproduced in Murobushi Tetsurō, ed., "Takabatake Kashō," special feature, *Purintsu 21: 21st Century Prints* 19, no. 3 (Autumn 2008), 13.

46 Matsumoto, *Takabatake Kashō: Taishō, Shōwa, retoro byūtī*, 53.

47 Reproduced in Takabatake Kashō Taishō Roman Kan, *Takabatake Kashō Taishō Roman Kan zuroku*, 106.

48 Reproduced in ibid., 101.

49 Reproduced in ibid., 107.

50 This image was used on the cover of a writing paper collection and is reproduced in Murobushi, "Takabatake Kashō," 12.

CHAPTER 9

~

Feminist Acts of Reading

Ariyoshi Sawako, Sono Ayako, and the
Lived Experience of Women in Japan

BARBARA HARTLEY

I N RECENT DECADES, revisionist feminist scholarship—scholarship
that revisits previous research with a view to identifying how women
have been elided—has retrieved the voices of many Japanese girls and
women subjugated by conventional academic activity. The narratives
of *komori*, child carers who were mere children themselves,[1] and *jokō*,
the young women whose arduous labor funded prewar Japanese state
excesses, are two groups whose previously unknown stories owe their
circulation to recent feminist activity. Similar work profiling individual women has ensured, for example, that the role of Kanno Suga (1881–
1911), the radical activist journalist murdered by the Japanese state, is no
longer concealed in the shadow of the Kōtoku Shūsui (1871–1911) legend.[2]

Some women's narratives, nevertheless, remain outside the sphere
of feminist endeavor, seemingly superfluous to a transnational movement, which, in the words of Chandra Talpade Mohanty, aims to highlight "a common context of struggles against exploitative structures and
systems."[3] This essay will discuss two post–World War II women writers, Ariyoshi Sawako (1931–1984) and Sono Ayako (b. 1931), whose textual contributions have been largely overlooked in revisionist feminist
inquiry. Sono, particularly, presents the conundrum of whether or not
feminist researchers should concern themselves with the activities of
women—often privileged—who hold political views that are violently
contrary to their own. Although politically inoffensive in this sense,

Ariyoshi has failed to capture the imagination of feminist scholars in the way that other literary women of her generation have.

In this discussion, I will argue for a feminist re-reading of the work of Ariyoshi and also of selected early texts by Sono. Since these narratives predate the transnational political consciousness that has informed Japanese feminist critiques of Japanese Imperial Army sex slavery policies, they may appear dated. Yet, Komashaku Kimi offers a feminist model for viewing such narratives as a way of "witnessing" women's subordination to patriarchal authority. In her 1984 discussion that demonstrates the demeaning inference in the term "office flower" (*shokuba no hana*), widely used in reference to women office workers,[4] Komashaku argues that postwar Japanese society forcibly categorized women as either prostitutes or wives. Each category derived from the same "source," namely misogynist social attitudes.[5] Observing how women were stripped of their humanity and thus objectified by the male gaze,[6] Komashaku noted that the literary narrative had the capacity to act as "witness" to the lived experience of this objectification.[7] This "witnessing" of women's marginalized social position occurs in many texts by Ariyoshi and in selected texts, particularly early texts, by the now reviled Sono.

In her 1994 discussion of high-speed economic growth and the postwar family, Ueno Chizuko noted what was basically the self-infantalizing quality of the postwar Japanese male,[8] who, she argued, regarded the husband/wife relationship as one of a mother and her son. If we overlay Ueno's ideas with those of Komashaku, we can only conclude that Japanese women at the time of high-speed economic growth were rendered as objects—either prostitutes or wives—by a powerful collection of self-infantalizing males. The texts of both Ariyoshi and the early Sono narrate the embodied experiences of these women. Ariyoshi's narratives, in particular, sit against and place in sharp relief a postwar background during which time, as Suzuki Yūko points out, the Occupation's "opportunistic" (*tsugōshugiteki*) promotion of the emperor developed into a form of "Shōwa Emperor adulation" (*Shōwa Tennō sanbi*).[9] This left the issue of Japan's wartime excesses destructively unresolved.

Suzuki's comments, however, are not confined to the activities of overt emperor system champions. She also critiques the wartime collusion of iconic prewar women's movement figures such as Hiratsuka Raichō (1886–1971), Ichikawa Fusae (1893–1981), and Takamure Itsue (1894–1964),[10] whose flagrant statements of support for the emperor and the war effort remained unquestioned following Japan's defeat.[11] Sono is no Hiratsuka, nor is she an Ichikawa. Nevertheless, given the fact that, in spite of the wartime failings of women such as Hiratsuka and Ichikawa, contemporary feminist scholars continue to assign value to their activities, there is surely value in these same scholars examining Sono's narratives to assess whether or not there are elements in this writer's works that can add to the feminist project.

Ultimately, regardless of the personal politics of individual women such as Sono, my discussion speaks to matters of feminist epistemology. I transfer to the Japanese context questions raised by Sandra Harding in her discussion of feminist practice and the construction of scientific knowledge.[12] Here, Harding asks: "Which kinds of knowledge projects have [significance for feminist researchers], which don't, and why?"[13] Echoing the approach of Gayatri Chakravorty Spivak, Chandra Talpade Mohanty, and bell hooks, Harding reminds us of the need to conduct research from the periphery and to consider a "logic" that will "start thought from marginalized lives."[14] This includes an investigative focus on "everyday [rather than heroic] life."[15] This task is not without problems. We know from Spivak's work that giving a voice to the marginalized can easily degenerate into the patronizing "speaking for" that is the hallmark of the hegemony.[16] Nevertheless, even as she articulates the contradictions involved, Spivak exhorts researchers to commit to this task.

Harding particularly advocates for an understanding of the fact that women's work involves the care of the bodies of "men, babies, children, old people, [and] the sick."[17] Since women are given "responsibility for local places where those bodies exist," they inadvertently free "men in the ruling groups to immerse themselves in the world of abstract concepts."[18] It is in the representation of the lived experiences of Japanese women with responsibility for the care of bodies in marginalized "local places" that the work of Ariyoshi and the early Sono can offer material for feminist consideration. We may question how a privileged ultra-conservative such as Sono can contribute to an understanding of the embodied experience of other women. Borrowing from the work of Ann Garry, however, Sakiko Kitagawa argues for a mode of feminism that permits an understanding of the "complex interconnectedness" of women's lives.[19] In other words, without in any way reverting to an essentialist interpretation of the idea of "women," Kitagawa implies that there are connections between various aspects of the lives of many if not all women. I would argue that the representation of this "complex inter-connectedness" between women's lives is a key feature of the narratives of Ariyoshi and the early Sono. Their texts are thus productive ground for considering the "exploitative structures and systems" that, recalling Mohanty, bring feminist praxis into play. I will argue this with reference to a number of works by Sono, while acknowledging the problems caused by this writer's more notorious ideological excesses. I will also argue for a re-reading of Ariyoshi while offering some thoughts on why she has failed thus far to rate as a candidate for feminist analysis.

Sono Ayako

There could be no figure more guaranteed to problematize the assumptions of feminist theory than Sono Ayako (b. 1931), the ultranationalist doyenne whose hard-right leanings saw her appointed education advisor to the second and current administration of Prime Minister Abe Shinzō.[20] Nevertheless, without valorizing her ultra-rightist activities, I argue that selected works by Sono have the potential to inform feminist research. While we may have little inclination to absolve the writer from responsibility for her excesses in the same way that postwar feminists overlooked the "serious wrong turn"[21] made by some prewar activist women, we should perhaps remember that even feminist icons can commit ideological error.[22] The reverse of this is that feminists might consider appropriating for their own use ideas that derive from the ideologically tainted.

Sono Ayako was not a wartime collaborator. She was a child in the early years of Japanese aggression in China and an adolescent during the Pacific War. She has, however, consistently offended with comments such as the claim that the forced suicides in Okinawa—"compulsory suicides" to borrow Norma Field's expression[23]—were carried out when "[f]athers and older brothers" acted "out of love" to "[end] the lives of their mothers and sisters."[24] While these and similar statements have made her a pariah among Okinawan activists, Sono was not always so strident. She first came to public notice in 1954 with the nomination of her short story, "Visitors from Afar" ("*Enrai no kyakutachi*"), for the Akutagawa Award. As Douglas Slaymaker notes, this powerful text, set in a Hakone hotel requisitioned by Occupation Forces, is "extraordinary for its time" in its scathing depictions of the "foibles and eccentricities, the complexes and anxieties, afflicting both Japanese and Americans."[25]

The narrative usually cited as the quintessential Occupation critique is Kojima Nobuo's 1954 work, "American School" ("*Amerikan sukūru*").[26] This work, I would argue however, is really little more than an account of the idiosyncrasies of the group of Japanese English-language teachers ordered to visit the eponymous school. In fact, the Occupation personnel and American teachers who feature in Kojima's text merely act as narrative ploys in order to profile all the more sharply the psychological state of the Japanese. This state ranges from the manic fear of the English language demonstrated by anti-hero "protagonist" Isa, to the inflated ego of the bullying Yamada who boasts both of his English-language skills and of his prowess in removing heads with a military sword following Japan's invasion of China.[27] In "Visitors from Afar," however, Sono's unforgiving eye relentlessly dissects the American presence. Among the memorable Occupation personnel drawn by the writer's incisive pen are the colorless Captain Diorio; the bullying commander, Captain Lynch, with his self-obsessed wife and petty shoplifting daughter; and the petulant young Texan barber, Sergeant Rose. Sono even takes a swipe at the iconic Helen Keller (1880–1968), who visited Japan in 1938 and then again in 1948.

Although she did not receive the prestigious literary award, the Akutagawa selection committee praised Sono's forthright account of the Americans who appear in "Visitors from Afar." In fact, several selection committee members noted the "new" or "fresh" approach taken by Sono, with Niwa Fumio commenting positively on the manner in which the narrator asserts herself as an equal in relation to the Americans in the text.[28]

An even more memorable aspect of Sono's narrative, however, is the derisive critique provided by the girl narrator, Namiko, of what she clearly regards as the pitiful inadequacy of her Japanese confreres. Namiko is especially contemptuous of Sakaguchi, the ex–Imperial Army sergeant in charge of the information desk at the hotel where she works. She is, in fact, completely devoid of sympathy for this middle-aged militarist whose precious ideals have been shattered by defeat. Given the strength of Namiko's disdain, readers at the time of the narrative's publication would have been hard-pressed to predict that this girl protagonist's creator would eventually emerge as Japan's fully fledged right-wing matrician. Similarly, Namiko's dismissal of the suffering of Kibe who, following the loss of her husband and child in Manchuria, commits double suicide with another hotel employee at the close of the text, suggests little empathy for the rightist-inspired victim mentality that eventually emerged in Japan. In fact, the incisive girl narrator's energy undercuts any sense of loss or grief, suggesting that the country's postwar future lies in the dynamism of its youth, who are untainted by the ideologies of the wartime era.

In addition to "Visitors from Afar," the young Sono produced other works that interrogated discourses supportive of the "emperor adulation" that Suzuki notes characterized the era. "Fire and Sunset" ("*Hi to yūhi*," 1957), for example, is an account of a fractious adolescent evacuated during the war, like Sono herself, to Kanazawa. As the narrative unfolds, the girl narrator realizes that her ailing grandmother is deeply loved by the elderly man who visits each day and who even assists the girl in her "body care-work" of washing her grandmother's diapers.[29] The narrative implies a sexual freedom on the part of women of the grandmother's generation during their girlhood in this region of prewar Japan, a freedom that subversively undermines the hegemonic demand imposed on girls of the time to preserve their chastity for marriage and to give their reproductive all to the state as a good wife and wise mother. Simultaneously, this depiction of the grandmother's response to the overtures of the elderly male visitor provides a remarkable affirmation of the sexual identity of the aging woman.[30] With its insights into the alternative gender and sexuality mores that operated behind the rigid norms imposed on prewar women, "Fire and Sunset" calls for a strong feminist reading. Similarly, feminist scholars can only applaud "Visitors from Afar" with its powerful girl protagonist whose incisive eye sees the shortcomings of both her Japanese and American confreres and who forthrightly gives voice to these shortcomings in a manner that, as Niwa's comments suggest, is very much on her own terms.

We might argue pragmatically against the study of women such as Sono—perhaps we just don't have the time. Isn't it better to retrieve the narratives of extraordinary women such as Kanno Suga or to tell the story of the mill girls whose embodied exploitation generated the capital through which the madness of Japanese militarism was unleashed? Yet, while she may fail abysmally as a model of feminism herself, Sono's texts can provide important insights into the experiences of women and girls. Brilliantly innovative scholarship may have excavated stories, such as those of Kanno and the mill girls, which were previously entombed in masculinist discourses. Yet Sono's early narratives, too, provide us with alternative accounts of women's lives that contest—while demonstrating the constraints that operated on women—the hegemonic assumptions that resulted in the erasure of both Kanno and the girls who worked the mills.

Ariyoshi Sawako

Ariyoshi Sawako's situation differs from that of Sono in that during her relatively brief life—cut short when she passed away in her sleep in 1984 at the age of fifty-three—she was never associated overtly with the political right. Ariyoshi's consignment to the margins of feminist research is, I would argue, related to negative reception patterns established by male *bundan* (literary establishment) scholars, patterns that have been inadvertently replicated in revisionist feminist analysis. Ariyoshi spent her professional life struggling to be recognized as a writer of serious literature. Women's literary recognition was often the function of a relationship to a powerful *bundan* man, particularly, as Rebecca Copeland and Esperanza Ramirez-Christensen point out, to a father with a literary background.[31] Ariyoshi, however, was not the daughter of a famous father, nor did she receive the unreserved accolade of any male critic. From a slightly different perspective, Chieko Ariga has noted in a discussion of mass-produced women's paperback literature that these narratives come to the reader through "the lens of [male] *bundan* critics." This, Ariga makes clear, leads to women's works "often becom[ing] framed in patriarchal discourses and appropriated for [the male critic's] purposes."[32]

Although Ariyoshi Sawako was one of postwar Japan's most prolific writers, assessment of her work most certainly was delivered in terms of Ariga's "patriarchal discourses." A novelist, short-story writer, essayist, and both kabuki and *bunraku* (puppet theater) playwright, she came to public notice in 1956 when, two years after Sono, one of her narratives was shortlisted for the Akutagawa Prize. While her work was not dismissed out of hand by the male selection committee, Ariyoshi committed the cardinal sin of setting her text in the traditional Japanese art world. As a result, her work was assessed as stale and out of date.[33] This was because mid-1950s Japan was a time during which "enlightened" (male) thinkers rejected traditional Japanese values as much as they rejected American cultural norms. That an interest in traditional Japanese themes was a violation of the standards that operated at the time is clear from Sono Ayako's observation that, in spite of her youth, Ariyoshi was often labeled in literary meetings as a middle-aged traditionalist.[34] Drawing inspiration from local sources, therefore, immediately marked Ariyoshi as unsuitable for recognition by the center of the Japanese literary community.[35] In spite of praise for her narrative ability, she became derogatively labeled as a writer of women's stories. Even those who commended her work did so conditionally. Okuno Takeo, for example, was often complimentary of Ariyoshi's achievements. To some extent, however, he saw her mainly as a young woman who could tell a good story.[36] Although he later relented and unreservedly praised the literary quality of her work, he also noted that he initially felt some resistance to Ariyoshi's narratives because they were read by so many of the women whom he knew.[37]

While Ariyoshi's work was included in early English-language compendiums of Japanese women's writing, and while a number of translations appeared of some of her best-selling novels,[38] there is little feminist scholarship that examines her narratives. Scrutiny of the women writers of her generation who have fired the imagination of feminist scholars— Kōno Taeko (b. 1926) and Kurahashi Yumiko (1935–2005), for example— indicates that these are writers whose work was the subject of discussion by members of the male-dominated *bundan*. Even if, as Atsuko Sakaki points out, Kurahashi had to defend herself from attacks by conservative commentators such as Etō Jun,[39] attacks that drove her to withdraw for a lengthy time from the public sphere, her work did at least draw the attention of powerful literary men. Relatively little attention, however, was given to Ariyoshi's material. While it is unlikely to be the result of deliberate intent, the fact remains that by overlooking Ariyoshi as a subject for their work, feminist researchers have duplicated the exclusionist tactics of *bundan* men. This is in spite of the fact that, as Yosano Keiko argues, Ariyoshi provided for Japanese women a "fluid (*jūnan*) and truly forward-looking image of womanhood" that was "not confined" by either time or circumstance.[40] Wendy Jones Nakanishi suggests, moreover, that Ariyoshi's style of writing has influenced the current generation of Japanese women detective writers.[41] Ironically, these latter have been the focus of much inspiring feminist scholarship.[42]

In many respects, Ariyoshi was a writer before her time. Her first long novel, *The River Ki* (*Ki no Kawa*, 1959), is the tale of three women of successive generations set against a backdrop of the changing social circumstances of modern Japan.[43] Based on the narratives of the women in her mother's family, the story is structured around the matriarch, Hana, and her fraught relationship with her eldest daughter, Fumio, a spirited young woman aligned with the prewar women's movement. A secondary theme of the novel is the strength of relationships between grandmothers and granddaughters—the text begins and concludes with the protagonist, Hana, as a granddaughter and grandmother, respectively. Three decades later, *The Joy Luck Club* (1987) and *The Kitchen God's Wife* (1991) by Amy Tan (b. 1952) became international best sellers. Each was more or less structured around generational relationships between women in one or more families in a manner similar to Ariyoshi's *The River Ki*. Tan, of course, is an extraordinary writer. Her texts, furthermore, have strong American content that attracts the first-language English reader. Nevertheless, there are enough similarities between the works of the two writers to suggest that Ariyoshi's material can be seen as a global precursor to the work of the American novelist. Had translations of her material been more thoughtfully marketed it is conceivable that Ariyoshi could have achieved a status in the West similar to that of Amy Tan's.

I would argue that one "problem" with Ariyoshi's material that has made her work unpalatable to both male writers and to some feminist scholars is an absence of the overt representation of sex. In the postwar era, at least, male critical admiration for a woman writer seems often to have been proportionate to the sexualized content, almost always understood in heterosexual terms, of the woman writer's work. (This was not necessarily the case in the prewar era when a woman's "worth" as a writer was often perceived as a function of her capacity to endure hardship.)[44] Thus, writers of highly sexualized material such as Kōno Taeko and Yamada Eimī (b. 1959)—both brilliant women—received accolades and close attention while Ariyoshi languished.

Certainly, Ariyoshi's depiction of sexual encounters can be bland. *The River Ki*'s Hana, for example, is the best wife and wisest mother in all of Ki Province. Nevertheless, she demonstrates a degree of remoteness toward Keisuke, her not unlikeable spouse, so that the affection she directs his way is curiously lacking in intensity. While the text suggests that Hana is physically aroused on her wedding night,[45] any intimation of sexual ardor is obliterated by her wooden performance of the act itself. Hana remains "rigid" in her husband's embrace, and even has the practical presence of mind to take care "not to ruin her elaborate coiffure."[46] It is, in fact, the moments in the text in which Hana interacts with those of her own sex that she most overtly evinces passion. I do not wish to imply a sexual relationship between Hana and other women in *The River Ki* or a sexual preference for women. On the contrary, she directs powerful, if clandestine, expressions of desire toward her brother-in-law, Kōsaku. Nowhere, however, does Hana clearly express toward any male the overt emotion that she shows early in the narrative toward her grandmother, Toyono, or later toward her granddaughter, Hanako. At the time of her departure as a bride from the family home, for example, readers are told:

> Toyono straightened Hana's kimono collar and whispered, "How enchanting you are!" Her eyes were wet with tears. Hana's eyes were also brimming and she held her breath lest she give way to her emotion.[47]

This depth of (albeit mildly saccharine) feeling demonstrated by both women might in other texts denote a separation of lovers.

Rather than avoiding the representation of sexuality, however, might it not be that Ariyoshi ultimately regards physical coupling with a male as a less compelling activity for a woman than other writers suggest? Hidaka Shōji has noted the tendency of Ariyoshi's male characters to be weak and ineffectual.[48] Should we be surprised, then, when her women protagonists decline to satisfy their carnal desires with these men? In other words, as Ann Sherif argues with respect to the novel *Kimono* by Kōda Aya (1904–1990), Ariyoshi's material can be read as a challenge to "the primacy of the heterosexual contractual relationship," emphasizing instead "the centrality of female bonds, primarily in a social and ideological sense, as a core aspect of subjectivity."[49]

Notwithstanding an absence of overt sex, Ariyoshi can nonetheless metaphorically suggest deep and transgressive emotions. One brilliant example occurs in *The River Ki* when, pre-empting the use of the raw egg as a metonym for passion by director Itami Jūzō (1933–1997) in the 1985 film *Tampopo*,[50] Ariyoshi has Hana consume a fresh egg she has bought as a gift for her brother-in-law with whom there is, for a time at least, a clear mutual attraction. Piercing the shell with a hairpin, she gently breaks the membrane of the egg, which she then throws "her head back" to consume.[51] The scene is quite voluptuous with intimations of masturbation—a private moment of personal pleasure connected by the metonym of the egg to Hana's embodiment, an association strengthened by the fact that she has only recently had a child. Nowhere in her work, however, do we see women who openly express their desires through, for example, Kōno's often discussed masochism or Yamada's attention-grabbing masturbation at an open window. This disinterest in the overt representation of women's sexual desire can create a misleading impression of conservatism and/or a lack of interest in women's corporeal experiences.

If Sono's early work demonstrates the potential for feminist endeavor in the writing of women authors who later cleave to the ultra-right, Ariyoshi, as is apparent in *The River Ki*, represents the experiences of many generations of women in Japan. Furthermore, there is a remarkable diversity to the content of her narratives, which range from the tale of the life of Izumo no Okuni (1572–?), the woman credited with "inventing" kabuki theater performance, to an account of the everyday struggle in New York's Harlem precinct of a Japanese war bride who returns to the United States with her African American husband.[52] Judging by the volume of the sales of her work, moreover, readers clearly understood the worth of her narratives. It is no accident perhaps that one of her highest-selling works, *The Twilight Years* (*Kōkotsu no hito*, 1972), which topped the 1972 best-seller list in Japan, was the narrative of a woman caring for the body of her aged father-in-law stricken with dementia—a clear "witnessing" of the work of a woman, recalling Harding, with responsibility for the welfare of a body in a highly localized place. Surely, Ariyoshi is one woman writer whose work demands a strong feminist reading and who deserves to be memorialized through robust feminist analysis.

Conclusion

Feminist methods have changed the course of scholarship inside and outside Japan across multiple fields of endeavor. I noted at the outset of this discussion that feminist scholars had retrieved voices subjugated or overlooked by conventional research activity. Yet these scholars have not been able to reverse fully the erasure of other women from the feminist public eye. This chapter has presented two women writers who, for markedly different reasons, have been overlooked in recent revisionist scholarship related to women in Japan. Yet I would argue that the work of both women can add value to feminist literary activity.

The emergence of Sono Ayako as a spokesperson for the ultra-right has led—understandably—to her complete exclusion from feminist scholarship. Nevertheless, scrutiny of this writer's early work demonstrates that the narratives of even a woman whose objectives are diametrically opposed to the feminist cause can contest the hegemonic assumptions that contribute to the social restraints imposed on many women in Japan. The assertive independence of the protagonist of Sono's "Visitors from Afar" drew the admiration of even the crusty male critics who judged the Akutagawa Prize–nominated short story. "Fire and Sunset" invokes the girlhood experiences of an elderly woman in a way that suggests considerable sexual license for the women of imperial Japan and that thereby interrogates, as successfully as more overtly feminist texts, the suffocating restrictions placed on these women by the asexual "good wife, wise mother" norm.

Ariyoshi's marginalization, on the other hand, is in many ways an unintended outcome of the manner in which literary production in Japan and elsewhere is often a highly gendered activity. Echoing Copeland and Ariga, Ueno Chizuko notes that the construction of gender in writing is a masculine endeavor and that women must comply with a writing style defined by men.[53] I would argue that similar constraints operate, in fact, on feminist scholars. In other words, despite the best attempts of researchers who seek to disrupt masculinist bias, given the all-encompassing nature of that bias and its associated discourses, it is perhaps to be expected that even revisionist feminist scholars have overlooked Ariyoshi's contribution. The mere volume of her output, however, which she produced in spite of her relatively short life, confirms that Ariyoshi's work demands close feminist investigation. Furthermore, this author's interest in narrating the lives of an extraordinarily wide variety of women located in an extraordinarily wide range of settings bears unequivocal witness not only, recalling Komashaku, to the "objectification" of women in Japan, but also to the remarkable way in which these women demonstrate agency and vitality in the face of social restraint.

166 BARBARA HARTLEY

Notes

1 For an account of *komori*, see Mariko Tamanoi, *Under the Shadow of Nationalism: Politics and Poetics of Rural Japanese Women* (Honolulu: University of Hawai'i Press, 1998), 55–84.

2 See the chapter on Kanno in Sharon L. Sievers, *Flowers in Salt: The Beginnings of Feminist Consciousness in Modern Japan* (Stanford, CA: Stanford University Press, 1983), 139–162.

3 Chandra Talpade Mohanty, *Feminism without Borders: Decolonizing Theory, Practicing Solidarity* (Durham, NC: Duke University Press, 2003), 46.

4 Komashaku Kimi, *Majo no ronri*, rev. ed. (Tokyo: Fuji Shuppan, 1984), 25–26. Here, Komashaku draws on the ideas of the German Marxist August Bebel (1840–1913).

5 Ibid., 25.

6 Ibid., 26.

7 Ibid., 27.

8 Ueno Chizuko, *Kindai kazoku no seiritsu to shūen* (Tokyo: Iwanami Shoten, 1994), 206–207. This book has also been published in English as *The Modern Family: Its Rise and Fall* (Melbourne: TransPacific Press, 2009).

9 Suzuki Yūko, *Feminizumu, tennōsei, rekishi ninshiki* (Tokyo: Inpakuto Shuppankai, 2006), 151.

10 Ibid., 35.

11 The issue of feminist collaboration with the state during wartime is discussed by Elyssa Faison in her chapter in this volume.

12 Sandra Harding, "Rethinking Standpoint Epistemology: What is 'Strong Objectivity?'" in *Feminist Epistemologies*, ed. and with intro. Linda Alcoff and Elizabeth Potter (New York: Routledge, 1993).

13 Ibid., 49.

14 Ibid., 50.

15 Ibid.

16 See Gayatri Chakravorty Spivak, *A Critique of Postcolonial Reason: Toward a History of the Vanishing Present* (Cambridge, MA: Harvard University Press, 1999).

17 Harding, "Rethinking Standpoint Epistemology," 55.

18 Ibid.

19 Sakiko Kitagawa, "Cultural Self-Understanding and Japanese Feminism," http://utcp.c.u-tokyo.ac.jp/members/pdf/kitagawa_east_asian _feminism.pdf, last accessed April 24, 2014. Kitagawa links this to the well-known feminist notion of "intersectionality," that is, "the set of

gender, race, social class and sexuality," but also notes that, while "the most impressive," this is not the only example of connectedness in women's lives.

20 Sono is a supporter of *oya gaku*, literally parental studies but implying a need to reject Western values and to suffuse a greater sense of prewar ideals into contemporary parenting. For information on *oya gaku*, see Matthew Penney, "Japan's Prime Minister and His Cabinet Members' Organizational Affiliation," *Peace Philosophy Centre*, February 21, 2013, http://peacephilosophy.blogspot.com.au/2013/02/japans-prime-minister -and-his.html.

21 Suzuki, *Feminizumu, tennōsei, rekishi ninshiki*, 35.

22 Instances of well-known feminist women failing to abide by industrial conditions for women whom they employ come to mind.

23 Norma Field, *In the Realm of a Dying Emperor: Japan at the Century's End* (New York: Vintage Books, 1993), 61.

24 I cite from Kamata Satoshi, "Shattering Jewels: 110,000 Okinawans Protest Japanese State Censorship of Compulsory Group Suicides," trans. Steve Rabson, *Japan Focus* 6, issue 1 (January 1, 2008), http://japanfocus.org /-Kamata-Satoshi/2625. The text referenced is the widely cited "epitaph" written by Sono, which accompanies a rock monument commemorating the Third Naval Attack Squadron, Third Battalion, on Tokashiki Island.

25 Douglas Slaymaker, *The Body in Postwar Japanese Fiction* (London: RoutledgeCurzon, 2004), 140.

26 Kojima Nobuo, "American School," in *Contemporary Japanese Literature: An Anthology of Fiction, Film and Other Writing Since 1945*, ed. Howard Hibbett (New York: Alfred A. Knopf, 1977). One discussion that cites this narrative as critical of the American presence is Edward Fowler, "Piss and Run: Or How Ozu Does a Number on SCAP," in *Word and Image in Japanese Cinema*, ed. Dennis Washburn and Carole Cavanaugh (Cambridge: Cambridge University Press, 2000), 285.

27 Kojima, "American School," 127.

28 Bungei Shunjū, "Akutagawa shō senpyō, no. 31," in *Akutagawa shō zenshū*, vol. 5 (Tokyo: Bungei Shunjū, 1982), 425.

29 Sono Ayako, "Hi to Yūhi," in *Shin Nihon bungaku zenshū*, vol. 20: *Sono Ayako shū* (1957; Tokyo: Shūeisha, 1963), 133.

30 Sono's valorization can only make us recall the 2001 denial of the old woman's worth made by Ishihara Shintarō (b. 1932), the then–Governor of Tokyo. For details, see the Committee on Elimination of Discrimination Against Women, "The Third Consideration of Japanese Governmental Report: Proposal of List of Issues for Pre-sessional

Working Group," January 27, 2003, http://www.jclu.org/katsudou/seimei
_ikensho/20030127e/03speech.html.

31 See Rebecca L. Copeland and Esperanza Ramirez-Christensen, eds., *The Father–Daughter Plot: Japanese Literary Women and the Law of the Father* (Honolulu: University of Hawai'i Press, 2001).

32 See Chieko M. Ariga, "Text versus Commentary: Struggles over the Cultural Meaning of 'Woman,'" in *The Woman's Hand: Gender and Theory in Japanese Women's Writing*, ed. Paul Gordon Schalow and Janet A. Walker (Stanford, CA: Stanford University Press, 1996), 353.

33 Selection panelists variously regarded the narrative as out of date, constrained by an "obligation/duty" theme, and a "re-hash" of the work of previous writers. See Bungei Shunjū, "Akutagawa shō senpyō No. 35," in *Akutagawa shō zenshū*, vol. 5.

34 Sono Ayako, "Ariyoshi-san no koto," *Bungakukai* 13, no. 3 (March 1959), 133.

35 Agawa Hiroki, Miura Shumon, and Okuno Takeo, "Ariyoshi Sawako: Hito to Bungaku," *Bungakukai* 38, no. 12 (December 1984), 173.

36 Okuno Takeo, *Nihon bungaku shi: Kindai kara gendai made* (Tokyo: Chūkō Shinsho, 1970), 227.

37 Okuno Takeo, *Joryū sakka ron: Shōsetsu wa honshitsuteki ni josei no mono ka* (Tokyo: Daisanbunmeisha, 1974), 194.

38 These include *The River Ki* (*Ki no kawa*), trans. Mildred Tahara (1959; Tokyo: Kodansha International, 1980); *The Doctor's Wife* (*Hanaoka Seishū no tsuma*), trans. Wakako Hironaka and Ann Siller Kostant (1967; Tokyo: Kodansha International, 1978); *The Twilight Years* (*Kōkotsu no hito*), trans. Mildred Tahara (1972; Tokyo: Kodansha International, 1984); and *The Kabuki Dancer* (*Izumo no Okuni*), trans. James A. Brandon (1969; Tokyo: Kodansha International, 1994).

39 Atsuko Sakaki, "(De)Canonizing Kurahashi Yumiko: Toward Alternative Perspectives for 'Modern' 'Japanese' 'Literature,'" in *Fiction in Contemporary Japan and Beyond*, ed. Stephen Snyder and Philip Gabriel (Honolulu: University of Hawai'i Press, 1999).

40 Yosano Keiko, "Josei bungaku no aratana uneri," *Bungaku* 9, no. 2 (March–April 2008), 79.

41 Wendy Jones Nakanishi, "Desperate Housewives in Modern Japanese Fiction," *Electronic Journal of Contemporary Japanese Studies*, May 14, 2007, http://www.japanesestudies.org.uk/articles/2007/Nakanishi.html.

42 See, for example, Amanda C. Seaman, *Bodies of Evidence: Women, Society, and Detective Fiction in 1990s Japan* (Honolulu: University of Hawai'i Press, 2004).

43 Ariyoshi, *The River Ki*.

44 See, for example, Agawa, Miura, and Okuno, "Ariyoshi Sawako," 174. Here Miura suggests that women such as Hayashi [Fumiko] and Hirabayashi [Taiko] could not have become writers without "the same sorts of arduous life experiences as men."

45 Ariyoshi, *The River Ki*, 23.

46 Ibid., 26.

47 Ibid., 17.

48 See Hidaka Shōji, "Jōkyō e no kakyō toshite: Ariyoshi Sawako to Kurahashi Yumiko," *Kokubungaku kaishaku to kyōzai no kenkyū* 25, no. 15 (December 1980), 105–106.

49 Ann Sherif, *Mirror: The Fiction and Essays of Kōda Aya* (Honolulu: University of Hawai'i Press, 1999).

50 Here, the young "gangster" character breaks a raw egg, which is then passed between his own mouth and that of his lover as the couple's passion heightens.

51 Ariyoshi, *The River Ki*, 71.

52 Ariyoshi, *The Kabuki Dancer*; Ariyoshi Sawako, *Hishoku* (Tokyo: Chūō Kōron Sha, 1964).

53 Ueno Chizuko, "Vernacularism and the Construction of Gender in Modern Japanese Language," *Proceedings of the Midwest Association for Japanese Literary Studies* 3 (Summer 1997), 10.

CHAPTER 10

~

Dangerous Women and Dangerous Stories

Gendered Narration in Kirino Natsuo's
Grotesque *and* Real World

KATHRYN HEMMANN

I N JULY OF 2003, former Japanese prime minister Mori Yoshirō stated that women without children should not receive welfare benefits. "It is truly strange that we have to use tax money to take care of women who don't even give birth once, who grow old living their lives selfishly and singing the praises of freedom," Mori explained in a speech addressing Japan's falling birthrate, which had reached an all-time low of 1.29 children per woman.[1] October of the same year saw the publication of the book *Howl of the Loser Dogs (Makeinu no tōboe).*[2] Its thirty-seven-year-old author, Sakai Junko, howled the praises of the freedom enjoyed by older unmarried women while attempting to dispel unpleasant stereotypes surrounding women who had left their twenties behind without marrying. Although women who fail to breed may indeed be seen as "loser dogs" by male politicians such as Mori, Sakai argues that the augmented incomes that accompany freer access to the working world have supported a revolution in women's lives. As a fortunate side effect, women are no longer pushed into undesirable marriages by economic necessity. Sakai's justifications for the pleasures of the single lifestyle touched a nerve in Japan, and her book quickly sold hundreds of thousands of copies.[3] *Howl of the Loser Dogs* is filled with bitter sarcasm and self-deprecating humor, and its author makes no move to identify her manifesto as a rallying cry for women of the twenty-first century. Nevertheless, Sakai is able to fashion a rational and reasonable rebuttal against the accusation that "selfish" women are responsible for perceived social ills such as falling birthrates and rising marriage ages.[4]

Anger at phallocentric discourse and the double standards imposed by a patriarchal society at the turn of the millennium found its way into feminist fiction as well. Kirino Natsuo (b. 1951) puts this sense of political frustration to literary use in her best-selling crime and suspense stories. After graduating with a law degree from Seikei University, Kirino began to write romance novels and won the Sanrio Romance Prize for *The Ways of Love* (*Ai no yukue*) in 1984.[5] By the early 1990s, however, Kirino had turned to crime fiction. Her 1993 debut mystery novel under her current pen name,[6] *Rain Falling on my Face* (*Kao ni furikakaru ame*), won the Edogawa Rampo Award for mystery fiction, but it was her 1997 novel *OUT* that became a breakout success, winning the Mystery Writers of Japan Award and being nominated for the 2004 Edgar Allen Poe Award of the Mystery Writers of America when it appeared in English translation.[7] Her novels have continued to be commercially successful while winning ever more prestigious literary awards, such as the Tanizaki Jun'ichirō Award for her 2008 novel *Tokyo Island* (*Tōkyōjima*) and the Murasaki Shikibu Literary Award for her novel *The Goddess Chronicle* (*Joshinki*), also published in 2008.[8]

This essay focuses on the novels *Grotesque* (*Gurotesuku*) and *Real World* (*Riaru wārudo*), which were both originally published to great acclaim in 2003 before going on to achieve international recognition in translation.[9] Through these stories, Kirino responds to several strands of discourse on women and social responsibility that shaped public policy in Japan at the turn of the century. By allowing women to narrate their own lives in these novels, Kirino explores both the agency and the deception involved in both personal and political storytelling. Even as her female characters claim the right to tell their own stories, their attitudes toward themselves and other women reflect misogynistic social discourse.

The traditions of mystery and detective fiction place great emphasis on first-person narrators, who exercise absolute control over what the reader knows and does not know. These narrators are also able to guide the reader's interpretations of events while influencing the reader's perception of other characters. Describing the role of the narrator in international crime fiction of the twentieth century, Rebecca Copeland writes, "Generally narrating his story from a first-person perspective, the private eye decides what constitutes truth. He locates it, names it, orders it, and acts on it."[10] Such privileges are typically considered to be masculine, Copeland argues; and, in much of the crime fiction of the twentieth century, the narrator is indeed a man. In *Detective Agency: Women Rewriting the Hard-Boiled Tradition*, Priscilla Walton and Manina Jones illuminate an alternate tradition of mystery novels narrated by female detectives, demonstrating that "when women's detective fiction uses the first-person perspective [. . .] the gaze and the voice is female."[11] The narrators in Kirino's *Real World* and *Grotesque* are not police officers or private investigators, however, but rather the accomplices and victims of the crimes around which both novels are centered. Kirino thus ascribes narrative agency to people who are typically treated as minor characters in someone else's story. Since the narration these characters offer may be their only way to achieve subjectivity, these women elucidate their justifications for their attitudes and behavior at length. Both the teenage narrators of *Real World* and the adult narrators of *Grotesque* seek to win the reader's sympathy and understanding as they attempt to explain their frustration with the social and economic systems that limit their ability to control their own lives. Even as Kirino gives her characters free rein to rant to their hearts' content, however, she also encourages the reader to be critical of the internalized misogyny expressed by her narrators.

Real Girls in *Real World*

Kirino's *Real World* has five narrator characters: a male high school senior who kills his mother, and the four female high school students who become involved with him as he flees from home immediately afterwards. These four young women, Toshi, Yuzan, Kirarin, and Terauchi, attend the same school and have been friends for years. They are drawn into the escape attempt of the boy, who attends a different high school, after he steals the bike and cell phone of Toshi, who lives next to him and indirectly witnessed the murder. Each of the novel's eight chapters is narrated by one of these girls or by the boy himself. At the end of the novel, Kirarin is killed in a car accident resulting from the boy's failed plan to hijack a taxi, and Terauchi is driven to commit suicide by the guilt she feels in the wake of the incident. The stress causes Yuzan to run away from home without graduating from high school, and a bitter and dispirited Toshi is left to pick up the pieces.

The male narrator of *Real World*, whom Toshi has unflatteringly dubbed "Worm," is loosely based on "Sakakibara Seito," the pen name of a fourteen-year-old junior high school student who killed an eleven-year-old boy in Kobe in 1997.[12] Three days after the murder, Sakakibara impaled his victim's head on the front gate of the boy's school along with a letter declaring his hatred of compulsory education and raucously celebrating the pleasure and release he found in killing. Sakakibara then sent a similar letter to the *Kobe shinbun* newspaper, taunting the police and justifying himself with confused statements such as "Maybe if I had been able to be myself since birth, I wouldn't have had to do things like leave the severed head in front of the junior high school's main gate."[13] After being captured by the police, Sakakibara confessed to four other attacks. The victims of these attacks were girls, one of whom was found bludgeoned to death. The violence of these crimes set off a debate in Japan concerning the vulnerability of girls and young women to male predators.[14] In *Real World*, Kirino similarly associates Worm, her Sakakibara stand-in,[15] with four young women, but each of these girls has her own story to tell about Worm. None of them is particularly frightened of him, and they do not consider themselves his victims. If anything, they are in turn amused and disgusted by his self-aggrandizing posturing, and each of them associates with him for her own purposes.

By demonstrating her female characters' surprising lack of concern regarding Worm's potential to harm them, Kirino turns the reader's attention to issues surrounding political notions of female vulnerability. In *Think Global, Fear Local*, David Leheny demonstrates that, although the 1999 Law for Punishing Acts Related to Child Solicitation and Child Pornography and for Protecting Children (Jidō kaishun jidō poruno kinshi hō)[16] was passed partly because of foreign criticism of Japanese sex tourism, it was also formulated in response to domestic fears concerning the breakdown of social order represented by the young women engaging in practices associated with "compensated dating" (*enjo kōsai*).[17] It was never entirely clear what these practices, which ranged from phone calls conducted through "telephone club" services to arranged visits to love hotels,[18] specifically entailed; but, as the legal age for sexual consent in Japan is thirteen, it would have been difficult to classify them as strictly illegal.[19] Measures taken to prevent compensated dating, such as increased police presence in youth centers like the Ikebukuro entertainment district of Tokyo, were less concerned with law and order than they were with protecting notions of childhood innocence associated with school-age girls. As Leheny explains, "Children are seen not just as vulnerable—and therefore in need of protection—because of their size and lack of experience, but also as innocent, and therefore less deserving of the world's myriad cruelties than adults."[20] Ideas regarding innocence and the necessity of protection were associated much more with young women than they were with young men, and the legislators who proposed and passed the 1999 law were much less interested in protecting young women (who often became its victims)[21] than they were with protecting their own image of young women as innocent and virginal.

Through its parallels to the Kobe Child Murders (*Kōbe renzoku jidō sasshō jiken*), *Real World* challenges such notions of youth vulnerability. In giving the young male murderer four outspoken female accomplices, Kirino overturns the concept of female innocence, demonstrating that young women are not sweet and pure but instead acutely conscious of social pressures and the disappointments of the adult world. By banding together into homosocial groups and rejecting the adult world, the four female narrators of *Real World* are not retreating into a fantasy of girlishness often associated with cute (*kawaii*) culture,[22] but instead are expressing their frustration and disappointment with the fate that awaits them as adult women, who are typified by the mother whom Worm despised.

Terauchi, the most emotionally astute of the four girls, commits suicide at the end of the novel upon realizing that, as a woman, she will never be able to live without compromising her identity as a rational thinker and critical observer given the social expectations surrounding young women, who experience strong pressure from their peers and employers to be innocent, sweet, and finely attuned to the needs of others.[23] In her suicide note to her friend Toshi, she describes the psychological anxieties arising from conflicting demands on women:

> I'm living in the middle of an unfamiliar transformation, I guess you'd call it, something mankind's never experienced before, with the role of family getting more messed up than anybody imagines, changing day by day, growing more complicated and individualistic, something nobody can really comprehend, and I have to pretend to fill all these roles every day. Otherwise I can't survive. That totally wears me out. In the reality of everyday

occurrences I've had to submit to people in order not to lose them.[24]

Toshi fully understands Terauchi's despair over the gendered expectations she must pretend to meet in order to be considered normal; not
only must she achieve the same measures of individualistic academic success as a male student, but she must also be attractive, approachable, and
friendly. If the life of a male student studying for college entrance exams
is stressful enough to drive Worm to homicide, then how much more
disheartening is the realization that the results of these exams are all but
meaningless to young women, who are still expected to become wives
and mothers while being systematically denied the same employment
opportunities as men.[25] Toshi's anger, Terauchi's suicide, Kirarin's death,
and Yuzan's rebellious flight from her family to live on her own in Tokyo
are characterized not as consequences of their involvement with Worm,
but rather as reactions against the alienation they experience at home, at
school, and within society at large. The unhappy endings of these girls'
stories may thus be understood as a form of literary attack against cultural double standards that allow no middle ground for young women to
negotiate their own identities as they move into adulthood.

Working Women and Working Girls in *Grotesque*

In *Grotesque*, Kirino focuses on what happens to high school girls after
they graduate and the adult women they become. By allowing her female
characters to narrate their own lives instead of acting as the victims or
villains in the lives of the men who surround them, Kirino removes these
women from the anonymity of statistics and endows them with agency
as individuals while simultaneously demonstrating their lack of freedom
within a phallocentric economy of desire. Within this social economy,
women measure themselves and each other according to their value to
men, either by means of their sexual desirability or by means of their
adherence to male standards of success that they can ultimately never
meet. Because women lose value as they get older, young women are dis-
dainful of older women, and older women attempt to preserve their youth
for as long as possible while resenting younger women. This real-world
unpleasantness is reflected in the narrative bitterness with which the

lives of the female characters of *Grotesque* are portrayed, and the novel's female narrators unwittingly internalize outward systems of misogyny as self-hatred. Like the teenagers of *Real World*, these narrators perceive high school as a dangerous environment for young women, who struggle to meet an impossible ideal of beauty and desirability whose logical conclusion is either prostitution of the body or prostitution of the soul. As they grow older, women are doomed to become disappointments if not outright failures. In *Grotesque*, Kirino thus reveals the system by which a woman's value is measured to be fundamentally flawed.

The primary narrator of *Grotesque* is an unnamed and unmarried thirty-nine-year-old woman who lives with her elderly grandfather in his government-funded apartment complex in "P Ward" on the east side of Tokyo.[26] She works part time in the ward office in the day-care section of the welfare division, where she investigates wait-listed applicants for the ward's forty-eight licensed day-care facilities, which are all operating at full capacity. Her story is set in motion by the death of her sister Yuriko, a prostitute who was murdered by an illegal immigrant named Zhang Zhe-zhong. Zhang also killed the narrator's former schoolmate Kazue, who, despite having graduated from a prestigious university and being employed at a large corporation, had also been working as a prostitute. The lives of these three women had been connected since high school, and *Grotesque* reveals how all of them have been betrayed by the phallocentric ideologies they unwittingly learned to embrace as teenagers.

Grotesque opens with the murder of Kazue, which parallels the TEPCO OL Murder Incident (*Tōden OL satsujin jiken*) of 1997, in which the body of a thirty-nine-year-old female office worker—or "OL"[27]—employed at Tokyo Power was found in an apartment in Shibuya's Maruyamachō love hotel district. Upon further investigation, the office worker, who had graduated from Keio Girls Senior High School (Keiō Gijuku Joshi Kōtō Gakkō), was revealed to have been a freelance street prostitute, and a thirty-year-old Nepalese man, supposedly one of her clients, was charged with her murder.[28] Adrienne Hurley cites Naitō Chizuko's *Empires and Assassinations* (*Teikoku to ansatsu*) as demonstrating how the media was able to create a story from the sparse facts concerning the case in order to entertain readers and viewers. For example, certain convenience store workers in Maruyamachō were familiar with the victim, telling police investigators that she would often buy low-calorie foods and that she was nothing but skin and bones.[29] From these sorts of second-hand observations came lengthy speculations on the woman's entire life history, and respected political opinion magazines such as *Bungei shunjū* and *Gendai* devoted entire issues to explications of the incident. Many fictionalized versions of the story, such as Sakabe Shūichi's manga *Backdoor Quota* (*Ura noruma*), quickly appeared on the shelves of bookstores and video rental stores.[30] Naitō argues that many of these publications, both highbrow and lowbrow, expressed excessive prurient interest in the love life of the victim, who was subjected to male fantasies of both the sexual and sociopolitical variety. Commenters overtly and obliquely suggested that her murder was a logical result of her perceived licentiousness and that her personal failings were a direct consequence of her career ambition.[31]

Kirino challenges this system of male-centered discourse in *Grotesque* by allowing the women involved to tell their own stories. The writer especially succeeds in deglamorizing phallocentric fantasies of prostitution by showing that, even as prostitution functions as a problematic means of self-expression for Kazue, it ultimately fails the narrator's sister Yuriko, for whom it temporarily served as a means of income and a signifier of prestige. By the end of the novel, the beautiful Yuriko, who dropped out of high school to become a model and hostess, trolls the same street corner of Shibuya that Kazue, the graduate of one of the nation's top universities, does. The two are equally unsuccessful as prostitutes, and they both compare themselves to an old woman they call "the Marlboro Hag," whose territory they have appropriated. The Marlboro Hag does not have a backstory, and she doesn't need one; it is implied that, without a man to support them, all women end up in the same situation: old, ugly, and ignored. Just as they are doomed to fail in a competition with men in the world of work, women are also doomed to lose to other women in the competition for male attention. According to the phallocentric economies of desire that constrain Kazue and Yuriko, women who cannot remain girls are doomed to failure. In the closing chapters of *Grotesque*, the narrator, who cares for her senescent grandfather and assumes custody of Yuriko's illegitimate son, prides herself on her usefulness as a feminine caregiver, but she continues to rate herself unfavorably against Kazue and Yuriko, blind to the misery caused by patriarchal hierarchies and competition between women.

Instead of living glamorous lives as economically successful "loser dogs" blithely thwarting conservative gender roles, the narrator of

Grotesque, as well as Kazue and Yuriko, demonstrates that societal norms of femininity and family are difficult to escape. The narrator's own problematic solution to the paradox of femininity is to remain a girl by remaining a virgin, thus retaining her value, if only at a symbolic level. At the end of the novel, she muses:

> Once I graduated from college I took a completely different path from my model-turned-prostitute younger sister. I chose to be inconspicuous. In my situation, inconspicuousness meant living forever as a virgin, a woman who would have no contact with men. . . . A permanent virgin. Do you know what this signifies? It may sound wholesome and pure to you, but that was not actually the case. Kazue articulated it brilliantly in her journals, didn't she: to miss the only chance one has to have power over a man. Sex is the only way a woman has to control the world.[32]

By renouncing her sexual identity as a woman, the narrator sees herself as giving up on competing in a male-dominated world. For her own personal satisfaction, however, she stays in her grandfather's apartment and continues to wear her class ring from her elite private high school, thus maintaining some remnant of her privileged status of "schoolgirl" while abjuring the abject identity of an adult woman. The narrator, Kazue, and Yuriko have internalized misogynistic phallocentric economies of desire that reward youthful beauty and heterosexual attraction. Since these women have realized that they will never be able to compete on a level playing field with men, they compete with other women for the attention of men, sometimes even within their own families. Since the female characters in *Grotesque* are too competitive with each other to communicate or to form alliances in the way that men do, their ultimate fate is to be either dead, as in the case of Kazue and Yuriko, or severely emotionally disconnected from the world, as in the case of the narrator. Within a male-dominated society, the pleasures of the independent woman are eclipsed by the nagging shame generated by every woman's inevitable failure to live up to unrealistic standards. By illustrating the effect of such impossible expectations on the lives of individual women in uncomfortably sharp detail, Kirino forces her reader to acknowledge their implicit misogyny.

Nevertheless, Kirino's characters are able to exercise a modicum of personal agency in *Grotesque* by telling their own stories. The novel's narrative viewpoint is fractured and more than likely edited not just by the main female narrator but by the secondary narrators as well, thus disallowing the possibility of any one definitive interpretation. Kikuchi Yumi has argued that the entirety of Kirino's novel functions as a conversation between the unnamed narrator and the writers of the documents she presents to the reader, which often flatly contradict the information the narrator has presented as fact. Although the primary narrator "asserts her subjectivity by claiming the authority to interpret the pasts of other people," she is clearly emotionally unbalanced and unreliable.[33] The firsthand accounts the narrator offers the reader, such as journals supposedly written by Kazue and Yuriko, are not any more trustworthy, however, as each narrator has a major stake in explaining and justifying her behavior both to the reader and to herself. Although all of the narrators of *Grotesque* deceive themselves and rely on misogynistic stereotypes to tell their stories, it is their prerogative to narrate their own lives from their own perspectives as individuals instead of as gendered embodiments of phallocentric anxieties concerning the roles of women in a changing society.

Telling Their Own Stories

In *Real World* and *Grotesque*, Kirino Natsuo critiques the contradictions inherent in phallocentric discourses on women in Japan by demonstrating their effects on the women themselves, who find themselves trapped in a cycle of outwardly imposed misogyny and internalized self-hatred that they in turn direct toward other women. By lifting female "characters" from public discourse and transforming them into independent subjects by granting them the ability to narrate their own lives, the author establishes fiction as a serious and effective channel of feminist activism. Kirino's novels have been received well by critics and have reached a large and diverse audience[34] despite the dark tone of her writing and the explosive volatility of the social and political topics she addresses. In a postmodern world dominated by a powerful and inexorable news media, stories have an incredible power to shape not just the lives of individuals but also the trajectories of societies, and Kirino's brilliant and compelling crime fiction demonstrates the ability of female-centric stories to provide a necessary alternative and counternarrative to mainstream discourses on women and gendered political issues in contemporary Japan.

Certainly, an author does not have the ability to shape legal and political discourses as directly as politicians or bureaucrats do, but many of the social issues currently being debated in Japan, such as the shrinking workforce, low birthrate, and aging population, directly concern women and the choices they make in their lives. By drawing her material from sensationalist news stories and hot topics in political debates, Kirino imbues her novels with the potential to shift public opinion and inspire the critical attitudes necessary to provoke social change. Fiction thus serves as a mirror in which women and men can scrutinize their lives, the limitations imposed on them, the future paths available to them, and the means by which they can shape the world to reflect their own identities and desires. The goals of feminist activism include not only social and political change but also the inseparable matter of cultural change, and rethinking literature by recovering and amplifying women's voices is a critical step in the transformation of the stories societies tell themselves about gender and equality.

Notes

1   Anthony Faiola, "Japanese Women Live, and Like It, On Their Own: Gender Roles Shift As Many Stay Single," *Washington Post*, August 31, 2004, http://www.washingtonpost.com/wp-dyn/articles/A47261-2004Aug30.html.
2   Sakai Junko, *Makeinu no tōboe* (Tokyo: Kōdansha, 2003).
3   Tomomi Yamaguchi, "'Loser Dogs' and 'Demon Hags': Single Women in Japan and the Declining Birth Rate," *Social Science Japan Journal* 9, no. 1 (2006): 109.
4   Married women with children have also been regarded as selfish by male pundits and policy makers, who view them as enjoying a carefree existence away from the pressures of the working world in a "woman's paradise" (*onna tengoku*). See Margaret Lock, "Centering the Household: The Remaking of Female Maturity in Japan," in *Re-Imaging Japanese Women*, ed. Anne E. Imamura (Berkeley: University of California Press, 1996), 82.
5   Kirino Natsuo, *Ai no yukue* (Tokyo: Sanrio, 1984).

6 "Kirino Natsuo" is a pen name for Hashioka Mariko. Earlier in her career, the writer also used the pen names Kirino Natsuko for romance fiction and Nobara Noemi for young adult fiction. In addition, she has used the pseudonym Morizono Miruku for her work as a script and scenario writer for a genre of women's (*josei*) manga referred to as "ladies' comics" (*redīzu komikkusu*, often shortened to *redi komi*), which are often stereotyped as disposable pornography for women in their twenties and thirties but frequently contain strong elements of social criticism.

7 Kirino Natsuo, *Kao ni furikakaru ame* (Tokyo: Kōdansha, 1993); Kirino Natsuo, *Out*, trans. Stephen Snyder (London: Vintage Books, 2006), originally published as *OUT* (Tokyo: Kōdansha, 1997).

8 Kirino Natsuo, *The Goddess Chronicle*, trans. Rebecca Copeland (Edinburgh: Canongate, 2012), originally published as *Joshinki* (Tokyo: Kadokawa Shoten, 2008); Kirino Natsuo, *Tōkyōjima* (Tokyo: Shinchōsha, 2008). Detailed information on Kirino's life and literary career can be found on her website, *Bubblonia* (http://www.kirino-natsuo.com). See also J. Madison Davis, "Unimaginable Things: The Feminist Noir of Natsuo Kirino," *World Literature Today* 84, no. 1 (2010): 10.

9 Kirino Natsuo, *Grotesque*, trans. Rebecca Copeland (London: Vintage Books, 2007), originally published as *Gurotesuku* (Tokyo: Bungeishunjū, 2003); Kirino Natsuo, *Real World*, trans. Philip Gabriel (London: Vintage Books, 2008), originally published as *Riaru wārudo* (Tokyo: Shūeisha, 2003).

10 Rebecca Copeland, "Woman Uncovered: Pornography and Power in the Detective Fiction of Kirino Natsuo," *Japan Forum* 16, no. 2 (2004): 251.

11 Priscilla L. Walton and Manina Jones, *Detective Agency: Women Rewriting the Hard-Boiled Tradition* (Berkeley: University of California Press, 1999), 14.

12 In the original Japanese, the nickname given to Worm by Toshi and her friends is "Mimizu," which refers specifically to an earthworm. In contrast, the self-chosen pseudonym "Sakakibara Seito" betrays an almost humorous degree of literary affectation and is written with characters suggesting a meaning along the lines of "the sacred drunken demon of the rose."

13 Adrienne Carey Hurley, *Revolutionary Suicide and Other Desperate Measures: Narratives of Youth and Violence from Japan and the United States* (Durham, NC: Duke University Press, 2011), 164.

14 David Leheny, *Think Global, Fear Local: Sex, Violence, and Anxiety in Contemporary Japan* (Ithaca, NY: Cornell University Press, 2006), 59–63.

15 Like Sakakibara, whose real name has been withheld from the media according to child protection laws, Worm is not given a real name in *Real*

World. Moreover, Toshi's unflattering description of Worm is uncannily similar to Sakakibara's photo, which was leaked to the press and is easily accessible through a quick search on the Internet. Kirino references the online discussions of the Kobe Child Murders when Terauchi's younger brother shows her a picture of Worm that he has found on an online message board.

16 In the title of this law, the term used to refer to prostitution, *kaishun*, was presumably chosen over the more common term *baishun* in order to emphasize the illegality of buying sex as opposed to selling sex, thus placing the onus of responsibility on the men who engaged the services of prostitutes, not the prostitutes themselves. This emphasis is consistent with the ostensible purpose of the law, which was to protect innocent young women from lecherous older men. There is ample evidence to suggest, however, that the youth surveillance recommended and justified by the law was focused on punishing "financial deviancy" on the part of young women. See Sharon Kinsella, *Schoolgirls, Money, and Rebellion in Japan* (New York: Routledge, 2014).

17 "Compensated dating" is not necessarily a euphemism for prostitution. As Leheny, in *Think Global, Fear Local*, and Kinsella, in *Schoolgirls, Money, and Rebellion*, explain, the activities to which the expression refers were never clearly specified, but the general understanding as advanced by both news and entertainment media was that the practice involved young women going on dates (either in public places, such as a coffee shop, or in more private spaces, such as a karaoke room) for pocket money.

18 A telephone club (*terekura*) service is a phone number that a patron dials (sometimes from a booth in a small store devoted to the purpose) to be connected with a person (usually female) who may then arrange to meet for a date or for paid sex. Love hotels are hotels in which guests can book rooms by the hour; they are convenient for couples because of the anonymous and frequently automated nature of the check-in process.

19 The age of consent is set in Articles 176 and 177 of the Penal Code of Japan. However, most prefectural-level laws raise the age to 16 or 18. The age of majority in Japan is 20, and local laws further regulate sexual behavior involving minors. Based on where the offense occurred, sexual activity with a minor would be treated differently by municipal or district laws. Nevertheless, 13 remains the national standard age of consent.

20 Leheny, *Think Global, Fear Local*, 54.

21 Young women became victims of the law in the sense that they were harassed by police officers (and, in extreme situations, incarcerated), whereas the men who paid for their services were not held accountable.

In other words, the law resulted in the policing of female rather than male behavior.

22 See Brian McVeigh, "Commodifying Affection, Authority and Gender in the Everyday Objects of Japan," *Journal of Material Culture* 1, no. 3 (1996); and John Whittier Treat, "Yoshimoto Banana Writes Home: *Shōjo* Culture and the Nostalgic Subject," *Journal of Japanese Studies* 19, no. 2 (1993).

23 See Alisa Freedman, "Bus Guides Tour National Landscapes, Pop Culture, and Youth Fantasies," in *Modern Girls on the Go: Gender, Mobility, and Labor in Japan*, ed. Alisa Freedman, Laura Miller, and Christine R. Yano (Stanford, CA: Stanford University Press, 2013).

24 Kirino, *Real World*, 183.

25 See Joyce Gelb, *Gender Policies in Japan and the United States: Comparing Women's Movements, Rights, and Politics* (New York: Palgrave Macmillan, 2003), 41–63; and Tachibanaki Toshiaki, *The New Paradox for Japanese Women: Greater Choice, Greater Inequality*, trans. Mary E. Foster (Tokyo: International House of Japan, 2010), 227–264.

26 Amanda Seaman describes the east Tokyo of Miyabe Miyuki's 1992 suspense novel *All She Was Worth* as a "working-class neighborhood circumscribed by the employment and lifestyle of its inhabitants. [It is] not the world of brand-name goods and foreign goods; rather, its inhabitants are focused on the needs and demands of everyday existence." In *Grotesque*, the narrator's description of "P Ward" as being right across the river from Chiba Prefecture suggests that the area is modeled after Edogawa Ward. See Amanda C. Seaman, *Bodies of Evidence: Women, Society, and Detective Fiction in 1990s Japan* (Honolulu: University of Hawai'i Press, 2004), 31.

27 The "OL" of "TEPCO OL Murder Incident" stands for "office lady," or female office worker. Although the designation "OL" previously referred specifically to a quasi-secretarial class of female workers expected to retire after getting married in their mid-twenties, the term has come to be applied to any woman who works in a formal office setting. This shift may be partially a result of the gradual elimination of nonessential staff in large companies in the post-bubble economy of the 1990s, as well as the gains made by women in the workplace in this environment.

28 After multiple hearings, Govinda Mainali was found innocent on the basis of DNA evidence and released from prison in 2012.

29 Hurley, *Revolutionary Suicide*, 200; Naitō Chizuko, *Teikoku to ansatsu: Jendā kara miru kindai Nihon media hensei* (Tokyo: Shinyōsha, 2005).

30 Sakabe Shūichi, *Ura noruma*, 3 vols. (Tokyo: Green Arrow Shuppansha, 2008–2009).

31 Hurley, *Revolutionary Suicide*, 200.

32 Kirino, *Grotesque*, 460.

33 Kikuchi Yumi, "Kirino Natsuo *Gurotesuku* ni okeru futatsu no monogatari: 'Kataru mono' no yokubō to 'katarareru mono' no teikō," *Kokubun* 114 (2010): 50.

34 Davis, "Unimaginable Things," 10.

PART IV

Rethinking Boundaries

THIS SECTION GATHERS CHAPTERS that investigate and redraw the boundaries between Japanese feminism and its various "others." Some of the binaries examined and challenged include Japan versus non-Japan, straight versus queer, and mainstream versus minority groups.

Sarah Frederick invites us to reconsider the figure of socialist feminist Yamakawa Kikue (1890–1980) through transnational boundary crossing and queer internationalism, specifically Yamakawa's translation of the writings of Edward Carpenter (1844–1929). Carpenter was a sexologist with a complex understanding of gender difference and androgyny, who believed that sexual relations could be one basis for social politics. In focusing on Yamakawa's translation of Carpenter, Frederick draws our attention to the unexpectedly queer and affective dimensions of the famed socialist feminist in early twentieth-century Japan.

Setsu Shigematsu reexamines the 1970s women's liberation movement in Japan known colloquially as *ūman ribu* (women's lib), interrogating its contradictory legacy in order to propose a new framework for critical transnational feminism. Noting in particular the Japanese women's liberation activists' engagement with the question of violence and imperialism, Shigematsu proposes critical transnational feminism to facilitate conversation between Japanese feminists and women of color, third world feminists, and postcolonial feminists.

Akwi Seo evaluates the activism of Korean women in Japan from the perspective of transnational and postcolonial feminism. Focusing on the group Uri Yeoseong (Korean Women) Network, which was active from 1991 to 1998, Seo analyzes its efforts to transcend multiple boundaries between women of different nationalities, political affiliations, and cultural backgrounds. These Korean women activists aspired to build a transnational feminist counterpublic addressing worldwide violence against women, in particular the issue of Japanese military "comfort women" during the Asia-Pacific War. Seo's chapter thus provides a concrete example of the kind of critical transnational feminism proposed by Shigematsu.

Finally, Keith Vincent takes up the possibilities of global alliances forged by prominent feminist and queer scholar, Takemura Kazuko (1954–2011). Takemura was a scholar of American and English literature and was instrumental in translating feminist and queer theory from English to Japanese. This chapter echoes Frederick's chapter in focusing on another high-profile Japanese feminist and her queer affiliations. It also shares the attention to transnational boundary crossing found in the other chapters. In showing how Takemura's work as a boundary crosser provides a model of engaged scholarship, Vincent's chapter also suggests ways forward for rethinking Japanese feminisms.

—AK

CHAPTER 11

~

Yamakawa Kikue and Edward Carpenter

*Translation, Affiliation, and
Queer Internationalism*

SARAH FREDERICK

Y AMAKAWA (AOYAMA) KIKUE (1890–1980) remains one of the most
famous figures in the history of Japanese feminism. She participated in important debates in Japanese feminist thought in both prewar
and postwar Japan, and her rigorous argumentation from a Marxist
feminist position stands as some of the most coherent and polemically
effective material in this history. Within the leftist community she was
particularly effective at bringing attention to gender issues, while among
feminists she constantly called attention back to issues of class and the
importance of economic independence for women in any vision of equality or liberation—positions discussed by Elyssa Faison in her chapter
in this volume. Yamakawa's work as a translator, however, has received
relatively little recognition, with most focus being on her translations
of August Bebel (1840–1913) and rarely on her important translations
of the more eclectic Edward Carpenter (1844–1929).[1] Carpenter was an
extremely influential contributor to world political and cultural thought
in the early twentieth century, particularly in his combined attention to
queer sexualities and socialism. In Japan, he was deeply influential and
known by most intellectuals in the 1910s and 1920s. While Carpenter was
seemingly known to all the major prewar Japanese feminists, he has been
rather seldom discussed in North American studies of Japanese feminism.[2] This chapter explores this history and the possible influences of

Carpenter on Yamakawa and Japanese feminisms more generally. It suggests also a need for broader attention to queer cosmopolitanism and to Carpenterian modes of queer affiliations, friendships, and cultural comparison in thinking about twentieth-century Japanese feminisms.

While no longer mentioned in most histories of early Japanese feminism, Edward Carpenter turns up frequently in 1920s writings in political philosophy and the arts.[3] It is difficult to quickly characterize the thought of this socialist, philosopher, poet, composer, historian and theorist of sexuality, and founder of the Fabian Society, but a few examples can illustrate the broad appeal of Carpenter. We see Yoshiya Nobuko invoke Carpenter in her important essay "Loving One Another" ("*Aishiau kotodomo*," 1921). Her main purpose was to push back against women's education experts during a panic about relationships among schoolgirls after several famous double suicide incidents. Yoshiya argued that rather than condemning such relationships on the basis of outlying incidents, educators should value them because the "friendship love" (*yūai*) at girls' schools could serve as a transportable skill when they reach adulthood. Yoshiya's account brings out one of the appeals of this socialist thinker for Japanese feminisms in the 1920s, with attention to the possibilities for adolescent girls (*shōjo*):

> In his "Affection in Education" (*Ai no kyōiku*), Edward Carpenter points to this sort of feeling, this friendship love. When it occurs between older girl (*nenchō no shōjo*) and younger girl (*nenshō no shōjo*), or else between an instructor and student, it can be extremely advantageous from an educational perspective, and immeasurably so. When this happens, the younger girl's feelings towards the older girl or the teacher she loves do not stop at taking her as a love object; she worships her as a sort of hero for her own spirit and imitates her. Meanwhile, the older girl is touched by the dearness of that younger girl and becomes her protector and helper, and almost without realizing it they both develop a beautiful ethical, social, and unselfish character.[4]

Wondering by what means Yoshiya came to learn of Carpenter's thought, I discovered that she made use of Yamada Waka's paraphrase of Edward Carpenter's "Affection in Education" (1899) in a 1920 Japanese volume. As Yoshiya made only the slightest of modifications to Yamada's account, in today's practice most would call this plagiarism. But this seems to have been a common practice at the time, and it is hard to know what went on behind the scenes in terms of personal exchanges of texts and translations. Yamada is using Carpenter to discuss a modern but still biologically grounded notion of gender difference.[5] Yoshiya's targeted change from Yamada is to use the word "*shōjo*" (girl) to replace "*shōnen*" (boy, or youth). This diverges from Carpenter's own focus on sexuality among schoolboys, to emphasize "pure" relationships among schoolgirls, which were under scrutiny at the time, though quite accepted among even quite conservative educators.

A standard reading is to focus on the "virginal," "pure," "spiritual," and "nonphysical" aspects of these relationships. Still, I would argue that Yoshiya is building on the embrace of same-sex sexuality as a part of social ethics in an established thinker to support her own view of passionate relationships among girls in her own time.[6] I think it is important not to underplay the extent to which these were represented by Yoshiya and others as having some physical elements and as erotic in nature, even if not considered "sexual" because they did not involve *heterosexual* sex. As Akaeda Kanako argues, it was also important that even as they used terms like "spiritual" they also were increasingly "including same-sex love in the category of sexuality" and that this "new knowledge" was related to the translation of Carpenter.[7]

Meanwhile, translator Tamura Hiroshi emphasizes instead the argument that "physical love and sexual love" (*nikutai ai to seishin ai*; glossed by the translator in his introduction with the English "sexual passion" and "spiritual love") are important parts of marriage and key to "liberation of women long-oppressed" (*sokubaku sarete kita onna no kaihō*); for this reason he chooses the title *Sexual Love Marriage: A Cry for Reform* (*Sei-ai kekkon: Kaizō no sakebi*) for *Love's Coming of Age*, and emphasizes the choice of one's own marriage partner.[8] We can see the ways that quite diverse feminisms were invoking Carpenter at this time with various nuances. By the time of her own translation in 1921, Yamakawa can easily write in her introduction that Carpenter "has a large number of books translated into Japanese, and his thought and the person are well known in Japan."[9]

As Jeffrey Angles discusses, Edogawa Ranpo and Hamao Shirō exchanged Carpenter's books along with those of John Addington Symonds as part of a passionate correspondence.[10] Somewhat earlier we see a major translation of many of Carpenter's writing on diverse subjects, including music, translated by Miura Kanzō (1883–1960). In his introduction Miura writes that for him Carpenter would be a "Bible for our times," bringing the "proper joy of sex (*sei*, glossed as *sekkusu*) and limitless empathy, together with a new vision for an eternally harmonious world." Miura was a Methodist minister and translator (from English versions) of works by diverse writers including Tolstoy, Kropotkin, and Tagore. (In the postwar period Miura also translated Helene Blatvatsky and formed a school of yoga).[11] But first the introduction cites a passionate and sympathetic review of Oscar Wilde's *De Profundis* by Tanaka Ōdō (1868–1932), who himself had referred to Wilde as this "Bible for modern times."[12] Like Yoshiya's citation of Carpenter, these references are not surprising given that all of these figures are commonly discussed in terms of "same-sex love" and queer sexualities.

As prefigured by Miura's comments on a "harmonious world" and connections to Tagore, more recently Carpenter has become an important figure for rethinking liberalism, colonialism, and queer internationalism, such as in discussions of his friend E. M. Forster's fiction, and particularly Carpenter's inspiring influence for *Maurice*. Lauren Goodlad writes that friendship among men was "upheld as a liberating alternative to the status quo," and that in *The Intermediate Sex* (1906) Carpenter explored a utopian vision "describing 'Love' as a 'binding and directing force' that could harmonize bonds of sex, nurture, brotherhood, and citizenship." Including in his vision working-class men, women, and colonized peoples, Carpenter saw "inequality as a 'democratic' spark for mutually uplifting desire."[13] Goodlad's interpretation gives us a good sense of the appeal of *The Intermediate Sex* for Yamakawa.

While many visions of late Meiji (1868–1912) and Taishō (1912–1926) era thought are often caught up in an "importation" model of Western thought, we see many Japanese progressive thinkers in the early twentieth century also writing and speaking in terms of a model of cosmopolitanism in their modes of boundary crossing rather than an East–West interaction. Sakai Toshihiko, who was probably the first to translate Carpenter (in 1895), writes with interest in the "cosmopolitan," seeking definitions in Japanese and English dictionaries, and with self-deprecating humor considering whether he might fit the definitions; he is most interested in the idea of being "free from local, or national ideas, prejudices, or attachments."[14]

It is worth noting that one area of boundary crossing between Carpenter and Japanese thinkers was quite literal. Carpenter corresponded with and met in person a significant number of Japanese people in the 1910s.[15] We see among these correspondents Noguchi Yonejirō (poet, critic, and father of Isamu Noguchi), Tomita Saika (translator and professor at Kansai Gakuen), Abe Isō (prominent thinker), and Itō Kei (aspiring woman novelist and comparative philosopher of religions who later published as Itō Megumu).[16] The most intense interaction was with Ishikawa Sanshirō, a Christian socialist involved in establishing the journal *Sekai fujin* (World women), who was also connected with figures involved in the High Treason Incident (*Taigyaku jiken*) of 1910.[17] In fact, it is likely that Ishikawa was spared prosecution because he had already been arrested for distributing Carpenter's ideas, which he had identified as an alternative to "mere mechanical materialistic socialism."[18] He wrote letters, often addressed, "My adorable Mr. Carpenter," and went to England to stay with Carpenter and joined various events and Fabian parties. Feminist Fukuda Hideko also wrote to Carpenter to thank him for helping Ishikawa while he was in England and for helping him find a supporter in Europe. After losing financial support in Japan, Ishikawa had gone "quite penniless and depressed" to Brussels, had been taken in as a helper to a friend of Carpenter's and was sustained by funds from Carpenter, and, it seems, bank transfers from friends such as Fukuda in Japan.[19] Ishikawa is also one of the links to Yamakawa, as he was a speaker at a forum on women's issues run by the feminist socialist group Red Wave Society (Sekirankai) that included Sakai Magara (Sakai Toshihiko's daughter), Yamakawa, and Itō Noe.

Carpenter sought news of and knowledge about Japan.[20] In response, Tomita Saika writes, for example: [sic] "It is my great pleasure to inform you your very recent work—translations of *Toward Democracy*—were found in here so remotest and farthest district of this country about seventeen hours' distance from the capital. A tea party with name of *TD* was took place by them last night."[21] Carpenter continued to ask these friends and translators about Japan, not only about his own reception there, but knowledge for the sake of his own thinking. He seems to have been aware of Mushanokōji Saneatsu's utopian socialist community New Village (Atarashiki Mura), which too was influenced by Carpentarian thought, as were some other nudist and utopian societies in Japan.[22] Carpenter in turn was fascinated by sexuality in Japan, as

introduced to him by the writings of late nineteeth-century resident of
Japan Lafcadio Hearn, translations of seventeenth-century writer Ihara
Saikaku, accounts of love among men in the samurai community, and
conversations with Ishikawa. He writes to Ishikawa expressing sympathy over the imprisonment of radicals in Japan together with requests for
more information about samurai love. Both of these affected Carpenter's
own thought significantly. In short, these figures were part of a cosmopolitan, international network of thinkers, discussing sexuality and
socialism across cultures.

While Carpenter corresponded directly with Olive Schreiner, who
was so influential in Japan, as well as Fukuda Hideko and Itō Kei, as
mentioned above, Japanese women were in contact with him primarily
via acts of translation, and their community was a local one interested
in socialism and feminism in the late 1910s and 1920s. Unfortunately, we
know of no letters from Yamakawa or her direct associates to Carpenter,
but I wish to take some inspiration from these connections and from
the fact that she translated one of his most important works about affin-
ity, love, and social change, *The Intermediate Sex*, to consider briefly the
possible roles of translation and interpersonal connection in this important feminist's thought. The purpose is not to simply reinsert a forgotten figure, or forgotten connection, back into the history to fill in a gap.
Rather it is to turn attention to the important roles that such connections,
including international ones, played in activism and in thought about
gender and sexuality in early twentieth-century Japanese feminism, and
world feminisms more generally. In particular, I mark the importance
of translation as a way for some women to participate in international
activist movements, and as a way to be engaged outside the structures
of marriage, especially when they lacked the resources to travel.[23] The
Public Order Law (Chian iji hō; enacted in 1900 and subsequently revised
various times) severely restricted women's public political speech, but
translating and discussing socialist writings from abroad was one area of
activity that remained possible.[24]

Yamakawa published translations of two of Carpenter's most influential works, *The Intermediate Sex* and *Love's Coming of Age*. The former
appeared in the journal *Safuran* founded by former Bluestocking Society
(Seitōsha) contributor Ōtake Kōkichi and the latter in an individual
volume titled, *A Theory of Love* (*Ren'ai ron*, 1921).[25] Yamakawa is known
for being devoted to keeping a discussion of women's position and gender

differences a part of Japanese socialism, and equally committed to keeping class analysis a part of Japanese feminism. But Carpenter's discourse on sexuality is not something frequently associated with Yamakawa Kikue's type of feminism. Given that apparent absence of association, what did Yamakawa acquire from this translation experience? While it is common to emphasize the way non-Japanese feminists influenced and enlightened Japanese feminists, bringing feminism to Japan via translation, the case of socialism is particularly important for disrupting that narrative. The point in Yamakawa's writing is not that there is a specific "Japanese" culture of capitalism or a "Japanese" oppression of women in capitalism, but that these dynamics have a cross-cultural universality. Her translations themselves are not to "introduce" Carpenter (or the important figure of Japanese socialist feminism, August Bebel) from "the West," but to convey multiple ways of looking at these dynamics across cultures. Yamakawa was given an opportunity to study at Columbia University with a scholarship but after thinking about whether she would learn more about socialism in Japan or America, she chose Japan.[26] This choice is part of her image as a not particularly "cosmopolitan" figure, despite her vast readings in international socialism. But while Yamakawa chose to stay in Japan and work closely with her surrounding community in the intellectual development of Japanese socialism and activism, her sense of the world had a certain cosmopolitan nature, created out of acts of translation. The translations were not done in back rooms as personal, intellectual projects. Rather, people like Sakai Toshihiko suggested texts. Around those texts, groups of feminists and socialists gathered, and their translation projects and related language study were part of their community building. Yamakawa tells of Kamichika Ichiko urging her to attend Ōsugi Sakae's French reading classes, where she met others in this community with whom she remained connected throughout her career. Though she notes that Ōsugi tended to fall asleep while teaching, a slight jab at him, the point is that the personal interactions, often surrounding foreign languages and texts, were key to the emergence of Japanese Marxian thought and the community of activists.[27]

In her translator's introduction to Carpenter's *Love's Coming of Age*, Yamakawa writes that she finds this the most "progressive" out of all of Carpenter's works, "with its theories of both sexes showing the richest degree of understanding and sympathy." Comparing Carpenter to Bebel, whom she was also translating and by whom she was heavily influenced, she writes that Bebel is "realistic, scientific, combative" while Carpenter is "dense with poetic, idealistic feeling."[28] Bebel's writing is backed up by facts and figures, Carpenter's by "finely detailed, meticulous observations of human emotion (*ninjō*)." In terms of "social facts" Bebel's writing is superior, but "for those who may be left unsatisfied by such logical writing, this book [by Carpenter] that has a greater sense of freedom, rich with special charms, will be more appealing."[29]

Her attention to this difference is refined. Yamakawa is a writer and activist who thinks strategically about audience. In women's magazines she focuses on class analysis as key to effective ways of thinking about what others saw as purely women's issues. Meanwhile, in socialist publications she argues for the *centrality* of attention to women for any effective workers' movement. Although people may not often think of Yamakawa as questioning categories of gender and sexuality, her writing across these audiences questions these categories, even as she seems to write "for men" or "for women." While her writing is always closer to Bebel's struggle-oriented and logical stances, her audience affects the framings and her way of pulling people in. For example, in the opening to what became her 1928 debate with anarchist Takamure Itsue, she vividly describes the photo essays of elite eligible bachelorettes. She uses this stunning detail to reveal the stylistic parallel between these descriptions and real estate ads. She thus draws in the audience of women for *Fujin kōron* (Women's forum), who would be familiar with the two genres of photo essays and real estate ads, demonstrating her sharp attention to modes of writing and their rhetorical and political effects.[30]

Attuned as well to the rhetorical style of thinkers in her time and language, she writes in her autobiography that anarchist Ōsugi Sakae and Sakai Toshihiko, both of whom supported the publication of translations of Carpenter, gradually transformed their own writing styles from 1910 to 1920, moving from difficult Sinified Japanese toward an "everyday, clear" tone for the masses.[31] Her experience translating Bebel and Carpenter may have helped to refine this sense of audience and the varied power of different rhetorical styles for different audiences.[32] Her essay "I, Me, Mine" ("*Ore ga ore no ore ni ore o*"), about gender and rhetoric in literary criticism and political philosophy, also displays this interest.[33]

These differences in rhetorical style emerge in the translations of Carpenter. Sakai produced an abridged translation of *Love's Coming of Age* in 1915, as *Relations Between Men and Women in a Free Society*

(*Jiyūshakai no danjo kankei*).³⁴ Yamakawa then does a complete version soon after. Sakai republished his own translation later, saying that although hers supersedes his, there still might be some value in his "pamphlet style" abridged translation for some readers, since after reading "any given line" they will be likely to want to read the whole thing. The stylistic difference between these translations is remarkable in many ways. Each might be considered quite close to the original in some sense, such as Sakai's literal translation of phrases like "coming of age." He notes that he has been looser with the title, saying vaguely that there were "various factors" that led him to change it to "Relations Between Men and Women in a Free Society," while Yamakawa's title (*Ren'ai ron*) focuses on "love."³⁵

There is an interesting challenge for the translators. Carpenter writes: "I would say that in the social life of the future this need will surely be recognized, and that (while there will be no stigma attaching to voluntary celibacy) the state of enforced celibacy in which vast numbers of women live to-day will be looked upon as a national wrong, almost as grievous as that of prostitution—of which latter evil indeed it is in some degree the counterpart or necessary accompaniment."³⁶ Sakai renders "enforced celibacy" as "being forced to live a single lifestyle" (*dokushin seikatsu o okuraseruru*) and continues on to say that prostitution is an "inevitable result" of so many "single women."³⁷ Interestingly, Sakai does not include the parenthetical statement about those who choose celibacy as having this right. Yamakawa at one point uses the term "state of forced singlehood" (*kyōseiteki dokushin jōtai*) but does not translate this as leading to prostitution; rather, she emphasizes that it is a sad situation equal to it, with the nuance being that either form of control on sexuality is undesirable. Unlike Sakai, and Tamura as well, Yamakawa does manage to include a term to indicate "celibacy": *hiseiteki keiken* (not having sexual experience) and is thus able to communicate more fully the force of Carpenter's suggestion that to suppress and control a woman's sexual desire in any way for the sake of her family or other social institutions was as oppressive as condoning or profiting from the prostitution of her body.

Yamakawa uses this category of "unmarried" woman to question the institution of marriage from the point of view of sexuality, in addition to the class analysis she uses in most other contexts to criticize the institution of marriage as it exists in feudal and capitalist societies. Yamakawa often also observed the sexism within the households of families on the left, and how this was often at odds with the ideals of their activism. Women who did not marry within the movement came to be ostracized, while those who stayed within became "wives" rather than comrades. Meanwhile, being a translator was a way to maintain a place within the movement as a woman, a place that could be maintained without sex or marriage relationships.

An interesting set of personal accounts surrounding Yamakawa's translations of Carpenter and the home life of feminists are her observations of Itō Noe, an editor of the feminist journal *Seitō* (Bluestocking), and lover of Ōsugi Sakae. Itō too was, in a very different sense, an "unmarried" (but certainly not "celibate") woman. Itō had several children with Ōsugi, who was also involved with feminist Kamichika Ichiko, in addition to having been married to Hori Yasuko.[38] Yamakawa had been very disturbed by public prostitution in Japan, and her accounts of why are focused on her personal encounter with the neighborhoods near her house and a visit to Fukagawa, where she was upset by the eerie atmosphere as young women from the countryside were bartered and stuck in the middle of arguments between capitalist owners and state officials.[39] Itō had written a piece about the ineffectual and puritanical nature of Christian anti-prostitution movements to which Yamakawa had written a sharp response, but one that began with an affection for her rhetorical style:

Dear Ms. Noe,

I have never had the pleasure of meeting you, but I often read what you have written. It is rare that I pick up *Seitō*, but when I do I always turn to your pieces. Rather than finding your arguments admirable, I am attracted instead by your wholehearted stances from which you hold your ground. Even if it be childish or sloppy, there is nothing more precious than a cry that comes from the heart. If there are weaknesses to be found in the premises on which your arguments are based, these are generally only subtle issues that might be argued over by intellectuals and scholars. For this reason I like you. But it is precisely because I like you that picking out some aspects of your recent piece that I think are not fully thought through gives me a feeling of disappointment.

And it is to contend with this sense of disappointment and address you with it directly that I write you this letter.[40]

For comparison, just a snippet of the earthy writing that Yamakawa had translated faithfully from Carpenter on prostitution:

It is certainly very maddening at times to think that the Destinies of the world, the organization of society, the wonderful scope of possible statesmanship, the mighty issues of trade and industry, the loves of Women, the lives of criminals, the fate of savage nations, should be in the hands of such a set of general nincompoops; men so fatuous that it actually does not hurt them to see the streets crammed with prostitutes by night, or the parks by day with the semi-lifeless bodies of tramps; men, to whom it seems quite natural that our marriage and social institutions should lumber along over the bodies of women, as our commercial institutions grind over the bodies of the poor, and our "imperial" enterprise over the bodies of barbarian races, destroyed by drink and deviltry.[41]

Yamakawa has similarly been struck by Sakai Toshihiko's statement that he did "not have an opinion" about prostitution. But Yamakawa's own writing style is much different from Carpenter's, focusing on logic rather drama.[42] What Yamakawa seems to appreciate in Itō, however, is the latter's Carpenterian ability to connect her passion to social ills. Carpenter expresses many of his opinions in this emotionally moving way, and it is this sort of passion and freshness that Yamakawa likes about Itō, even if Itō writes in a different mode than she herself would. Yamakawa's experience of translating a large amount of Carpenter's writings may, I would argue, have helped her recognize the value of Itō's approach.

After reading her response to Itō, Ōsugi invites Yamakawa to their home because he thinks she and Itō "should become good friends."[43] While Yamakawa waits to debate prostitution with Itō, the latter is busy serving sake and food to the male activists who are hanging out in the house. Yamakawa impatiently waits the whole time, observing this young woman "with a small body, large bun in her hair, and a baby on her back," cutting an image so different, Yamakawa remarks, from Itō the activist at *Seitō* magazine.[44] While lugging dishes back and forth, Itō gives a casual reply that she has not really thought about her differences in opinion with Yamakawa very much. On their way out, Ōsugi confides to Yamakawa that his lover is not yet very enlightened, and invites Yamakawa to help her—this is one basis for their work together in the Red Wave Society. Later Yamakawa sees Itō at the theater when Ōsugi is home babysitting for her. Itō seems like a different person than in her home, "like a country schoolgirl" with "the freshness of a wildflower."[45] Just one month after Itō and Ōsugi's death, she writes in *Fujin kōron* that Itō was not some sort of "hero," and, rather than being "driven by logic," her thought had been "instinctual," "simple," "wild," and "primitive." But Itō had been the best fit for Ōsugi because she contained "nothing bad" and her naive and open personality allowed them both an unfettered range of complex ideas, a potential cut short by their assassination; Yamakawa's criticism of their murder in the woman's magazine is all the more powerful because of her personal account of their warmth and foibles.[46] Here, various person-to-person interactions, such as mentor and intellectual (or even intellectual and prostitute) might—via personal communication, language study, and translation—create a bond leading to a transformed social vision and ethical connection. Ōsugi's invitation to Yamakawa to become a sort of productive big sister to Itō suggested the ways that, as Carpenter put it, heterosexual men look toward women "generally with a proprietary sort of love."[47] But Yamakawa and Ōsugi's observations of inequality (both between herself and Itō, and between Ōsugi and Itō) and experience of inequality was also a "spark"—to quote again from Goodlad—toward social change, and might have even been part of the flame that the police wanted to put out through their murder. We see in these writings a direct, "emotional" way of understanding the ethics of the moment. And yet in polemical writings for magazines about prostitution, Yamakawa translates this into the "logical, concise, combative" style of Bebel.

As Goodlad argues in her examination of E. M. Forster's "queer internationalism," politically charged encounters with the other can create a not unproblematic but sometimes ethically significant "view" from which to "open oneself to the world's multifarious disclosures: to cultivate an ethos of ongoing epistemological revision and embodied encounter."[48] It may be a strange approach to attempt to attach these nonerotic encounters of Yamakawa's within the city of Tōkyō with this vision, but my sense is that it is important to include these forms of internationalism via translation and personal encounter in our understanding of canonical Japanese feminism. I think these are not unrelated to the ways that Japanese feminists developed interest in other forms of inequalities, such as the link Yamakawa makes in her autobiography between subjects of discrimination such as the Burakumin (a group of people historically discriminated against in Japan) and Jews, or between her circle of Japanese feminists and women in the Japanese Empire—often these were problematic or articulated in ways that might feel uncomfortable to us now. But these encounters, wherever they took place, were inspired by movement of texts and people around the world at this time, and were always disruptive of the epistemological status of the categories in question.[49] Yamakawa's goal in translating Carpenter was certainly to bring feminism and the problems of women to Japanese socialism. But (or "and"), her insertions were inspiring at key moments, bringing insight into the complexity of gender categories. These moments in her thinking affected and often inspired how she invoked the category of "woman," a central category of her analysis of society and in her activism.

Notes

1   A recent work closely related to this article is Michiko Suzuki, "The Translation of Edward Carpenter's *The Intermediate Sex* in Early Twentieth Century Japan," in *Sexology and Translation: Cultural and Scientific Encounters Across the Modern World, 1880–1930*, ed. Heike Bauer (Philadelphia: Temple University Press, 2015). The influence of Yamakawa's translation of Carpenter on the understanding of hermaphroditism in Japan is discussed in Leslie Winston, "The Trope of the Hermaphrodite in Modern Japan," *Harvard Asia Quarterly* 16, no. 3 (2014). My chapter focuses on Yamakawa's translations of Edward Carpenter. Another fruitful area of inquiry would be her first translations, which were short stories by Vladimir Korolenko, including the 1885 story "Son Makara" (Makar's dream).

2   A Japanese published series of translations related to the women's movement does include Carpenter and many male figures: Mizuta Tamae, ed., *Sekai joseigaku kiso bunken shūsei*, 15 vols. (Tokyo: Yumani Shobō, 2001). It is important to acknowledge people who have worked on sexology, including Sabine Frühstück, *Colonizing Sex: Sexology and Social Control in Modern Japan* (Berkeley: University of California Press, 2003); and Ronald Loftus, "The Inversion of Progress: Taoka Reiun's Hibunmeiron," *Monumenta Nipponica* 40, no. 2 (July 1985).

3   The textual history of Carpenter translations to Japanese is complex
      and at moments hard to determine. The earliest I have found is Sakai
      Toshihiko's translation of *Civilization: Its Cause and Cure* as *Bunmei
      no hei oyobi sono kyūchi: Edowādo Kāpentā no chosaku o shōkai shita
      mono* (Tokyo: Min'yūsha, 1895), and later his translation of Carpenter's
      Love's Coming of Age (New York: M. Kennerly, 1911) as *Jiyūshakai no
      danjo kankei* (Tokyo: Tōundō Shoten, 1915). Poet Tomita Saika translated
      Carpenter's *"Demokurashī no hō e"* (Towards democracy), in *Waseda
      bungaku* 116, no. 7 (1915). Another translation of *Love's Coming of Age*
      is *Seiai kekkon: Kaizō no sakebi*, translated by Tamura Hiroshi (Tokyo:
      Mita Shoten, 1921). Yamakawa also makes reference to having seen
      translations of Carpenter texts in a pamphlet called *Kakumei fujin*, a
      special issue of *Chokugen* in her "Shakaishugi fujin undō to Sekirankai,"
      Yamakawa Kikue shū, vol. 3 (Tokyo: Iwanami Shoten, 1982), 2, though I
      could not find any reference to Carpenter in the *Kakumei fujin* pamphlet,
      which introduces figures such as revolutionary Catherine Breshkovsky
      (1844–1934). I was unable to locate any issue of *Chokugen* that included
      Carpenter. Yamakawa also mentions "learning about Bebel and
      Carpenter" from the magazine *Kindai shisō*, and, although these are not
      in the table of contents of *Kindai shisō*, he is likely mentioned, as is his
      supporter Ishikawa Sanshirō. Sakai Toshihiko's *Shinsekai* magazine also
      discussed Carpenter, and Yamakawa mentions reading this as well. See
      Yamakawa Kikue, *Onna ni dai no ki* (Tokyo: Heibonsha, 1972), 165–166.
      According to Sheila Rowbotham, Carpenter was translated into Japanese
      for a magazine among the Japanese community in Los Angeles in 1919.
      See Sheila Rowbotham, *Edward Carpenter: A Life of Liberty and Love*
      (New York: Verso, 2008), 348.

4   Yoshiya Nobuko, "Aishiau kotodomo," in *Senzenki dōseiai kanren bunken
      shūsei*, ed. Furukawa Makoto and Akaeda Kanako, vol. 3 (Tokyo: Fuji
      Shuppan, 2006). This essay was originally published together with
      one by Kamichika Ichiko in *Shinshōsetsu*, in January 1921. Yoshiya
      rewrote the essay later as "Dōsei o ai suru saiwai," in *Akogare shiru koro*
      (Tokyo: Kōransha, 1923). This is the starting point of my attention to
      Carpenter and Yamakawa Kikue. Meanwhile, Michiko Suzuki's focus
      is on Yoshiya's development of Carpenter's ideas for the purpose of
      discussing love among girls, another important part of this conversation
      about translations of Carpenter. See Suzuki, "The Translation of
      Edward Carpenter."

5   Yamada Waka, *Ren'ai no shakaiteki igi* (Tokyo: Tōyō Shuppanbu, 1920),
      284–285. The original passage from Carpenter refers to "boyhood or
      girlhood"; the closest passage in the original essay is: "School friendships

of course exist; and almost every one remembers that they filled a large place in the outlook of his early years; but he remembers, too, that they were not recognized in any way, and that in consequence the main part of their force and value was wasted. Yet it is evident that the first unfolding of a strong attachment in boyhood or girlhood must have a profound influence; while if it occurs between an elder and a younger schoolmate, or—as sometimes happens—between the young thing and its teacher, its importance in the educational sense can hardly be overrated." See Edward Carpenter, "Affection in Education," *International Journal of Ethics* 9, no. 4 (July 1899), reprinted in *The Intermediate Sex: A Study of Some Transitional Types of Men and Women* (London: George Allen & Unwin, 1908). Meanwhile, the chapter called "The Intermediate Sex" was originally printed in *Love's Coming of Age* (1896) and then reappears in *The Intermediate Sex* in 1908, giving it its title. The Japanese translations of *Love's Coming of Age* often do not have the chapter "The Intermediate Sex," making Yamada's gloss an important part of the textual history.

6   Nuanced readings in this vein include Deborah Shamoon, *Passionate Friendship: The Aesthetics of Girls' Culture in Japan* (Honolulu: University of Hawai'i Press, 2012); and Suzuki, "The Translation of Edward Carpenter," 208.

7   Akaeda Kanako, *Kindai Nihon ni okeru onna dōshi no shinmitsu na kankei* (Tokyo: Kadokawa Gakugei, 2011), 94.

8   Carpenter, "*Seiai kekkon*," i.

9   Yamakawa Kikue, "Yakusha yori," in Edward Carpenter, *Ren'ai ron* (translation of *Love's Coming of Age*), trans. Yamakawa Kikue (Tokyo: Daitōkaku, 1921), 1; reprinted (facsimile) as *Sekai joseigaku kiso bunken shūsei*, vol. 13, ed. Mizuta Tamae (Tokyo: Yumani Shōbo, 2001).

10   Jeffrey Angles, *Writing the Love of Boys: Origins of Bishōnen Culture in Modernist Japanese Literature* (Minneapolis: University of Minnesota Press, 2011), 156–157. See also, Michiko Suzuki, "Writing Same-Sex Love: Sexology and Literary Representation in Yoshiya Nobuko's Early Fiction," *Journal of Asian Studies* 65, no. 3 (August 2006). Eve Kosofsky Sedgwick also compares Symonds and Carpenter in *Between Men: English Literature and Male Homosocial Desire* (New York: Columbia University Press, 1985).

11   Edward Carpenter, *Sei ni tessuru geijutsu*, trans. Miura Kanzō (Tokyo: Kōshin Bungakusha, 1917). The above quote is from page 9. One example of his Tagore writings from the same period is Miura Kanzō, "Tagore no jinseikan," *Dai san teikoku* 70 (June 1916).

12   Tanaka was trained at the University of Chicago by John Dewey and was known for his work on pragmatism.

13 Lauren Goodlad, "Where Liberals Fear to Tread: E. M. Forster's Queer Internationalism and the Ethics of Care," *Novel* 39, no. 3 (Summer 2006).

14 Sakai Toshihiko, *Sakura no kuni jishin no kuni, Gendai yūmoa zenshū*, vol. 2 (Tokyo: Gendai Yūmoa Zenshū Kankōkai, 1928), 508–510.

15 Sheffield City Libraries, Fabian Economic and Social Thought Series 1, *The Papers of Edward Carpenter, 1844–1929, from Sheffield City Libraries* (Marlborough, Wilshire, England: Adam Matthew, 1994) (microfilm). Most correspondence with Japanese individuals is on reel 9. Some translations into Japanese are also found in this archive. An index is included in reel 1.

16 Itō, who is generally catalogued as Itō Megumu, wrote a book about Buddhism and Japanese culture in 1942 that seems to me to very much fit in with Kyoto School Philosophy in both erudition and fascism: Itō Megumu, *Nihon bunka to Nihon bukkyō* (Osaka: Shinshindō, 1942). She is also the author of *Saikin rinrigaku* (Tokyo: Nisshindō, 1922). I thank Kristen Williams for helping me to identify the author of these letters to Carpenter as Itō Megumu.

17 This was an apparent plot to assassinate the emperor; a total of twenty-four individuals were sentenced to execution in early 1911, though most had little or no connection to the plot itself.

18 In Chushichi Tsuzuki, "'My Dear Sanshiro': Edward Carpenter and His Japanese Disciple," *Hitotsubashi Journal of Social Studies* 6, no. 1 (November 1972): 3.

19 Fukuda Hideko to Edward Carpenter, November 14, 1914, in Sheffield City Libraries, *The Papers of Edward Carpenter*, reel 9, MSS 380–42.

20 Yamakawa Kikue et al., *Yamakawa Kikue no kōseki: "Watakushi no undōshi" to chosaku mokuroku* (Tokyo: Domesu Shuppan, 1979), 19.

21 Tomita Saita to Edward Carpenter, July 13, 1916, in Sheffield City Libraries, *The Papers of Edward Carpenter*, reel 9, MSS 380–11.

22 An early translation of a short selection from Carpenter's *Angel's Wings* appears as "'Jiga' no hyōgen to jiyū," trans. Nagashima Naoaki, *Atarashiki mura* 4, no. 3 (March 1921). Nagashima Naoaki was an active Taishō-era (1912–1926) translator who did work for the *Shirakaba* and *Atarashiki mura* journals. He also translated Balzac's *Pere Goriot*, works of August Strindberg, and was one of the translators for the Shinchōsha collected works of Dostoevsky.

23 This is not meant to dismiss the restrictions on an imprisoned figure such as Ishikawa discussed earlier, or, on the other hand like Itō Kei, the extent to which many educated women *were* traveling and studying internationally in the 1910s and 1920s, to a degree often forgotten in scholarship.

24 Even translation remained an area of some controversy. Research has shown that the attribution of a translation by Yamakawa Kikue was suppressed by educator and feminist Tsuda Umeko because of her association with the left. See Yamakawa Kikue et al., *Yamakawa Kikue no kōseki*, 100.

25 Edward Carpenter, *Ren'ai ron* (Love's coming of age), trans. Yamakawa Kikue (Tokyo: Daitōkaku Shoten, 1921); Edward Carpenter, "Chūseiron" (*The Intermediate Sex*), trans. Aoyama (Yamakawa) Kikue, serialized in *Safuran*, nos. 3–5 (1914), facsimile reprints in *Safuran*, 2 vols. (Tokyo: Fuji Shuppan, 1984). Yamakawa's *The Intermediate Sex* translation was retitled "*Dōseiai*" (Same-sex love) and reappeared in combination with a portion of *Pure Sociology* by Lester Ward to form a volume called *Josei chūshin to dōseiai* (Gynocentricism and same-sex love) (Tokyo: Ars, 1919). The shift in titles is important, as discussed by Suzuki, "The Translation of Edward Carpenter," 201–205. Although the "Gynocentricism" portion of the title represents the Ward section of the volume, the use of "*dōseiai*" (same-sex love) was increasingly associated with love among girls in the 1910s, even at the same time as it was coming to be used more frequently to translate the English word "homosexuality." On the one hand, the term associated same-sex sexuality more closely with sexological discourse and less with the historical term of *nanshoku* (erotic relations among men). At the same time, many have also referred to *dōseiai* as being more "spiritual," as discussed in Suzuki, and also in J. Keith Vincent, *Two-Timing Modernity* (Cambridge, MA: Harvard Asia Center, 2012), 32, 48. It is possible that the Yamakawa–Ward volume was simply marketing the word that was more familiar by 1919. "*Chūsei*" much better reflects the originality and queerness of Carpenter's term "intermediate."

26 Yamakawa Kikue, *Onna ni dai no ki* (Tokyo: Heibonsha, 1972), 176–177.

27 Ibid., 166. The text they were reading was *Les lois sociales* by Jean-Gabriel de Tarde.

28 Yamakawa, *Ren'ai ron*, 1–2.

29 Ibid., 3.

30 Yamakawa Kikue, "Keihin tsuki tokkahin toshite no onna," in *Yamakawa Kikue shū*, vol. 5, 2.

31 Yamakawa, *Onna ni dai no ki*, 166.

32 An important aspect of thinking about feminist writing is certainly writing style, such as in Yamakawa's debates with feminist, anarchist writer Takamure Itsue, whose intensely passionate and serpentine sentences and logic contrast with Yamakawa Kikue's rigorous and crisp, clear logical argumentation.

33 Yamakawa Kikue, "Ore ga ore no ore ni ore o," in *Yamakawa Kikue shū*,

vol. 1, 83–87. The gendered aspect of *"ore,"* a casual, masculine first-person pronoun, is used here in several different cases of grammar to suggest a tone of masculine egotism among some critics. The essay provides criticism of both escapist sentimentalism and of macho posturing found in masculinist political philosophy.

34 Edward Carpenter, *Jiyūshakai no danjo kankei* (Love's coming of age), trans. Sakai Toshihiko (Tokyo: Tōundō Shoten 1915); republished as Edward Carpenter, *Jiyūshakai no danjo kankei*, trans. Sakai Toshihiko (Tokyo: Bunkagakkai, 1925).

35 Carpenter, *Jiyūshakai no danjo kankei* (1925), frontmatter. The remarks are found in this 1925 version, but not in the 1915 version.

36 Carpenter, *Love's Coming of Age* (New York: M. Kennerly, 1911), 9. In the original, it is clear that Carpenter is discussing women's sexual needs, while Sakai's translation renders it more vague.

37 Carpenter, *Jiyūshakai no danjo kankei* (1925), 3.

38 Another of Ōsugi's lovers had been Kamichika Ichiko, who is also part of the story of the translation of Carpenter. As Akaeda points out, Kamichika writes in *Safuran* about discussing the translation with Yamakawa and the fact that they had been talking about "same-sex love" (*dōsei ren'ai*) when she was doing the translation of *The Intermediate Sex*. See Akaeda, *Onna dōshi no shinmitsu na kankei*, 92–93.

39 Yamakawa, *Onna ni dai no ki*, 167.

40 Yamakawa, "Nihon fujin no shakai jigyō ni tsuite Itō shi ni atau," in *Yamakawa Kikue shū*, vol. 1, 2.

41 Edward Carpenter, *Love's Coming of Age* (New York: M. Kennerly, 1896), 34–35.

42 Yamakawa, *Onna ni dai no ki*, 178.

43 Ibid., 167.

44 Yamakawa, "Noe to Ōsugi," in *Yamakawa Kikue shū*, vol. 8, 58.

45 Yamakawa, *Onna ni dai no ki*, 169.

46 Yamakawa, "Noe to Ōsugi," in *Yamakawa Kikue shū*, vol. 8, 64–65.

47 Gay Wachman, *Lesbian Empire: Radical Crosswriting in the Twenties* (New Brunswick, NJ: Rutgers University Press, 2001), 69.

48 Goodlad, "Where Liberals Fear to Tread," 330.

49 To see Yamakawa's thoughts on Buraku issues and Jews, see Yamakawa, *Onna ni dai no ki*, 239–241. Pages 315–368 in the same volume discuss her interactions with various groups across Asia and Europe.

CHAPTER 12

~

Rethinking Japanese Feminism and the Lessons of *Ūman Ribu*

Toward a Praxis of Critical Transnational Feminism

SETSU SHIGEMATSU

T HIS ESSAY REFLECTS on the lessons of the 1970s Japanese women's liberation movement as a means to rethink Japanese feminism in relation to transnational feminism. By revisiting the history of this women's liberation movement—known as *ūman ribu*—I reflect on its contributions, limits, and contradictions as an example of radical Japanese feminism. More specifically, this chapter revisits *ūman ribu*'s approach to women and violence and considers how it contributes to rethinking power differences among feminists. The second half of the essay discusses Japanese feminism more broadly in relation to race, nationalism, and imperialism and interrogates the status of Japanese feminists in relation to non-Japanese feminists within Japan. By examining the lessons of *ūman ribu* and the limits of Japanese feminism, I put forward some notes toward a praxis of critical transnational feminism (CTF). This essay discusses the need for a critical transnational feminism to address power and hierarchies among feminists and feminisms. It is my hope that CTF can be a means to reflect on the methodologies and racialized epistemologies we utilize to research, represent, and exchange knowledge about Japanese feminism, and by extension, Japan and its (post) colonial conditions.

Ūman Ribu and Transnational Feminism

The rise of *ūman ribu* marked a watershed in the history of postwar feminism in Japan. Its newness or break from previous Japanese women's movements was characterized by its militancy against Japanese patriarchy, emphasis on women's sexuality, and women-centered cultural transformation, all of which are characteristics of radical feminism.[1] A new generation of Japanese women protested the sexist constraints of both existing student movements and New Left radicalism, and heralded an unprecedented gender critique of Japanese postwar society and the Japanese Left.[2]

From the beginning, activists adopted the loosely transliterated English phrase *ūman ribu* (woman lib) and *ribu* (lib) to name their movement, signaling their solidarity with other liberation movements as well as a turn toward the transnational. Although there were existing Japanese terms for women's liberation (*josei kaihō* and *fujin kaihō*, both combining terms meaning "woman" with a term meaning "liberation"), the utilization of this foreign *katakana* phrase *ūman ribu* marked a connection with, and a desire to be part of, a broader range of liberation movements that extended beyond Japan. Activists of the *ribu* movement engaged with feminists in the United States, Europe, and Asia. Their multiple modalities of cross-racial and cross-linguistic exchange included forms of recognition, (dis)identifications, solidarity, dialogue, interactions, and formal translation that can be understood as material and experiential practices of transnational feminism. This radical feminist movement was thus a hybrid formation constituted by domestic political conditions but also informed by the transnational and transcultural practices and movements of feminist knowledge.[3]

Over the last few decades, transnational feminism has been an expanding contemporary feminist paradigm that engages with global forces of capitalism, imperialism, and colonial modernity. Ongoing discussions and debates surrounding transnational feminism provide a productive arena to examine how the lessons and limits of *ūman ribu* and Japanese feminism can, in turn, illuminate our understanding of diverse feminisms as transnational and transcultural movements.

Transnational feminism, conceived as a critical response to Western cultural imperialism, builds on a genealogy of women of color, third world feminism, and postcolonial feminism.[4] Paradigm-shifting interventions by feminists such as Cherríe Moraga and Gloria Anzaldúa's *This Bridge Called My Back: Writings by Radical Women of Color* (1983), Valerie Amos and Pratibha Parmar's "Challenging Imperial Feminism" (1984), and Chandra Mohanty's "Under Western Eyes: Feminist Scholarship and Colonial Discourse" (1991), are foundational works that articulate how racism, classism, heteronormativity, and geopolitical hegemony have constituted many Euro-American middle-class feminist endeavors and practices.[5] Building on this feminist genealogy, which includes the work of Angela Davis, Gayatri Spivak, Kimberlé Crenshaw, M. Jacqui Alexander, and others, I take transnational feminism to involve an *intersectional* approach to feminist practice that accounts for how gender, race, ethnicity, class, and nation are constituted by imperialism and colonial modernity.[6] That said, the question of how transnational feminism negotiates the material and institutional structures of first world power-knowledge formations, as well as Euro-American and Anglocentric epistemic hegemonies, requires further examination. Inderpal Grewal and Caren Kaplan noted in 2001 that the very term "transnational" "has become so ubiquitous in cultural and critical studies that much of its political valence seems to have become evacuated."[7] In the context of neoliberal globalization, feminists continue to debate the efficacy of the terms "transnational" and "transnational feminism."

Critical Transnational Feminism as Praxis

In their introduction to *Critical Transnational Feminist Praxis*, Richa Nagar and Amanda Lock Swarr emphasize the need to reassess the limits and contradictions of transnational feminism. This collection recognizes that transnational feminism "always runs the risk of unwittingly reinforcing the deeply problematic power relations that it seeks to disrupt."[8] The editors advocate critical transnational feminism as an "inherently unstable praxis whose survival and evolution hinge on a continuous commitment to produce self-reflexive dialogic critiques of its own practices.[9]

Building on such understandings of transnational feminism, in what follows I elaborate a praxis of *critical transnational feminism* in dialogue with Japanese feminism. In my elaboration of critical transnational feminism, I underscore the criticality of the power differences within feminism. The *criticality* of power not only implies *persistent critique*, but also recognizes that transnational feminism faces an imminent crisis due to the unexamined violences within its own system(s). The full recognition of power and aggression among feminists as constitutive and potentially abusive is vital. This criticality of power involves, on the one hand, a continual analysis of the material effects and personal impact of power differences and hierarchies among feminists/feminisms. On the other hand, this critical praxis emphasizes the imperative to openly address and (re)negotiate power differences. CTF acknowledges power differences and structural hierarchies as the extant condition of social relations, therefore endorsing the collective creation of discourses and practices to deal with the conflicts and ruptures that often arise due to power differences, aggression, racism, ableism, elitism, and heteronormativity among feminists.

CTF thus encourages dialogue between diverse feminisms and feminists in Japan, including non-Japanese feminists and other feminist/queer discourses. By engaging in dialogue with other feminisms in a transnational frame, we can place *ūman ribu* and Japanese feminism in conversation with queer women of color feminism and decolonial feminism. Such conversations raise the following questions: How are Japanese feminisms/feminists situated within a critical transnational feminist paradigm? How does Japan's history and status as a non-Western imperial power shape Japanese feminism (and its heternormative/queer history)? How are different feminist subjects in Japan situated within larger global economies of race, nation, ethnicity, gender, and class, across the first world and third worlds, and do such questions matter?[10] To what extent do the majority of feminists in Japan, as members of the ethnically and racially dominant group within the country, occupy a positionality analogous to that of white feminists in the United States? Are Japanese feminists in Japan similar to middle-class Euro-American feminists in terms of their relative privilege and racialized position? These kinds of questions engage with the critiques that have been posed by third world feminists, queer and women of color feminists, post- and decolonial feminist theory, and inform my understanding, positionality, and rethinking of Japanese feminism and transnational feminism.[11]

CTF encourages dialogue about differences of power between U.S.-based knowledge production in English, and Japan's relative status as a regional and global power. How does Japan's historical relationship to the United States involve racialized forms of knowledge production? To what extent have scholars assessed how Japan Studies (as a historically white- and male-dominated field) functions as an orientalizing discourse that racializes the Japanese within a global schema of race, whereby whiteness is still considered a "universal" vantage point that produces dominant discourses, putative objectivity, and "truth"? Have we adequately addressed how Japan is interpreted or co-figured, to recall Naoki Sakai's analysis, through racialized discourses in relation to the West; how Japanese subjects and subjectivities can be caught in a conflicted desire to imitate, subvert, and overcome the whiteness of the West?[12] What are the political and discursive effects of an enduring legacy of knowledge production that remains predominantly Eurocentric in its utilization of theory?[13] By moving out of area studies/nation-based models into a paradigm of CTF, we can raise different questions that hitherto have been deemed out of bounds, and, thereby, interrogate power and hierarchy within feminisms in Japan and beyond.

Nearly fifty years have passed since the emergence of *ūman ribu*. These decades have witnessed the diverse production of feminist discourses, debates, exchanges, and reflections on the legacy of the movement.[14] In what follows, I begin by elaborating how *ūman ribu*'s lessons about women, feminism, and violence contribute toward a praxis of CTF. Then in the second half of this essay, I discuss Japanese feminism in relation to imperialism and race, informed by lessons from women of color and decolonial feminism. In doing so, I begin to answer some of the questions posed above. I hope that these provisional notes toward a praxis of CTF can be fruitful in rethinking Japanese feminism in a transnational frame.

A Self-Reflexive Feminist Analytics of Violence

The writings from the *ūman ribu* movement document moments of conflict and harm that enable an interrogation of hierarchical feminist relations as dynamic formations of solidarity and difference in power. The history of *ūman ribu*'s engagement with the problem of violence contributes to a praxis of CTF, not only because its activists challenged violence against women by men and the imperial-capitalist state, but because they engaged with violence *by* and *among* women. In *Scream from the Shadows: The Women's Liberation Movement in Japan*, I describe the conditions of violence by and among women and feminists as an aporia of feminist thought.[15] I contend that the manifestation of violence within, among, and by women has not received adequate attention thus far in feminist studies due to the ways in which feminism has largely posited women as victims of patriarchal, masculinist, and sexist violence, and not its primary agents or key perpetrators. Insofar as women are ontologically situated within and also constituted by larger structures of patriarchal, capitalist, imperialist, racial, and gendered violence, women can and do engage and participate in violence and resistance to violence, often simultaneously. The following cases provide examples of how *ūman ribu* embraced the manifestation of violence among and by women as feminist concerns.

From the early years of the movement, *ribu* activists critically engaged with the phenomena of mothers who kill their children (*kogoroshi no onna*) and violence executed by women revolutionaries (in the United Red Army). Not only did *ribu* activists interrogate, connect with, and transform the discourse about maternal infanticide, but Tanaka Mitsu (b. 1943), *ūman ribu*'s most publicly visible activist, went so far as to frame abortion as a form of child killing.[16] In doing so, she argued that what is commonly understood within feminist discourse as a "women's right" involves violence by women.[17] Tanaka criticized the assumptions of liberal feminism, which has focused on a politics of rights and equality with men without often acknowledging the violent effects of asserting women's rights over others. The tenets of liberal feminism that promote and prioritize gender equality are often universalized as feminism. While liberal feminism has become the dominant form of feminism in the United States, many Japanese feminists have not necessarily aimed at equality with Japanese men as their political goal.[18] According to influential narratives of Japanese feminism, progress from grassroots activism (such as *ūman ribu* in the 1970s) to the rise of academic and state feminism in the 1980s is often cast as a positive development.[19] However, in our rethinking of Japanese feminism, we must be cautious of the compromises Japanese feminists make with the state.[20] Liberal reforms for women's equality have been selectively incorporated to serve capitalist and nationalistic economic agendas.[21] Indeed, what was notable about *ribu*'s politics in its early phase was its critique of liberal feminism and its rejection of the state's strategies to control and police bodies, rejecting both the sexist gender binary and the ableism demanded by a capitalist state.

Ūman ribu's rejection of the state's dominant gender logic can be seen in its support of the women of the United Red Army, specifically its female leader Nagata Hiroko. Despite the shocking impact of Nagata's leading role in killing fourteen of her comrades, *ribu* activists nonetheless embraced the manifestation of women enacting violence as a feminist concern.[22] Even though they did not support Nagata's violence toward her comrades, they critiqued how society prohibits women from expressing violence and thus treats violent women as more heinous, criminal, and "inhuman" compared to men who engage in violence. By not positing women exclusively or primarily as nonviolent victims, but by recognizing their potential to be aggressors and capable of violence, *ūman ribu*'s approach to women and their violence can contribute to a praxis of CTF. By establishing an understanding of women's participation and complicities in structures, systems, discourses, and acts of violence, this approach enables us to complicate our theorization of women, possessing various capacities and degrees of power to reproduce, perpetuate, prevent, disrupt, and resist various forms of violence and aggression.

Violence between Feminists as Contradiction? Micro-violence and Heteronormativity

In *To Women with Spirit: Toward a Disorderly Theory of Women's Liberation* (*Inochi no onnatachi e: Torimidashi ūman ribu ron*, 1972), Tanaka Mitsu describes a moment of physical harm and violence she inflicted on another young activist named Sayama Sachi. Sayama joined *ribu* after running away from an abusive mother. In the early 1970s, Tanaka and Sayama lived with other activists as members of *ribu* communes. On one occasion, Tanaka hit Sayama for not properly turning off the gas.[23] At the time, Tanaka was twenty-seven and Sayama was nineteen. According to Sayama, Tanaka never apologized for how she treated her and the harm she experienced in their relationship was never addressed or resolved. A de facto power hierarchy in the movement arose despite *ribu*'s anti-hierarchical feminist politics.[24] Sayama's experience of the power dynamics between them, as unequal and even abusive, continued decades later when *ribu* activists reunited to work on publishing documents from the movement.[25] In this case, the differences of power between Tanaka and Sayama were not racial, ethnic, or national, since both activists were Japanese women. However, their relative age, experience, writing skills, and prestige in the nascent movement constituted differences of power. These power differences were also gendered insofar as Tanaka became regarded as "the man" (a domineering authority) and was called the "*tennō*" (emperor) of the movement by other feminists. After Tanaka left the movement to live in Mexico, Sayama and several other women began to identify as lesbians.[26] They felt freer to do so because previously Tanaka's authority had maintained the heteronormative dominance within the movement. The homophobia and heteronormativity were forms of micro-violence and aggression among *ribu* activists addressed by James Welker's chapter in this volume.

Feminist leaders can become very invested in their authority and use aggression and deploy other tactics to preserve their power. The root conflict between these two feminist activists was not in their age/gender difference or relative difference of power per se, but how that difference of power was expressed and negotiated. In many cases, the differences of power a priori are not the source of the concern, but rather, what is troubling is how power differentials are a means to (mis)treat, (dis) respect, and (de)value the other. Power difference is not always an inherent problem; what is needed is the continual assessment of the effects of power differences. How are power differences addressed, negotiated, and articulated, and an opportunity for mentoring or abuse? The inability and refusal to work through, confront, take account of, and heal from such conflictual incidents remain a feminist conundrum that causes the breakdown of relations in feminist movements. Therefore, feminists need to openly acknowledge and assess how power differences constitute intrafeminist relations. More importantly, a *praxis* of CTF is necessary to prevent, acknowledge, and reduce harm from these power differences and conflicts. CTF should entail a practice of open and continual discussion to decrease harm and to strategically negotiate and utilize power differences to achieve shared goals.

The commitment to analyze and address the complex conditions of violence and harm among women and feminists will be key in further developing a paradigm of CTF. If we assume that women are constituted within and through structures of violence (such as colonialism and racism), we can analytically move from the macro-structures of violence to micro-interpersonal instances of violence to better understand how they are inter-constituted. We can then assess how women's complicities and contradictions are not necessarily anti-feminist per se, but an ineluctable part of any liberation struggle. A praxis of CTF should examine and work through various kinds of microaggressions and macro-relational violences, whether they are physical, economic, psychological, symbolic, racial, or gendered. CTF thus advocates a self-reflexive feminist analytics of violence whereby subjects are understood as variously constituted through interlocking systems and histories of imperialism, capitalism, nationalism, racism, classism, ableism, and heteronormativity. CTF is therefore committed to illuminating the aporias of feminist thought and praxis even when this involves exposing the contradictory and conflictual contours of feminist histories and movements. In the next section, I address the macro-structures of national-imperial violence that divide and hierarchize women.

Japanese Imperialism, Feminism and Race

In *Feminism in Modern Japan*, Vera Mackie writes,

> Feminist consciousness in Japan was forged as part of the development of a specific form of modernity. . . . Japanese modernity was also, however, a specific form of colonial modernity. Japanese culture was imbued with the features of a colonial and imperial power, and the identity of Japanese people was the identity of imperial subjects.[27]

Following from an understanding that Japanese feminist consciousness was concomitant with the emergence of modern Japan as an imperial nation, we should ask how Japanese feminism has been shaped and constituted by Japanese imperialism.[28] If the very production of modern Japanese subjects has been entangled with Japanese imperialism, which in turn was a response to Western imperialism, then we can understand Japanese feminism as the product and outcome of a hybrid modernity forged within a global history of competing racialized national-imperialisms.[29] Indeed, the racialized dimensions of Japanese national-imperialism as it relates to Japanese feminism has been undertheorized. Since "Japanese" has been predominantly understood to constitute a national identity, the *racialized* identity of the Japanese has often remained unexamined and underarticulated in Japan Studies. To grasp the ideological roots of the racialized identity of the Japanese, it is useful to cite Bruce Armstrong's "Racialisation and Nationalist Ideology":

I wish to suggest that the concept of a national family, which was central to Japanese nationalism, contained the potential for the racialization of the imagined community which represented the Japanese nation. The notion that every Japanese subject was related "by blood" to all other Japanese subjects and that all members of the national family were collectively related "by blood" to the Emperor implied that the criteria for membership of the national community were both cultural *and* biological. With the appropriation, by theorists of Japanese colonialism, of racist arguments developed in the West, these criteria came to be understood as the defining features of the Japanese "race."[30]

Drawing on Robert Miles, Armstrong discusses how "racism and nationalism can be articulated such that a 'race' category and a national category effectively overlap or coincide."[31] Based on Japan's history as a non-Western imperial power, Japan occupies a unique racialized position in a global schema of race and white supremacy. Although Japan attempted to challenge the white supremacist order of the British Empire and the United States as part of its propaganda, Japanese imperialists themselves produced discourses of Japanese racialized supremacy.[32] Imperial-colonial discourses and practices of racial superiority were part of Japan's propaganda and strategy to justify themselves as the supreme nation/race (*minzoku*) within a hierarchy of Asians. These racialized modalities of power were constitutive of Japanese conceptions of their status and identity in the world.[33]

Despite the centrality of race to the modern global order, the racialized status of the Japanese has often been understudied as an aspect of Japanese identity and gender ideology.[34] To highlight the raciality of the Japanese as a non-white/yellow/East Asian competing (former) imperial power brings attention to the whiteness of the United States as the superpower of the West.[35] In regard to these racial tensions in the postwar period, Yukiko Koshiro writes that Japanese and American racism was not eradicated, but that the U.S. Occupation in many ways reinforced a racial hierarchy despite its implementation of a new system of democracy intended to properly modernize the Japanese.[36]

The imperialist agenda of the United States and its brand of limited democracy significantly informed postwar Japanese feminism (and catalyzed *ūman ribu*).[37] The U.S. imperial agenda in East Asia brought decades of militarization and war, while espousing "freedom and democracy." Lisa Yoneyama has argued that the democratization policies and propaganda during the U.S. Occupation of Japan created an image of the United States as a liberator of Japanese women. Although the postwar Constitution and education system designed by the Americans asserted that men and women were entitled to equal political rights, these unprecedented civil rights were bestowed on Japanese women at the same time that formerly colonized populations in Japan were excluded from such political rights. Yoneyama writes,

> the hypervisibility of Japanese women's enfranchisement under the occupation was achieved *in exchange with* the invisibility of the disenfranchisement and elimination of the social and political rights of women and men from Japan's former colonies, including their right to be considered Japanese nationals.[38]

Yoneyama here reminds us that the relative "liberation" of Japanese women enabled through U.S. military occupation was achieved at the same time that former colonial subjects were summarily disenfranchised from their rights.[39] Yoneyama's argument thus highlights how Japanese women were relatively empowered by enforcing a nationalist exclusion, imposed by the imperial power of the United States that re-divided and hierarchized Japanese women and colonial subjects.[40]

Japanese thus functions not only as a nationality, but also as a *racialized* signifier of power and privilege that has been produced discursively and materially through historical structures of imperialism and capitalism. Koshiro writes that race came to have a double meaning, "race as manifested by physical appearance, and race as an explanation of national power and status in the world."[41] After its postwar recovery, Japan's rising economic power through the 1960s secured its recognition as an advanced first world nation. The treatment of Japanese as "honorary whites" in apartheid South Africa in the 1960s attests to how Japan's imperial legacy and relative global economic power manifest through racial logics.[42] The treatment of Japanese as whites by white South Africans demonstrates how whiteness as property and identity operates through logics of inclusion and exclusion. As Cheryl Harris has stated, "The right to exclude was the central principle, too, of whiteness as identity, for whiteness in large part has been characterized not by an inherent unifying characteristic but by the exclusion of others deemed to be 'not white.'"[43] Japan's proximity to whiteness within a global racial order can be further elaborated in relation to the racialized status of Japanese women in Japan compared with non-Japanese subjects.

The Racialized Ethnic Status of Japanese Women: Exclusivity and Hierarchy

As a researcher of Japanese feminism, I have been asked by scholars in other fields whether Japanese women are analogous in their racialized position within Japan to that of white women in the United States. If Japanese women occupy or approximate such a privileged status, what are the implications in regards to Japanese feminism? This question about Japanese women's relative whiteness and racialization is *not exclusively* about the phenotype of Japanese vis-à-vis other races and Asians, but is also about relative power and status.[44] For example, in contrast to visible phenotypic or epidermal distinctions between South Asians and Southeast Asians, such racial markers do not necessarily apply among Chinese, Japanese, and Koreans. Rather, racialization here operates *discursively*, producing political logics that are linked, in this context, with socioeconomic privilege and civil rights of Japanese women as members of the dominant ethnic majority in a postcolonial society. To date, these issues have not been addressed with frequency in academic work or feminist literature; however, scholars such as Sonia Ryang, Jung Yeong-hae, and Kim Puja have addressed such dynamics in this national-racialized feminist power structure.

Taking a postcolonial feminist perspective, Sonia Ryang has critiqued how Japanese feminism has tended to exclude non-Japanese women and reinforce the myth of homogeneity. Ryang writes,

Contemporary Japanese feminism has long been predominantly "nation-focused" and ethnocentric, concerned mainly with Japanese women in Japan. . . . By not focusing properly on discriminations based on gender *and* ethnicity, Japanese feminism has effectively condoned the dominant Japanese ideology of national homogeneity.[45]

Following Ryang, to focus on the *single axis of gender* and to ignore other power axes such as ethnicity and race produces a feminist hierarchy. This hierarchy privileges the kind of feminism that prioritizes gender issues for Japanese women, without marking Japanese as a specific ethnic/racial identity. This is analogous to white feminism in the United States. Similar to women of color in the United States, colonized subjects such as Ainu (indigenous people of the north of Japan), Okinawans, Korean, Chinese, and Taiwanese residents continue to face various forms of racialized and class discrimination within Japan, making their struggles intersectional, involving multiple discriminations, as documented by Akwi Seo's chapter. The ways in which Japanese feminists can focus on and often limit their concerns to gender issues is a result of a structure of ethnic and class privilege. One Okinawan feminist states,

> [Many Japanese] feminists have not acknowledged their privilege and historical oppression against Okinawans. They are sensitive about it and struggle to face their privilege. A conversation about the fact that Japan is a heterogeneous nation that colonized other nations needs to continue among transnational Japanese feminists so that they can be better allies to non-Japanese.[46]

In response to such criticisms, Japanese feminists have sought to mitigate such limits and exclusions by including the voices of "minority women" and "minority feminist criticism" in their publications.[47] The inclusion of "minority women" within a nation-state-based paradigm, however, results in the continued structural and discursive dilemma whereby the majority dominates and dictates who the minority is. Insofar as transnational feminism does not necessarily disrupt the logics of the nation-state that often privilege dominant ethnic groups within a national framework, CTF calls for a fundamental questioning and unsettling of the assumptions of nationalism and the analytic boundaries of the nation-state and its logic.

In "Racism Among Feminists," Jung Yeong-hae forwards a powerful argument against feminists who label the other as a minority. She opens her essay with incisive questions that continue to have relevance for dominant paradigms of Japanese feminism. Jung asks, "Who decides 'who is the minority?' Those who self-identify as the 'minority'? Or those who call the other the 'minority'?" Jung argues that those feminists who call the other the minority are deploying a "mechanism and power structure that give themselves the superior and universal position."[48] This indictment would apply to many Japanese feminists (myself included) who have re-produced this naming and labeling of "minority" while belonging to the majority.

Jung goes on to decry the reproduction of "white supremacy" (*haku-jin shijōshugi*) in feminism that claims that the origins of modern feminism lie with white middle-class feminism based on Eurocentric narratives about first- and second-wave feminism.[49] Jung demonstrates how racism has operated among U.S. white middle-class feminists to exclude black feminists and she posits Japanese women in Japan as analogous to white women in the United States in terms of their civil rights.[50] Tomomi Yamaguchi and Becky Thompson have also pointed out the problems of using the term second wave, noting how it privileges white middle-class feminists as the pivotal agents of feminist history.[51]

Hegemonic feminist paradigms about first and second wave have been adopted and canonized within Japanese academic feminism. For example, the opening volume of Iwanami Shoten's series, *Feminism in Japan*, begins by placing *ūman ribu* as the beginning of "second-wave feminism" (*dai ni ha feminizumu*) in Japan.[52] This collection, edited by influential feminist scholars Ehara Yumiko, Inoue Teruko, and Ueno Chizuko, (re)produces the dominant master narrative of white-feminist waves and categorizes colonized subjects in Japan as "minorities." The adoption and investment in paradigms of white middle-class feminism by Japanese feminists is also then related to questions of translation. As part of the theory of CTF, I would underscore the importance of further analyzing how racialized economies of translation operate in conjunction with modalities of imperialism and axes of race, ethnicity, class, and gender. What kind of hierarchies are reinforced through economies of translation and publication?[53] Do Japanese feminist exchanges and translations that privilege Euro-American feminism reinforce first world hegemonies?

Given this kind of criticism, what changes can scholars of Japanese feminism and (Japanese) feminists make? CTF emphasizes greater dialogue and solidarity between different forms of feminist discourse, in this case, between Japanese feminists and non-Japanese feminists in Japan, as well as with feminists beyond Japan. Queer women of color feminism in the United States and non-Japanese/ethnic feminists illuminate the limits, exclusions, and hierarchies (re)produced by dominant paradigms of white/Japanese feminism. Rather than reproducing the categories of majority versus minority feminism, a paradigm of CTF would interrogate how transnational feminism can perpetuate (neo)imperial-colonial relations and/or commit to an anti-imperialist or decolonial politics.

Since the late 1970s, one ongoing trajectory of Japanese feminism has been Pan-Asian feminism, which has aimed to support and build solidarity with Asian women from Japan's former colonies. Although lines of cross-ethnic solidarity were not immediately cultivated during the early 1970s, an anti-imperialist understanding has shaped how many *ūman ribu* activists and other Japanese feminists have invested in solidarity work with third world Asian women. By the mid-1970s, for example, *ribu* activists and other Japanese feminists protested against Japanese men who were going to Korea on sex tours. They did this as an expression of their anti-imperialist feminism and as an act of solidarity with Korean women who were protesting in Korea.[54] The Asian Women's Association (AWA) emerged from coalitional feminist organizing against sex tourism in Asian countries by Japanese businessmen.[55] Matsui Yayori (1935–2002) was a leader in founding the AWA in 1977 and a key feminist leader in organizing the Women's International War Crimes Tribunal for the Trial of Japanese Military Sexual Slavery.

During the 1990s, the debates surrounding the "comfort women" marked a turning point in Japanese feminism. According to Ulrike Wöhr, during the 1990s, "Just as 'white' feminists in North America and Europe have had to face the challenge of postcolonial feminisms, mainstream Japanese feminists could no longer evade the questions put to them by women of other ethnicities and nationalities residing within Asia, and even within Japan."[56] The feminist debates about the "comfort women" were very complicated and highlighted divisions among feminists in Japan. Wöhr describes how these divisions also came to represent debates among "majority Japanese feminists" like Ueno Chizuko vis-à-vis feminists such as Kim Puja, who argued from the perspective of a Korean feminist living in Japan. Ueno was accused by other intellectuals and activists of espousing "universalist" views and advocating a feminist hierarchy that places the importance of gender *above* ethnicity.[57] In contrast, Kim Puja represented a Korean-Japanese standpoint arguing for the recognition of colonial violence, and that "sisterhood" and "solidarity" would only be possible after Japanese women admitted their guilt and complicity as daughters of the colonizing nation.[58] Recognizing the ongoing historical effects of colonialism is a vital foundation for understanding the politics of decolonial feminism.

Feminism, Anti-imperialism, and the Decolonial

Contemporary critiques of Japanese feminism's national-racialized exclusivity are also pertinent to *ūman ribu*'s limitations in its early stage. Although many *ūman ribu* activists were informed by the anti-imperialist discourse of the New Left, seeking solidarity with colonized women within Japan was not considered imperative to Japanese women's liberation during the early 1970s. Many felt that the first step was to liberate themselves; therefore, organizing with women who are ethnic Korean, Ainu, Okinawan, or Buraku (a traditionally discriminated against caste) was not initially integral to *ribu*'s politics. Among *ribu* activists I interviewed, there was suspicion about "fronting" a rhetoric of solidarity with these groups in reaction to how such practices characterized the male dominated New Left student movements that *ribu* women deemed hypocritical due to their sexism.[59] Rather, some *ribu* activists identified themselves as analogous to these oppressed groups and went so far as to describe Japanese women as "colonized slaves" within the imperial nation of Japan.[60] Citing Angela Davis, a pamphlet by Group of Fighting Women (Gurūpu Tatakau Onna) describes the relations between Japanese women and Japanese men as that of a "slave" and "slave master."[61] This was similar to how radical white feminists adopted the language of African Americans and saw themselves as oppressed by men (as "slaves" to men) and targets of their sexual violence.[62] The circulation and resignification of such political discourse is also an example of transnational flows of feminist discourse from the United States to Japan that gloss over and/or ignore racial differences.

White feminist discourses that privilege gender over racial/ethnic difference would characterize Japanese feminism as it developed into liberal feminism and academic feminism during the late 1970s and 1980s. Yoko Ono is an apt example of this form of universalizing global feminism and a transnational symbol of the merging of Euro-American and Japanese feminist discourses that appropriate black experiences. She famously stated in 1969 that "Woman is the nigger of the world" and later released a song with John Lennon with this title and theme. Echoing the discourse of Euro-American abolitionists and suffragettes, Ono's statement at once conflates the oppression and de facto enslavement of Africans with the oppression of *all women*, and appropriates this suffering to render the plight of all women as somehow commensurate, similar, or analogous. Moreover, in 1972 the National Organization of Women (NOW) presented Ono and Lennon with the "Positive Image of Women" award for the song's "strong feminist statement." Ono's discourse and recognition from NOW highlight a convergence of white feminism and Japanese raciality. Ono's image decorated the cover of Japan's inaugural edition of the first commercial feminist magazine, *Feminisuto* (Feminist), which sold 22,000 copies in 1977. Founder and editor of *Feminisuto*, Atsumi Ikuko, describes this new Japanese feminist magazine as "five years behind American feminists," referring specifically to the publication of *Ms.* Magazine in 1972.[63] This Japanese-English bilingual publication was representative of the transnational circuits of Japanese feminism that invested in connections with Euro-American feminists. As arguably the most famous Japanese woman across the United Kingdom, United States, and Japan at the time, Ono's discourse and image symbolize the multivalent *transnational* connections between Euro-American feminism and Japanese feminism.

Thus, a vital question that CTF raises is the following: When does the transnational function to normalize the status quo, and when does it serve to decolonize power relations?[64] Following from this question, an analytical distinction to make is whether the *trans* in transnational feminism is queer/(non)heteronormative and guided by an anti-imperialist politics or a desire to further strengthen one's position by an appeal to the cultural capital of the West. When transnational feminist solidarities remain between first world nations, we might ask if these connections reproduce imperial forms of power. If transnational feminist practices are not anti-imperialist or decolonial, do they run the risk of reproducing neo-imperial forms of feminism?

As a final point, I make an analytical distinction between Japanese first world anti-imperialism and decolonial praxis.[65] I make this distinction because the former did not necessarily translate into anti-imperial solidarity work with other colonized women in Japan. A decolonial feminist politics would involve solidarity work with (formerly) colonized women/feminists, whereby first world (Japanese) feminists would *support* rather than lead and determine the political agenda. Hence CTF advocates a shift from an open-ended transnational perspective, which often reproduces the dominant logics of the nation-state, to a decolonial feminist trajectory, which focuses on solidarity that traverses and unsettles axes of power and (post)colonial logics of violence. Decolonial feminism recognizes that colonial logics structure, contour, and haunt contemporary conditions and that the process of decolonization is unfinished, always imperfect, and requires creative and strategic alliances.

Conclusion

These preliminary thoughts about a praxis of CTF are indebted to lessons drawn from the *ūman ribu* movement. By revisiting *ūman ribu*'s limits and seeming contradictions, we are reminded that various forms of violence within and among feminists can be productively reconceived as opportunities to better address power abuse and aggression among women. Such a feminist politics would involve an understanding that these kinds of constitutive contradictions contribute to a better praxis of CTF *if* feminists prioritize the importance of communicating openly about existing structural conflicts, and *create effective ways* to work through them. Differences of power and hierarchy need not be deemed antithetical to feminism and obscured, but rather should be openly discussed as the extant material conditions that require transformation. CTF thus aims to practice and theorize counter-hegemonic logics without presuming an absence of contradiction and conflict. By analyzing and working through the multiplicity of violences within feminist formations and histories, we may discover a new approach to power within feminism. Power differences among feminists within a transnational context need not be an impediment to coalition, but rather provide a basis for a praxis of CTF that recognizes exposing and harnessing the potential violence of feminist power as imperative for the future of feminisms.

Notes

I thank Ayako Kano, James Welker, Tamara Ho, Dylan Rodriguez, Akwi Seo, Tomomi Yamaguchi, and Ayano Ginoza for their comments on this chapter.

1   *Ūman ribu*'s call for comprehensive political, economic, social, cultural, and sexual revolution, constitutes what has been defined as "radical

feminism." See Machiko Matsui, "Evolution of the Feminist Movement in Japan," *National Women's Studies Association Journal* 2, no. 3 (1990).

2 Setsu Shigematsu, *Scream from the Shadows: The Women's Liberation Movement in Japan* (Minneapolis: University of Minnesota Press, 2012).

3 In part 1 of *Scream from the Shadows*, "Genealogies and Violations," I elaborate multiple domestic and transnational political genealogies that intersected to shape the emergence of the *ribu* movement.

4 Inderpal Grewal and Caren Kaplan ask "how to link diverse feminisms without requiring either equivalence or a master theory . . . without replicating cultural and economic hegemony." See "Introduction," in *Scattered Hegemonies: Postmodernity and Transnational Feminist Practices*, ed. Inderpal Grewal and Caren Kaplan (Minneapolis: University of Minnesota Press, 1994), 19.

5 Cherríe Moraga and Gloria Anzaldúa, *This Bridge Called My Back: Writings by Radical Women of Color* (New York: Kitchen Table, 1983); Valerie Amos and Pratibha Parmar, "Challenging Imperial Feminism," *Feminist Review*, no. 17 (Autumn 1984); Chandra Talpade Mohanty, "Under Western Eyes: Feminist Scholarship and Colonial Discourse," in *Third World Women and the Politics of Feminism*, ed. Chandra Talpade Mohanty, Ann Russo, and Lourdes Torres (Bloomington: Indiana University Press, 1991).

6 Angela Davis, *Women, Race and Class* (New York: Vintage Books, 1983); Kimberle Crenshaw, "Mapping the Margins: Intersectionality, Identity Politics, and Violence Against Women of Color," *Stanford Law Review* 43, no. 6 (1991); M. Jacqui Alexander and Chandra Talpade Mohanty, eds., *Feminist Genealogies, Colonial Legacies, Democratic Futures* (New York: Routledge, 1997); Gayatri Chakravorty Spivak, "Three Women's Texts and a Critique of Imperialism," *Critical Inquiry* 12, no. 1 (Autumn 1985); Gayatri Chakravorty Spivak, "Women in Difference," in her *Outside the Teaching Machine* (New York: Routledge, 1993), 77–95.

7 Inderpal Grewal and Caren Kaplan, "Global Identities: Theorizing Transnational Studies of Sexuality," *GLQ: A Journal of Lesbian and Gay Studies* 7, no. 4 (2001).

8 Richa Nagar and Amanda Lock Swarr, "Introduction: Theorizing Transnational Feminist Praxis," in *Critical Transnational Feminist Praxis* (Albany: State University of New York Press, 2010), 17.

9 Ibid., 9.

10 In her "Under Western Eyes Revisited," in *Feminism Without Borders: Decolonizing Theory, Practicing Solidarity* (Durham, NC: Duke University Press, 2003), 227, Chandra Mohanty complicates the usage of the terms first world and third world to account for the socioeconomic differences,

social majorities, and social minorities within these sites. However, I chose to continue to use the terms first world and third world, despite their limitations, for their political significance about the legacy and ongoing conditions of colonialism.

11 As a scholar born in Japan to Japanese parents, but raised and educated in England, Canada, and the United States, I am invested in feminism as a transnational and decolonial political project for gender liberation. I have learned and benefited from the movements of women's liberation across North America and Japan, and have been formed by these genealogies of struggle. I write as part of these genealogies and self-reflexive of my own power position within this global framework as someone situated in the U.S. academy who publishes primarily in English as an imperial language.

12 Naoki Sakai, "The Problem of 'Japanese Thought': The Formation of 'Japan' and the Schema of Cofiguration," in his *Translation and Subjectivity: On "Japan" and Cultural Nationalism* (Minneapolis: University of Minnesota Press, 1997), 40–71.

13 Ayako Kano, "Toward a Critique of Transhistorical Femininity," in *Gendering Modern Japanese History*, ed. Barbara Molony and Kathleen Uno (Cambridge, MA: Harvard University Press, 2005). Kano cites from a collection of letters Ueno Chizuko exchanged with philosopher Nakamura Yūjiro included in Ueno Chizuko, *'Ningen' o koete: Idō to chakuchi* (Tokyo: Seidosha, 1989), 207–209.

14 *Inpakushon*, no. 73, "Ribu nijū nen," special issue (1992); Onnatachi no Ima o Tou Kai, ed., *Zenkyōtō kara ribu e* (Tokyo: Inpakuto Shuppankai, 1996); Kanō Mikiyo, *Ribu to iu kakumei: Kindai no yami o hiraku* (Tokyo: Inpakuto Shuppankai, 2003), 57–69.

15 Shigematsu, *Scream from the Shadows*, 14.

16 Tanaka Mitsu, "Aete teiki suru = chūzetsu wa kitoku no kenri ka?" in *Shiryō Nihon ūman ribu shi*, vol. 2, ed. Mizoguchi Akiyo, Saeki Yōko, and Miki Sōko (Kyoto: Shōkadō Shoten, 1994), 63.

17 Shigematsu, *Scream from the Shadows*, 28.

18 Alexander and Mohanty contrast their approach to feminism with the "liberal-pluralist understanding of feminism" which they describe as "an inheritance from the predominantly liberal roots of American feminist praxis." See Alexander and Mohanty, "Introduction," in their *Feminist Genealogies, Colonial Legacies, Democratic Futures*, xvi. See also Yoshie Kobayashi, *A Path Toward Gender Equality: State Feminism in Japan* (New York: Routledge, 2012).

19 Ehara Yumiko describes the development of Japanese feminism from the 1970s to the 1990s in terms of three major phases: "the era of liberation" (1970–1977), characterized by activism, including *ūman ribu*; the

"emergence of Women's Studies" (1978–1982); and an "era of celebrated feminists and feminist debate" that followed. Ehara's narrative points to some of the historical tensions between *ūman ribu* activists and academic feminists, and some of the hierarchies and conflicts within Japanese feminism that have often juxtaposed academia versus activism and theory versus practice. See Ehara Yumiko, "Japanese Feminism in the 1970s and 1980s," trans. Yanagida Eino and Paula Long, *U.S.–Japan Women's Journal*, no. 4 (1993). I also address these tensions in my "Epilogue" to *Scream from the Shadows*, 171–175.

20 Such compromises and the dangers thereof are discussed in chapters by Elyssa Faison, Ayako Kano, and Tomomi Yamaguchi in this volume.

21 Patricia Boling, "State Feminism in Japan?" *U.S.–Japan Women's Journal*, no. 34 (2008). See also Kano's comments regarding Abe Shinzo's "womenomics" in the conclusion to this volume.

22 Setsu Shigematsu, "The Japanese Women's Liberation Movement and the United Red Army," *Feminist Media Studies* 12, no. 2 (2012).

23 Shigematsu, *Scream from the Shadows*, 160; Tanaka Mitsu, *Inochi no onnatachi e: Torimidashi ūman ribu ron* (Tokyo: Kawade Shobō, 1972), 98–99; Sayama Sachi, interview with author, San Francisco, June 7, 2001.

24 Sayama, interview, June 7, 2001.

25 Sayama Sachi, personal correspondence and interviews, 2010–2015.

26 In contrast with U.S. and other radical feminist movement(s), Tanaka did not promote "lesbian love"—a term sometimes used in Japan in the early 1970s—as an alternative to compulsory heterosexuality. As noted in James Welker's chapter in this volume, lesbians were marginalized within the *ribu* movement. This was also one of *ribu*'s limitations despite its central slogan that called for the liberation of eros. Tanaka and other activists I interviewed spoke of the irony of Tanaka becoming "the man" and "*tennō*" (emperor) of the movement insofar as she became the dominant authority and decision maker in the movement.

27 Vera Mackie, *Feminism in Modern Japan: Citizenship, Embodiment and Sexuality* (Cambridge: Cambridge University Press, 2003), 2–3.

28 Suzuki Yūko, *Feminizumu to sensō: Fujin undōka no sensō kyōryoku* (Tokyo: Marujusha, 1997); Kanō Mikiyo, *Josei to tennōsei* (Tokyo: Shisō no Kagaku, 1979).

29 Vera Mackie, *Feminism in Modern Japan*; Sharon L. Sievers, *Flowers in Salt: The Beginnings of Feminist Consciousness in Modern Japan* (Stanford, CA: Stanford University Press, 1983).

30 Bruce Armstrong, "Racialisation and Nationalist Ideology: The Japanese Case," *International Sociology* 4, no 3 (1989): 338.

31 Ibid., 340.

32 John Dower, *War Without Mercy: Race and Power in the Pacific War* (New York: Pantheon, 1987); Gerald Horne, *Race War! White Supremacy and the Japanese Attack on the British Empire* (New York: New York University Press, 2004).

33 Japan's relative whiteness and its shifting racialized discourses changed over the course of its empire-building project. See Yukiko Koshiro, *Trans-Pacific Racisms and the U.S. Occupation of Japan* (New York: Columbia University Press, 1999), 7; and Takashi Fujitani, *Race for Empire: Koreans as Japanese and Japanese as Americans During World War II* (Berkeley: University of California Press, 2013).

34 Gerald Horne, "The Asiatic Black Man? Japan and the 'Colored Races' Challenge White Supremacy," in *Black Renaissance/Renaissance Noire 4*, no. 1 (2002): 26–37.

35 Moon-Kie Jung, Joao H. Costa Vargas, and Eduardo Bonilla-Silva, eds., *State of White Supremacy: Racism, Governance and the United States* (Stanford, CA: Stanford University Press, 2011). Dylan Rodriguez has argued that we are no longer in an era of "'classical' white supremacy as a model of dominance based on white bodily monopoly" but that it is a "sophisticated, flexible, 'diverse' (neoliberal)" form of multicultural white supremacy that selectively incorporates people of color to further its logic of violence. See Dylan Rodriguez, "Inaugurating Multicultural White Supremacy," *Journal for Critical Alternatives*, November 9, 2008, http://criticalalternatives.blogspot.com/2008/12/inaugurating-multicultural-white.html.

36 Koshiro, *Trans-Pacific Racisms*, 16; Gerald Horne, *Race War!*; Maruyama Masao, *Thought and Behavior in Modern Japanese Politics* (New York: Columbia University Press, 1995); Jodi Kim, "Asian America's Japan: the Perils of Gendered Racial Rehabilitation," in *Ends of Empire: Asian American Critique and the Cold War* (Minneapolis: University of Minnesota, 2010), 95–142.

37 The postwar Constitution and education system designed by the Americans asserted that men and women were entitled to equal political rights. In spite of legal equality, these formal rights were mitigated and undermined by limited reforms of the Civil Code, the family registration system (*koseki seido*) and sociocultural discourses that continued to regulate and reproduce patriarchal gender norms and other forms of discrimination. These contradictory conditions catalyzed the rise of *ūman ribu*.

38 Lisa Yoneyama, "Liberation Under Siege: US Military Occupation and Japanese Women's Enfranchisement," *American Quarterly* 57, no. 3 (2005): 905 (emphasis in the original).

39 See Akwi Seo's chapter for more details on Koreans' loss of rights during the U.S. Occupation.

40 When we consider the rise of feminism in the United States and Japan as part of modern histories of imperial powers, we can compare how colonized people became "minoritized" within these nations.

41 Koshiro, *Transpacific Racism*, 3.

42 Masako Osada, *Sanctions and Honorary Whites: Diplomatic Policies and Economic Realities in Relations between Japan and South Africa* (Santa Barbara, CA: Greenwood Publishing, 2002), 145. Although the term "honorary whites" was never used in official or legal language in South Africa, it began to be widely used to describe the exceptional treatment that Japanese received in South Africa, such as being allowed to live in white-only areas.

43 Cheryl Harris, "Whiteness as Property," in *Critical Race Theory: The Key Writings That Formed the Movement*, ed. Kimberle Crenshaw, Neil Gotanda, Gary Peller, and Kendall Thomas (New York: The New Press, 1995), 283.

44 Setsu Shigematsu, "Intimacies of Imperialism and Japanese-Black Feminist Transgression: Militarised Occupations in Okinawa and Beyond." *Intersections: Gender and Sexuality in Asia and the Pacific* 37 (2015), http://intersections.anu.edu.au/issue37/shigematsu.pdf.

45 Sonia Ryang, "Love and Colonialism in Takamure Itsue's Feminism," *Feminist Review* 60 (1998): 2 (emphasis in the original).

46 "A-san," interview, January 1, 2016. Suzuki Mieko, a Buraku activist, similarly states, "I think that Japanese feminists have a limited perspective. . . . The economic and social background of these 'middle-class feminists,' and, consequently, their perspectives, are also very different from those of the Buraku women. Recognizing these differences is crucial. I think that feminists in Japan are lacking in terms of their understanding of minority issues and the structure of discrimination." See Suzuki Mieko, "Commitments to Women's and Buraku Issues," in *Voices from the Japanese Women's Movement*, ed. AMPO, *Japan Asia Quarterly Review* (Armonk, NY: M. E. Sharpe, 1996), 156.

47 For example, in AMPO, *Voices from the Japanese Women's Movement*, three out of twenty-six chapters provide women's perspectives from Buraku, ethnic Korean, and Ainu communities.

48 Jung Yeong-hae, "Feminizumu no naka no reishizumu," in *Wādomappu feminizumu*, ed. Ehara Yumiko and Kanai Yoshiko (Tokyo: Shinyōsha, 1997), 89. I thank Ayako Kano for directing me to this important essay on racism within feminism.

49 Jung, "Feminizumu no naka no reishizumu," 97. See also Becky

Thompson, "Multiracial Feminism: Recasting the Chronology of Second Wave Feminism," *Feminist Studies* 28, no. 2 (2002).

50 Jung, "Feminizumu no naka no reishizumu," 100.

51 I thank Tomomi Yamaguchi for raising this point in 2000 when we were part of an *ūman ribu* research group in Tokyo. See also, Thompson, "Multiracial Feminism."

52 Ehara Yumiko, Inoue Teruko, and Ueno Chizuko, eds., *Nihon no feminizumu*, vol. 1: *Ribu to feminizumu* (Tokyo: Iwanami Shoten, 2009), i. This series is also discussed by Ayako Kano in her chapter in this volume.

53 Questions about English-language hegemony and translation are raised by the very language and form of this essay, but it is beyond the limits of this essay to address them adequately.

54 *Ribu* activists embodied and lived their politics for decades and many committed to Pan-Asian feminist practice that was intended to build solidarity with women from nations formerly colonized by Japan. For example, Kuno Ayako, editor of *Women's Mutiny* (*Onna no hangyaku*), a *ribu* publication (*minikomi*) that continued for forty years, became a volunteer at a shelter specifically for Filipina women living in Japan. Miki Sōko, another veteran *ribu* activist, became very involved in supporting Korean women's filmmaking during the 1990s and early 2000s.

55 See the Asia–Japan Women's Resource Center's website: http://www .ajwrc.org/eng/index.php, last accessed March 10, 2015. The Asia–Japan Women's Resource Center continues this legacy of Pan-Asian Japanese feminist practice. The anti-imperialist feminist politics that shapes the Pan-Asian feminist movement of groups, such as AWA and AJWRC, involves a sustained practice of anti-imperialist feminism.

56 Ulrike Wöhr, "A Touchstone for Transnational Feminism: Discourses on the Comfort Women in 1990s Japan," *Japanstudien* 16 (2004): 66.

57 Oka Mari, "Watashitachi wa naze mizukara nanoru koto ga dekiru no ka: shokuminchishugi-teki kenryoku kankei ni tsuite no oboegaki," in *Shinpojiumu: Nashonarizumu to 'ianfu' mondai*, ed. Nihon no Sensō Sekinin Shiryō Sentā (Tokyo: Aoki Shoten, 1998), 221–223.

58 Ikeda Eriko, Kim Puja, Nishino Rumiko, Nakahara Michiko, and Matsui Yayori, "Zadankai: Naze 'josei kokusai senpan hōtei' o hiraku no ka," *Onnatachi no 21seiki* 17 (January 1999): 6.

59 Gurūpu Tatakau Onna, "Naze sei kaihō ka: Josei kaihō no mondai teiki," in *Shiryō Nihon ūman ribu shi*, vol. 1, ed. Mizoguchi Akiyo, Saeki Yōko, and Miki Sōko (Kyoto: Shōkadō Shoten, 1992), 212.

60 Gurūpu Tatakau Onna, "Naze ribu wa nyūkan o tatakau ka," in *Shiryō Nihon ūman ribu shi*, vol. 1.

61 Ibid., 238.

62 Sara Evans, *Personal Politics: The Roots of Women's Liberation in the Civil Rights Movement and the New Left* (New York: Vintage Books, 1980). Evans' work is an example of this form of white feminism.

63 Kathryn Tolbert, "Feminist Magazines Appear in Japan," *Herald Tribune*, November 25, 1977, 17B.

64 M. Jacqui Alexander and Chandra Talpade Mohanty, "Cartographies of Knowledge and Power: Transnational Feminism and Radical Praxis," in *Critical Transnational Feminist Praxis*, 24.

65 For a further distinction between Japanese anti-imperial feminism and decolonial feminism, see Shigematsu, "Intimacies of Imperialism and Japanese-Black Feminist Transgression."

CHAPTER 13

~

Toward Postcolonial
Feminist Subjectivity

Korean Women's Redress Movement
for "Comfort Women"

AKWI SEO

In the course of finding commonality in our difficulties and shar-
ing awareness, we encountered the issue of the "comfort women." We
found our way in the resolution of this issue. . . . In other words, we
found the "comfort women" issue to be the epitome of our problems.
We have engaged with it to reflect our way of life and to change our
society, in the belief that this will relieve the souls of the "comfort
women" who died in silence or live today.

—Kim Puja et al., "Atogaki"[1]

JAPANESE MILITARY SEXUAL SLAVERY was first politicized as a matter
of the human rights of women in the early 1990s in South Korea. The
issue soon went beyond war compensation between Japan and Korea,
paving the way for transnational efforts to abolish violence against
women in all conflicts. The redress movement for "military comfort
women" (in Japanese, *jūgun ianfu*) in Korea also galvanized women's
organizing in Japan. In its early phase, groups of ethnic Korean women
in Japan advocated for "comfort women," thus building bridges between
social movements in Japan and Korea. The activism of Korean women in
Japan, conducted through the Korean Women's Network on the Comfort
Women Issue (Jūgun Ianfu Mondai Uri Yoson Nettowāku), hereafter Yeoseong-Net,[2] was distinct as it addressed the intersectionality of

colonialism and gender, based on participants' experiences of multiple oppressions as women of the colonial diaspora.

Yeoseong-Net's contribution to create a framework of transnational feminist activism has been explored in detail as a structural transformation taking place within the framework of majority-minority women, as well as within the larger context of a globalizing Asia.[3] Also, some Yeoseong-Net members' individual memoirs were published in English.[4] In this chapter, I focus on Yeoseong-Net to explore the process of identity formation and expression of political agency, which signaled the emergence of a new postcolonial feminist subjectivity. Here I apply Inderpal Grewal's conceptualization of a subject that is heterogeneous as well as political, that destroys binaries and is inclusive, in opposition to a conventional notion of the subject as created out of the binaries of Self/Other, Subject/Object in the Western philosophical tradition. The new subject provides a constant critique of nationalist and even insurgent agendas, and of power relations that structure global economic flows—a critique that will never be complete.[5] This nonessentialist heterogeneous subject is useful for analyzing the creative meaning of Yeoseong-Net. Korean women in Japan were able to articulate their identities and share their insights about the socioeconomic structure surrounding them, thereby starting a new form of transnational feminist activism based on their agency as postcolonial diasporic women. It must be noted that they had little intention to maintain Yeoseong-Net as an organization (it dissolved in 1998), and resisted basing the organization on so-called "identity politics." Nonetheless, Yeoseong-Net helped to clarify their identities as Korean women in Japan (as distinct from Japanese women), Koreans in Korea, and new immigrants from Korea in Japan. This enabled them to forge solidarity and become active participants in politics, resisting multiple layers of oppression.

Feminists in each racial/ethnic group are affected by their race and class status, by their own experiences within their racial/ethnic movements, and by the structure of political choices for activism available at that time, so that organizationally distinct racial/ethnic feminisms emerge.[6] With this in mind, I examine here how and why the issue of forced military prostitution mobilized Korean women in Japan, and catalyzed the establishment of the first organization of Korean women in Japan that explicitly addresses women's liberation. In the following section, I examine the postcolonial diasporic conditions in which Korean women in Japan have been positioned, and their strategies for participating in the political sphere at the organizational level. Then, I explore Korean women's involvement in campaigns for redress for "comfort women," analyzing the narratives of former Yeoseong-Net members based on personal interviews. Lastly, I discuss the multiplicity of efforts made by Korean women in Japan to challenge structural oppression.

Engendering Korean Diaspora in Japan

As a result of Japanese colonial rule in Korea (1910–1945), there were approximately two million Koreans in Japan at the defeat of the Japanese Empire. Two-thirds of them returned to a liberated homeland, but postwar political instability on the Korean peninsula, which was intensified by the Cold War, made an estimated 600,000 Koreans decide to postpone their repatriation in anticipation of a Korean unification that still has not occurred. The Korean diaspora in Japan is characterized by the insecurity and political ambiguity of their status as former colonial subjects who are perceived as temporary residents, sojourners, and exiles.[7]

The postwar restructuring of Japanese nationhood gradually yet systematically excluded former colonial subjects from its membership. Technically speaking, people from the colonies (the Korean peninsula and Taiwan) initially had Japanese nationality, but were subjected to a newly introduced alien registration system in 1947. Upon ratification of the San Francisco Peace Treaty in 1952, the Japanese government unilaterally revoked their Japanese nationality. Koreans in Japan were suddenly made stateless. This institutional arrangement reflecting an ethnically exclusive concept of nationality was then used to justify the exclusion of Koreans as "foreigners," disentitling them from social welfare services such as public housing, the national pension plan, national health insurance, voting rights, and employment in public service.[8] In the private sector, discrimination was rationalized against even subsequent generations of Koreans, who had acquired Japanese language and culture. This rationalization was based on their lack of Japanese nationality. It was not until normalization of the diplomatic relationship between Japan and South Korea in 1965 that Koreans in Japan were entitled to permanent residency on the condition of their affiliation to the Republic of Korea (ROK), while the legal status of those Koreans not supporting the ROK was not stabilized until the early 1980s.[9]

Displaced from mainstream Japanese society as outsiders, Koreans developed a self-sufficient ethnic community that included banks, schools, businesses, culture and media institutions, and religious associations. They were typically employed as casual laborers or worked in small-scale family businesses such as restaurants, pachinko parlors, junk dealerships, and plastic factories. Postwar economic growth accelerated to improve their economic condition. In spite of their long-term residence in Japan, and the fact that Japan-born generations fluent in Japanese language and culture increasingly constituted the majority of these communities, Koreans remained invisible, or outsiders to Japanese society without proper recognition, not even as second-class citizens in their country of residence.[10] These conditions reinforced ethnic family and community relationships including their patriarchal structure.

The two ideologically opposing states in the postwar Korean peninsula reconstructed ethnic identity as a replacement for enforced Japanese colonial modernity. They did so by using Confucianism as a governing idea, at the center of which was patriarchy with specific gender norms.[11] Such state ideologies based on premodern Confucian values were readily accepted by people of the Korean diaspora in Japan during the decolonialization process, who had been yearning for national belonging in the postwar world order. Patriarchal values were further strengthened in their attempt to reconstruct family and community as a fortress against oppression imposed on them by Japanese society.[12] Unstable status and oppressive conditions in the country of residence affected women in particular, leaving them little choice but to depend on their families and their community, and thus suppressing their aspirations for gender equality.[13]

Women's Ambiguous Position in Ethnic Organizations

Ongoing uncertainties related to nationality and citizenship gave Koreans an unstable mentality, characterized by an endless search for self. The division of the Korean peninsula as a result of the Korean War further increased the uncertainty of their status. Uncertainty in national belongingness predisposed Koreans in Japan to become profoundly involved in nationalist politics, as well as in protests against repression by the Japanese authorities. The Korean community in Japan was ruptured along the same 38th parallel as the Korean peninsula, torn between those affiliated with the General Association of Korean Residents in Japan (the pro–North Korean state association known as Chongryun)[14] and the Korean Residents Union in Japan (the pro–South Korean state association known as Mindan).[15]

For most of the postwar period, political involvement by Korean women in Japan has been conducted under the umbrella of these two ethnonational organizations.[16] The women's association of Mindan is called the Association of Korean Women in Japan (Puin-hoe) and that of Chongryun is called the Democratic Union of Korean Women in Japan (Nyeomaeng).[17] In spite of their ideological differences, these associations are alike in adopting the conventionally feminine ideal of the patriotic "dutiful wife and devoted mother."[18] This model enabled women's political participation in nationalist projects, while reinforcing the gendered structure of Korean diaspora politics. The women's associations were expected to contribute to the decisions of male-dominated organizations, while women's aspirations to liberation were overshadowed by issues of ethnic liberation.[19]

As Japan-born generations came to comprise the core of the ethnic Korean community, the focus of ethnic movements shifted from nationalism to grassroots activism advocating human rights, based on their self-identification as "residents" in Japanese society rather than expatriates. The Korean civil rights movements first emerged through the cooperation between Koreans and Japanese in Kawasaki City, supporting a lawsuit by a young second-generation Korean man against a large electric corporation that discriminated against him in employment. Following Kawasaki, grassroots organizations advocating human rights for Korean residents appeared in cities with large Korean communities like Osaka, Kyoto, and Tokyo. Korean women organized their own civil rights groups like Kawasaki Omoni no Kai (Korean Mother's Association in Kawasaki) and Meari Kai (Association Echo) in Kyoto.[20] They organized from the standpoint of "mothers" advocating for their children's rights to have their ethnic background and identity respected in Japanese public schools. Emerging out of Korean mothers' self-help groups, these grassroots associations produced a new agency as community leaders imbued with ethnically specific identities as mothers, linking political subjectivity across private and public spheres.[21] Their political agency is evident in the fact that some members later were acknowledged as representatives of Korean residents in public committees sponsored by local governments.

These cases imply that femininity and motherhood were crucial to Korean women's political participation and were reinforced by ethno-national and civic movements. Although women were always active in Korean movements for justice, their position as activists was ambiguous. That is because the "political" has historically been defined as inherently masculine, as numerous feminist critiques have demonstrated. Women actively participated in political campaigns, but were marginalized in the male-dominant organizations. Therefore women's agency needed to be expressed through gender-specific roles such as child-rearing, which nonetheless enabled them to participate in the political sphere. Their active agency based on motherhood was not just a strategy but also reflected a major aspect of Korean women's reality, namely their devotion to family, especially to children.

The 1970s era of women's liberation in Japan, discussed in this volume in chapters by Setsu Shigematsu and James Welker, consequently had little impact on the vast majority of Korean women, due to the large disparity between Japanese and Korean women in terms of civil rights and economic, social, and political status, as well as a sense of distrust on the part of Korean women toward Japanese society, including Japanese women.[22] There were a couple of cases where Korean women took part in the Japanese feminist movement as individuals, but these were rare exceptions; women on both sides failed to understand each other in a way that recognized the different positionality between them.

Feminist Aspirations of Korean Women in Japan

As I have illustrated, Korean women remained invisible and marginalized in movements in which they participated. It was not until the 1980s that Korean women's feminist aspirations became salient, expressed sporadically and individually in minor ethnic or Japanese feminist media, suggesting the gradual incorporation of second-generation Korean women into Japanese public discourse.

As for collective activity, the Association of Korean Women in Japan for Democracy (hereafter Yeoseong-hoe)[23] was launched in 1987 by female activists who were members of Hantongryun (the Korean Democratic Reunification Union),[24] an organization supporting democratic movements against dictatorship in South Korea. Influenced by the rise of the women's movement in South Korea protesting violence against women, Korean female activists in Japan formed their own association addressing gender equality within the Korean ethno-national movement. Another example of this kind of organization was the formation of a young women's reading circle in 1984,[25] known as the Chōsen Joseishi Dokushokai (Association for Reading Korean Women's History).[26] The members met to read and translate masterpieces of Korean women's history published by Ewha Women's University.[27] They published the newsletter *Josei tsūshin* (Women's communication), compiling women's bold criticism of patriarchy in Korean society, including their ethnic community and family. Although members in Dokushokai did not set out to create a movement, *Josei tsūshin* provided a discursive space in which Korean women discussed women's liberation, mediating Korean women divided by different organizational affiliations. In other words, *Josei tsūshin*, published quarterly in the Japanese language, opened a kind of counterpublic for Korean women aspiring for liberation. It was at the moment of the politicization of Japanese military-imposed forced prostitution in South Korea during World War II that these women recognized a common interest in women's liberation and took collective action.

In December 1990, Yoon Jung-ok, head of the Korean Council for the Women Drafted for Military Sexual Slavery by Japan (hereafter the Korean Council), the leading organization of the movement for redress, came to Tokyo. Women who had contributed to the above-mentioned *Josei tsūshin*, activists who had withdrawn from Yeoseong-hoe, and several individual activists got together for a closed-door discussion with Yoon.[28] Seventeen women attending the session were inspired by Yoon's reinterpretation of "comfort women" as victims of patriarchy, not just colonialism, which had shamed the victims and had discouraged them from making complaints. They decided to take action in Japan for the redress of these victims. They started with translations of Yoon's interviews with survivors and published them as a booklet: *We Never Forget: Korean Military Comfort Women* (*Watashitachi wa wasurenai: Chōsenjin jūgun ianfu*). In 1991 they held a camp at the National Women's Education Center (NWEC) in Saitama in which about fifty Korean women participated. Yeoseong-Net was officially launched in Tokyo in November of the same year.[29] The following is a part of their inaugural statement:

> Reproduction of racism and oppression continues without the resolution of past colonial rule. In addition, women have been bound by the patriarchal structure. Without settling these problems, can there be any liberation for women? The issue of comfort

women represents the suffering of Korean women in Japan. We are beginning to make a belated effort to confront this problem, and take action from the perspective of Korean women in Japan. We are ashamed of ourselves for having avoided this issue until now. Nonetheless, we are finally able to approach this issue after forty-six years of struggle for the unification of our homeland, protesting racism and empowering ourselves. We encountered each other when we decided to confront the oppression of women.[30]

The statement exemplifies the merging of a critique against colonialism and patriarchy, articulated through a confrontation with the "comfort women" issue.

The Emergence of Yeoseong-Net

The military brothels had been known in postwar Japan, primarily by former Japanese soldiers who had been sent to battlefields. In the 1970s, the stories of "comfort women" appeared in the media, with journalists portraying the women as victims of Japanese military aggression, but not from the perspective of violence against women. From the feminist perspective, the issue was taken up by the Japanese women's liberation movement and groups such as Shinryaku=Sabetsu to Tatakau Ajia Fujin Kaigi (Asian Women's Conference Fighting Against Invasion=Discrimination) and Ajia no Onnatachi no Kai (Asian Women's Association), as well as described in documentaries and in nonfiction. But "comfort women" had not been perceived as a concrete agenda for political action in these movements.

Thus, Yeoseong-Net launched into action to shape public opinion on "comfort women" in Japanese society, addressing it as a real and urgent issue for resolution. One month after its inauguration, Yeoseong-Net held a rally for the testimony of Kim Hak-sun, the first survivor who came out as a victim of Japanese military sexual slavery and who brought her case to the Tokyo District Court along with two other women survivors. The rally was held at the Korean YMCA in Tokyo, in which 450 people participated. In January 1992, Yeoseong-Net organized a three-day hotline in cooperation with three women's associations, Nihon no Sengo o Hakkiri Saseru Kai (Association for the Clarification of Japan's Wartime

Responsibility), Jūgun Ianfu Mondai o Kangaeru Kai (Association to Think through the Comfort Women Issue), and Yeoseong-hoe. The hotline received testimonies from 235 people, including former Japanese soldiers. At the time of Prime Minister Miyazawa Kiichi's visit to Seoul, Yeoseong-Net appealed to the Japanese government to respond to the Korean Council's requests, namely for an official apology and full accounting of the facts, the building of a monument to the "comfort women," compensation, and education about the history of the "comfort women" in Japanese schools. Yeoseong-Net produced a number of publications, including a co-edited book with Yoon Jung-ok, a translation of the survivors' testimonies (1993), material for schools to use on this issue, and the newsletter *Allim*.[31] They conducted research overseas using historical records and interviews with survivors, and gave lectures on the issue. Yeoseong-Net gave presentations at the Asian Solidarity Conference on Japanese Military "Comfort Women" Issues, organized a workshop at the Fourth World Conference on Women in Beijing in 1995, and submitted a counter-report to the United Nations Committee on the Elimination of Discrimination Against Women in 1994. The activities of Yeoseong-Net were multilingual and extended overseas, intermediating among advocacy groups in South Korea, Japan, China, Canada, and other areas, which demonstrates the diversity of Yeoseong-Net members in terms of language and connection.[32]

I interviewed thirteen former Yeoseong-Net members in 2004. They were mostly second-generation resident Koreans. Twelve out of thirteen were of South Korean nationality, among whom three had changed their national affiliation from Chōsen (this term is associated with "North Korea" but in fact signifies the women are stateless). In terms of educational background, half of them had university diplomas and the rest were high school graduates at the time when they became involved in Yeoseong-Net. Eight had studied in the Japanese school system, one in an ethnic Korean school system, three had studied in both school systems, and one grew up and studied in Korea. Some women worked for Chongryun as office staff. One graduated from a Korean school in Japan, studied for a university degree in the United States, and had worked in New Zealand and Britain. Their occupations were varied, including a dentist, translator, interpreter, childcare worker, pharmacist, writer, photographer, housewife, and graduate student. Eleven of the women were married to ethnic Korean men and had children.

Their previous activist histories were diverse; they had participated in Dokusho Kai, Yeoseong-hoe, Puin-hoe, Ajia no Onnatachi no Kai, a documentary production on Koreans in Japan, the Korean Student League in Japan, and a local group devoted to reporting on the massacre of Koreans during the Great Kanto Earthquake of 1923. Together with their multilingualism, their experiences in social movements provided them with resources in organizing rallies, workshops, publishing, and networking. Considering that the majority of younger generations study in Japanese public schools, understand only the Japanese language, use Japanese (passing) names and get married to ethnic Japanese, Yeoseong-Net members were exceptionally rooted in their ethnic community. They could be considered ethnic intellectuals, but as women they had experienced marginalization in the gendered hierarchy of the Korean ethnic community in Japan.

Convergence on the Redress for "Comfort Women"

As demonstrated in its inaugural statement quoted above, intersectionality is the key concept of Yeoseong-Net activism. At an individual level, participants in the redress movement interpreted the structural oppression of Korean women in Japan by linking "comfort women" and first-generation women familiar with their situation. Shin Minja had known about "comfort women" from books. She considered it a tragedy that happened to women under colonial rule, and as an extreme case. She felt that her mother or other first-generation female relatives could have been forced to be "comfort women" were it not for the fortune of circumstance. On the other hand, she felt guilty because she avoided contemplating the issue of "comfort women." As sexual matters were regarded as taboo, she did not want to discuss it. Her attitude changed when she participated in the camp at the NWEC in 1991, where she shared this ambivalent feeling with other Korean women in Japan. She enhanced her understanding of the issue, finding a link between "comfort women" and the circumstances of her first-generation female relatives who were born to poor farmers and had no education.

Many Yeoseong-Net members had complaints about sexism within their families and their ethnic organizations, and their interest in feminism grew through reading *The Second Sex* by Simone de Beauvoir, for example. So why did they choose an ethnic organization through which to channel their activism? In an interview conducted in 2004, Kim Yeong-hee explained to me that she was influenced by the Japanese women's liberation movement of the 1970s, a time when domestic duties were imposed on her but not on her brothers. She complained about male dominance in Korean families, taking *jesa*, a Korean ceremonial ritual to honor one's ancestors, as an example: "Though women prepare food and all other things for *jesa*, they are excluded from the service, which was held by only men. There is no 38th parallel in terms of women's sacrifice." Like many Japan-born Koreans, she was educated in the Japanese school system and incorporated into Japanese society, using a Japanese name in daily life. She experienced a crisis between Japanese society and her ethnic identity. To resolve this identity problem, she became involved in an organization of young Koreans at her university, where she felt "liberated." She came out as "Korean," by abandoning her Japanese name and instead using her Korean name publicly.[33] She was concerned about human rights and engaged in advocacy for her brother-in-law, who was a political prisoner of the Korean dictatorship. But in the Korean student organization to which she belonged, it was believed that women's liberation was much less of a priority and would be realized only after Korean reunification. She was interested in the Japanese women's liberation movement, but she did not join, because in her view the movement failed to be aware of the history of Japanese colonialism and invasion in Asia. In order to pursue gender equality through an ethnic movement, she founded the women's group Yeoseong-hoe with other women members in Hantongryun (mentioned above). But she was faced with the difficulty of expanding women's autonomy under Hantongryun, and left soon thereafter to look for a way to consolidate her activism in human rights, ethnic rights, and women's liberation. When she encountered the redress movement for "comfort women," she thought of it as "a gift from heaven," as it might lead to an original movement by Korean women in Japan transcending difference in nationality (North and South Korean, and Japanese), organization, class, and generation. She said that though it presented a serious problem for them, the issue of "comfort women" created a space where various Korean women could encounter each other and forge solidarity. She compared the 1991 NWEC camp of Korean women in Japan concerning "comfort women" with the women's liberation camp in the early 1970s initiated by well-known radical feminist

Tanaka Mitsu. "Around fifty Korean women participated from all over Japan, with glittering eyes and passion," she recalled.

In the words of Park Hwami, the issue of "comfort women" connected Korean women in Japan, who had been fragmented and invisible in different but similarly male-dominated organizations. Yeoseong-Net activism represented a collective identity for Korean women in Japan. In Yeoseong-Net, the members found common ground in their frustration against sexism in ethnic movements. Reframing the issue of "comfort women" from a gender perspective encouraged them to reinterpret their situation as intersectional oppression characterized by both racial and gender hierarchies. This concept allowed them to reconsider their experience through mutually affecting, reinforcing, and constructing oppressions of race, class, gender, and sexuality.[34]

Korean women in Japan are first categorized as "former colonial subjects," and then as "foreigners" rather than as "women." Some members approached the Japanese women's liberation movement only to be marginalized. Kim Puja criticized Japanese feminists for their tendency to identify themselves as "victims," rather than oppressors, within the current structure of gender. She cited a case in which a Korean woman raised the postcolonial issue at a Japanese feminist group meeting on the topic of Alice Walker. She pointed out that it was strange that Japanese feminists identified themselves with "black women," because they belong to the majority group in Japanese society in terms of ethnicity. No one at the meeting responded to her statement.

On an organizational level, I would like to stress that before Yeoseong-Net, the members chose to be activists in the context of ethnic movements rather than women's liberation movements. It may be because of the very nature of modern notions of citizenship and political activism that the nation-state constitutes the horizon and the boundaries of political action.[35] Moreover, they were afraid to be stigmatized as traitors and worried that their criticism of sexism would undermine these ethnic movements, which were already vulnerable to oppression from the Japanese state. In this sense, alliance with the women's movement in Korea, their homeland (though only the southern half), justified Yoeseong-Net's activism, providing them legitimacy and autonomy as political actors, and as a distinct movement organized by Korean women in Japan.

Here a question arises. Was Yeoseong-Net a movement complicit with nationalism? Yeoseong-Net expressed oppositional views to male-dominant ethnic organizations in Japan as well as to the redress movement by South Korean women. In my interview, one member said that she was indirectly pressured to quit the Yeoseong-Net movement by a conventional ethnic organization through her husband who was employed by the organization. She interpreted this pressure to mean that the organization considered Yeoseong-Net to be dissident. Later the organization changed its attitude when the redress movement was reported by mass media. Most of all, Yeoseong-Net members came into conflict with the "false" dichotomy dividing "comfort women" by nationality, a notion largely shared by Korean activists, let alone Korean society, as well as the ethnic community in Japan. In this dichotomy, Korean "comfort women" are understood to have been virgin girls who were forced to work in the "comfort stations," while Japanese women are assumed to have been prostitutes who agreed to work under the state-regulated prostitution system. Yeoseong-Net members contested this sharp differentiation between "comfort women" and women in "voluntary prostitution," due to the slave-like conditions under which both groups served.[36] It is clear that Yeoseong-Net had an independent position in their approach to the "comfort women" issue, demanding the restoration of the dignity of all victims of Japanese military sexual slavery regardless of their nationality, former profession, and sexual experience. Thus, its political approach demonstrated how to lead the way to a new transnational feminist activism.

Divergence of Activism

Within a couple of years, Yeoseong-Net had accomplished their goal of reshaping public opinion about the redress of victims in Japan. As several support groups for the redress movement were subsequently created in Japan, Yeoseong-Net came to lose its distinctiveness by the mid-1990s. Yeoseong-Net was formally dissolved in 1998, as a result of the diversification of interests among its members. Respect for individual diversity and nonhierarchical horizontal relations between members were principles of Yeoseong-Net, as expressed in their symbol of the Setton, the traditional Korean combination of five colors. The celebration of diversity and loose organizational network had implicit meaning as a protest against the centralized bureaucratic system of conventional ethnic organizations. Also, the degree of commitment to feminism and ethnicity was different for individual members. For the members with feminist leanings, Yeoseong-Net activism appeared nationalist, while members focusing on ethnicity may have felt that their activism inclined too much toward feminism. Thus, the dissolution of Yeoseong-Net was inevitable in some sense, considered a positive and constructive consequence by the members. In what directions did the members diverge? Why did a body representing collectivity of Korean women in Japan become unnecessary?

Yang Ching-ja says that the dissolution had its roots in the two competing objectives that characterized Yeoseong-Net from its inception. One of these objectives was to focus on the single issue of redress for the victims of forced military prostitution. In 1993, Zainichi no Ianfu Saiban o Sasaeru Kai (Association to Support the Lawsuit by the Korean Victims in Japan—hereafter Sasaeru Kai) was established, composed of both Korean and Japanese women.[37] Some core members of Yeoseong-Net moved to Sasaeru Kai. Yang recalled that when she joined Yeoseong-Net, she had thought of herself as being on the side of the "comfort women" because she was a Korean woman in Japan, a postcolonial diasporic woman. But when she met the "real" victims in Korea, she realized there was a huge gap in the extent of victimization between "comfort women" subjected to enormous violence by the state military, and Korean women in Japan. This encounter made her reconsider her commitment to the redress movement. Yang realized she was as responsible for the issue as the Japanese because she also had lived in Japanese society without knowing about a first-generation Korean woman in Japan, Song Shin-do, who had come out as a "comfort women" survivor. The disjuncture between herself and the "comfort women" had enabled her to cooperate with Japanese society while living in the country of the perpetrator.

Another example of multinational activism was the Violence Against Women in War Network (VAWW-Net) Japan, which included Yeoseong-Net members and the late Matsui Yayori, a well-known Japanese feminist and founder of Ajia no Onnatachi no Kai. Matsui raised the idea of the women's tribunal to respond to the victimized women's claim for justice, from the consciousness of being feminists in the nation of the "perpetrator." With the Korean Council and ASCENT, VAWW-Net Japan held the Women's International War Crimes Tribunal on Japan's Military Sexual Slavery in Tokyo in 2000, which involved sixty-four victims from eight countries. The organization Ridoresu Kokusai Kyanpēn

(Redress International Campaign) was built by Yeoseong-Net member Kim Yeong-hee as a form of transnational activism in support of the victims. This demonstrates that the members' interests shifted from searching for self-identity to transnational activism.

Group Chame (a Korean word meaning "sisters") exemplifies another of these objectives; it was created in 1997 as a self-help group for Korean women in Japan. The founder, Park Hwami stated that her desire was to create a space where individual Korean women in Japan could talk about themselves, not as a theoretical enterprise, but in order to share time and space among women in the same circumstances, who experience the same difficulties and marginal status: "Not just for confirmation of our collective identity, but to prepare a condition freeing us for different goals."[38] Park is opposed to conceptualizing a solid and stable collective identity, but says it is necessary to secure a space where Korean women are respected as individuals and are not marginalized. In such a place the women can explore their own identity and representation.

Conclusion

Yeoseong-Net activism embodied a new political agency to position Korean women as creators of social change. It encouraged drastic change in their relationships, and a transcending of boundaries separating them from women in Japan (the host society) and Korea (the homeland), and from men in the Korean diasporic community in Japan. Thus despite its dissolution, the new subjectivity embodied by this group lived on in Korean women's activism in different fields, and maintained its efficacy in building transnational feminist solidarities. Kim Puja, a member of the governing board of VAWW-Net Japan, said that transnational feminist activism embodied in the Women's International War Crimes Tribunal became possible because Japanese feminists recognized the different positionality between Japanese and Koreans, the difference between the colonizer and the colonized.[39]

Using Nancy Fraser's notion of the "counterpublic," Vera Mackie illustrated organizational networks of activists in different countries against military prostitution, sex tourism, and exploitation of migrant women as a process of creating a "transnational feminist counterpublic" in opposition to the mainstream communication channels of the United Nations or related agencies and committees.[40] Yeoseong-Net was the fruit of women's effort to transcend ideological borders within the Korean diaspora community, and a space where individual Korean women in Japan who had been divided and marginalized in conventional organizations encountered each other and rediscovered themselves, found what they wanted to do, and dispersed in diverse directions. Yeoseong-Net was a counterpublic of Korean women in Japan that found the right words to express their thoughts, reframing their situation through the concept of intersectionality, and proposing counter-discourses to mainstream public space. Their practice of traversing intra-ethnic group differences empowered them to resist multiple forms of oppression, and nourished their capacity to create transnational activism cross-cutting ethnicity and nationality, country of residence and language, overcoming differences between the "colonizer" and the "colonized," "majority" and "minority." The position of Korean women in Japan is not single, but changes in various contexts; they belong to an ethnic "minority" group in Japan, situated at the "periphery" in relation to the "homeland" Korea, and they are also residents in the "colonizer" country. As postcolonial transnational feminists, their new subject position is enabled only through their efforts to articulate their intersectional positionality and to overcome these binaries at the same time.

It is not my intention to celebrate Yeoseong-Net as an example of a diasporic women's counterpublic. However, their marginalized position led them to initiate a new transnational activism linking feminisms that had been divided by nation-states. As bell hooks argues, understanding marginality as a position of resistance and power is crucial for oppressed, exploited, and colonized people.[41] These margins have been both sites of repression and sites of resistance. Thus they are also sites of possibility that offer radical perspectives from which to imagine alternatives. At the margin, these women created a new site of resistance, allowing the entrance of women from different backgrounds who expressed solidarity toward the mutual goal of liberation.

Notes

A great debt of gratitude for time and generosity is due the former members of Yeoseong-Net whom I interviewed. Special thanks go to Kim Puja, who introduced me to former Yeoseong-Net members and offered insightful advice. This chapter was written based on my dissertation research on Korean women's movements in Japan. I am thankful to my PhD advisor, Prof. Ito Ruri and my committee member, Prof. Jung Yeong-hae. Research for this article was carried out through an F-Gens research grant sponsored by Ochanomizu University.

1   Kim Puja et al., "Atogaki," in *Chōsenjin josei ga mita "ianfu mondai,"* ed. Yoon Jung-ok et al. (Tokyo: San-ichi Shobō, 1992), 278–279.

2   *"Uri yeoseong"* is a Korean word meaning "our (Korean) women." In Japanese *"yeoseong"* (women) is pronounced *"yoson,"* but in this chapter, I am Romanizing it based on the word's Korean pronunciation.

3   See Vera Mackie's writing on the topic: "Dialogue, Distance and Difference: Feminism in Contemporary Japan," *Women's Studies International Forum* 21, no. 6 (1998); "The Language of Globalization, Transnationality and Feminism," *International Feminist Journal of Politics* 3, no. 2 (2001); *Feminism in Modern Japan: Citizenship, Embodiment and Sexuality* (Cambridge: Cambridge University Press, 2003); and "Shifting the Axis: Feminism and the Transnational Imaginary," in *State/Nation/Transnation: Perspectives on Transnationalism in the Asia-Pacific*, ed. Brenda S. A. Yeoh and Katie Willis (London: Routledge, 2004). See also Ulrike Wöhr, "A Touchstone for Transnational Feminism: Discourses on the Comfort Women in 1990s Japan," *Japanstudien* 16 (2004).

4   Kim Puja, "Looking at Sexual Slavery from a Zainichi Perspective," in *Voices from the Japanese Women's Movement*, ed. AMPO, *Japan Asia Quarterly Review* (Armonk, NY: M. E. Sharpe, 1996); Kim Puja, "Global Civil Society Remakes History: 'The Women's International War Crimes Tribunal 2000,'" *positions: east asia cultures critique* 9, no. 3 (Winter 2001); Yamashita Yeong-ae, "Revisiting the 'Comfort Women': Moving Beyond Nationalism," in *Transforming Japan: How Feminism and Diversity Are Making a Difference* (New York: The Feminist Press, 2011).

5   Inderpal Grewal, "Autobiographic Subjects and Diasporic Locations: *Meatless Days* and *Borderlands*," in *Scattered Hegemonies: Postmodernity and Transnational Feminist Practices*, ed. Inderpal Grewal and Caren Kaplan (Minneapolis: University of Minnesota Press, 1994), 234–235.

6   Benita Roth, *Separate Roads to Feminism: Black, Chicana, and White Feminist Movements in America's Second Wave* (Cambridge: Cambridge University Press, 2004), 5.

7   Sonia Ryang, "Introduction: Between the Nations: Diaspora and Koreans in Japan," in *Diaspora without Homeland: Being Korean in Japan*, ed. Sonia Ryang and John Lie (Berkeley: University of California Press, 2009); Sonia Ryang, *Writing Selves in Diaspora: Ethnography of Autobiographics of Korean Women in Japan and the United States* (Lanham, MD: Lexington Books, 2008).

8 Institutional discrimination against foreign residents in social welfare was mostly abolished after Japan ratified the U.N. Universal Declaration of Human Rights in 1979 and the International Refugee Convention and Protocol in 1982.

9 The majority of Korean residents hold the special permanent residence status available to colonial-era immigrants and their descendants. As Japanese nationality law is based on *jus sanguinis*, which grants nationality only to those who were born to nationals, foreigners including Koreans born in Japan remain foreign unless they undergo naturalization. Until the 1980s, naturalization was permitted to applicants only upon verification of their assimilation. For example, they were required to adopt Japanese-sounding names. In recent years the number of ethnic Koreans with Japanese nationality has been increasing. This is due to the increase in naturalization as well as in intermarriage with Japanese nationals, whose children acquire Japanese nationality from birth. See Chikako Kashiwazaki, "The Foreigner Category for Koreans in Japan: Opportunities and Constraints," in *Diaspora without Homeland*.

10 Sonia Ryang, "Introduction," 16. These harsh circumstances led to the repatriation of nearly 90,000 Koreans from the late 1950s to the 1970s. There were also hundreds of Japanese wives of Koreans who repatriated to North Korea, expecting a better life, education, and employment. Most Koreans repatriating to North Korea originally came from what is now South Korea.

11 Song Yeon-ok, "Zainichi Chōsenjin josei to wa dare ka," in *Keizoku suru shokuminchishugi*, ed. Iwasaki Minoru et al. (Tokyo: Seikyūsha, 2005), 262–263.

12 The following are examples of state oppression of Korean family and community. Producing Korean alcohol called *makgoli* was a typical form of livelihood for impoverished Korean families in the years immediately following the war, and an activity in which women played a significant role. Because such alcohol production was unlicensed and illegal, producers were often subject to police raids. Another example is the hundreds of Korean-language schools that were built in the postwar period to prepare Korean children for repatriation. Because most of these schools were affiliated with the ethnic organization supporting the communist faction in Korea, they were forcibly closed by the Japanese Ministry of Education under the command of the General Headquarters of Allied Powers (GHQ) in the late 1940s. These raids and closures were often violent and even resulted in deaths. Such experiences of oppression increased the cohesion of ethnic organizations and their resistance against Japanese authority.

13 According to the survey *Zainichi Chōsenjin no seikatsu no jittai*, conducted by the Japanese Red Cross in the mid-1950s, the unemployment rate among Koreans in Japan was eight times that of Japanese nationals, and those who had steady jobs were engaged in construction, collecting scrap metal, taxi driving, and working in restaurants and bars. Women were invisible in these statistics but were engaged in the informal sector, contributing to family-run businesses typically owned by men. Cited in Song Yeon-ok, "'Zainichi' josei no sengo shi," *Kan* 11 (2002): 170.

14 The official name of Chongryun in Japanese is Zainihon Chōsenjin Sōrengōkai.

15 The official name of Mindan in Japanese is Zainippon Daikanminkoku Mindan.

16 One organization concerned with women's liberation was Nyeomaeng, the first association of Korean women in Japan, established in February 1946 in Arakawa, Tokyo. It ran evening Korean literacy classes for women and intervened in family conflicts such as domestic violence. However, since grassroots Nyeomaeng members were united under the umbrella of Joryun, the predecessor of Chongryun, their aspirations for women's liberation were superseded by the priorities of liberation as a nation. See Kim Yeong and Kim Puja, *Dainiji sekai taisen (kaihō) chokugo no Zainichi Chōsenjin josei undō* (Tokyo: Tokyo Women's Foundation, 1993).

17 The official name of Puin-hoe in Japanese is Zainippon Daikanminkoku Fujinkai. The official name of Nyeomaeng in Japanese is Zainihon Chōsen Minshu Josei Dōmei.

18 Sonia Ryang deploys gendered analysis of North Korean nationalist identity in Japan. See Sonia Ryang, "Nationalist Inclusion or Emancipatory Identity? North Korean Women in Japan," *Women's Studies International Forum* 21, no. 6 (1998).

19 Kim Yeong and Kim Puja, *Dainiji sekai taisen.*

20 For more detail, refer to Song Yeon-ok, "Zainichi Chōsenjin to wa dare ka"; Kang Yeong-ja, "Jimichi na gaikokujin kyōiku no torikumi o," in *Zainichi no omoni wa ima*, ed. Zenkoku Zainichi Chōsenjin Kyōiku Kenkyū Kyōgikai (Kyoto: Zenchōkyō, 1995); and Kawasaki Kodomo o Mimamoru Omoni no Kai, *Hikari ni mukatte: 20-shūnen kinenshi* (Kawasaki: Kawasaki Kodomo o Mimamoru Omoni no Kai, 1995).

21 For a similar case, see Kathleen M. Coll, *Remaking Citizenship: Latina Immigrants and New American Politics* (Stanford, CA: Stanford University Press, 2010).

22 Song Yeon-ok, "Zainichi Chōsenjin josei to wa dare ka." As Setsu Shigematsu explores in this volume, a segment of the women's liberation movement addressed the "comfort women," indicating a postcolonial

moment in their feminism. Vera Mackie has traced Japanese women's efforts to understand differences among women and their search for transnational solidarity with Asian women, including Koreans. See Mackie, "Dialogue, Distance and Difference"; and Mackie, *Feminism in Modern Japan*. There was also a Japanese women's group that supported a Korean woman who criticized the patriarchal nature of Korean families, in the course of a protest against fingerprinting for foreign registration in the 1980s. Non-Japanese women remained as "others" to most Japanese feminists, although there were some Japanese women who supported, understood, and included these "other" women.

23 The official name of Yeoseong-hoe in Japanese is Zainichi Kankoku Minshu Josei Kai.

24 The official name of Hantongryun in Japanese is Zainichi Kankoku Minshu Tōitsu Rengō.

25 Many of the women members received their primary education in the Chongryun school system and later studied at Japanese universities.

26 Many Korean ethnic organizations use Korean terms in their organization names or combine Korean and Japanese terms, but that was not the case for Chōsen Joseishi Dokushokai, which used only Japanese terms. A former member of Dokushokai explained that this reflected the lived reality of later generations of Koreans who grow up speaking Japanese.

27 As the first educational institution for women established in Korea, Ewha has been leading the field of women's studies as well as producing women leaders in every social arena.

28 The discussion was made possible by a member of Dokushokai, Yamashita Yeong-ae, who had been a graduate student of women's studies at Ewha Women's University. Yamashita played a significant role in introducing the Korean redress movement to Korean women in Japan, though she herself was not a Yeoseong-Net member.

29 In Osaka, a similar organization of Korean women in Japan dealing with the "comfort women" issue, named Chōsenjin Jūgun Ianfu Mondai o Kangaeru Kai (Association on the Issue of "Comfort Women"), was established. Kangaeru Kai and Yeoseong-Net worked together at their events, collaborating to invite "comfort woman" survivor Kim Hak-sun as well as a theater group from South Korea that dramatized the issue.

30 Jūgun Ianfu Mondai Uri Yoson Nettowāku, *Kono "han" o toku tame ni: "Moto jūgun inanfu Kim Hak-sun-san no hanashi o kiku tsudoi" o oete* (Tokyo: Jūgun Ianfu Mondai Uri Yoson Nettowāku, 1992), 40–41.

31 *Allim* published seventeen issues between 1992 and 1996. The circulation in 1992 was 1500. See Jūgun Ianfu Mondai Uri Yoson Nettowāku, *Yoson*

netto nenji hōkokusho 1992 (Tokyo: Jūgun Ianfu Mondai Uri Yoson Nettowāku, 1993), 15.

32 Kim Puja, "Zainichi Chōsenjin josei to Nihongun 'ianfu' mondai kaiketsu undō: 1990-nendai no Yoson Netto no undō keiken kara," *Sensō to sei* 28 (2009).

33 Many Koreans in Japan use *tsūmei*, or "passing" Japanese names, in everyday life to avoid discrimination. These *tsūmei* are a legacy of the colonial-era policy of *sōshi kaimei*, according to which Koreans had to adopt Japanese names. In contrast to *tsūmei* are *minzokumei* (ethnic names) or *honmyō* (real names), which are the Korean names listed in official documents such as foreign registration cards and driver's licenses. The issue of names has been crucial for the identity politics of Koreans in Japan.

34 Kimberle W. Crenshaw, "Demarginalizing the Intersection of Race and Sex: A Black Feminist Critique of Antidiscrimination Doctrine, Feminist Theory and Antiracist Politics," *University of Chicago Legal Forum* 139 (1989).

35 Mackie, "Shifting the Axis: Feminism and the Transnational Imaginary," 243.

36 See Park Hwami, "Sei no nijū kihan kara 'guntai ianfu mondai' o yomitoku," in Yoon Jung-ok et al., *Chōsenjin josei ga mita "ianfu mondai,"* 222–225; Song Yeon-ok, "Chōsen josei no feminizumu ni tsuite," *Allim* 9 (1994); Yamashita, "Revisiting the 'Comfort Women,'" 217–220; and Kim Puja, "Josei kokusai senpan hōtei ga norikoeta mono to norikoenakatta mono," in her *Keizoku suru shokuminchishugi to jendā* (Yokohama: Seori Shobō), 139–159.

37 Yeoseong-Net included Japanese and male members at the rank of "observers."

38 Gurūpu Chame, *Zainichi Korian josei no tame no enpawāmento wākushoppu hōkokusho* (Tokyo: Gurūpu Chame, 1997), 9.

39 Kim Puja, "Josei kokusai senpan hōtei," 155.

40 Mackie, "The Language of Globalization, Transnationality and Feminism"; Mackie, "Shifting the Axis."

41 bell hooks, "marginality as site of resistance," in *Out There: Marginalization and Contemporary Cultures*, ed. Russell Ferguson et al. (Cambridge, MA: The MIT Press, 1990).

CHAPTER 14

~

Takemura Kazuko

On Friendship and the Queering of American and Japanese Studies

J. KEITH VINCENT

TAKEMURA KAZUKO (1954–2011) was a key figure at the intersection of feminist and queer thought between Japan and the United States from the early 1990s until her death in 2011 at the age of fifty-seven. She was well known as a scholar of nineteenth- and twentieth-century American and British writers including Henry James, Virginia Woolf, Louisa May Alcott, Ernest Hemingway, and William Faulkner, as well as Hollywood film. A prolific translator of work by Judith Butler, Gayatri Spivak, Trinh T. Minh Ha, and Slavoj Žižek, she was also a tireless facilitator and mentor of others working on gender and sexuality studies in Japan.

Takemura was also an old friend of mine. We often joked about the fact that as a Japanese Americanist she spent her time studying the literature of my country while I, as an American Japanologist, spent mine studying hers. What brought us together was our common interest in and commitment to feminism and queer theory, so this difference in our particular fields of specialization never seemed to matter much. And yet now that she is gone, I find myself regretting not reading more of Takemura's work while she was alive. I also find myself asking why I did not. I do make it a point to read work about American literature that has to do with gender and sexuality, so I had no good reason not to read it. I suppose I thought if I were going to take the trouble to read something *in Japanese*, it would make sense for it to be *about Japan*.

I am embarrassed to admit this, but it was just such a calculation that kept me from learning more about Takemura's work. As someone who writes about Japanese literature in English, I really should know better; to the extent that if such a policy is applied in the other direction, it can only invalidate my own work. Why read what a white American man like me has to say about gender and sexuality in Japanese literature when one can go "directly to the source"? This sort of attitude is not at all uncommon in Japan, and in the United States for that matter, and it is one that I am always eager to denounce as narrow-minded and essentialist. And yet, with regard to Takemura's work, I was clearly not practicing what I was preaching.

I am grateful to have this essay included in this volume because it has given me the chance not only to go back and read more of Takemura's work, but to think more broadly about what Japanese Americanists and American Japanologists have in common, and how feminism and queer theory might help us to articulate those commonalities. It has also been a pleasure to re-acquaint myself with, and in many cases to learn about for the first time, aspects of the history of feminism and queer theory in the United States, through Takemura's eyes. Thanks to her 2012 book *The Challenge of the Power of Literature* (*Bungakuryoku no chōsen*) I now know, for example, that Louisa May Alcott's *Little Women* can be read as a queer text.[1] I learned that Kate Millet's classic 1970 work of feminist literary criticism *Sexual Politics* ends with a chapter in which she writes approvingly of the gender politics of Jean Genet, and that Millet's analysis of homophobia and misogyny in D. H. Lawrence presages the work of Eve Kosofsky Sedgwick fifteen years later in *Between Men*.[2] In a brilliant chapter on American anti-intellectualism, Takemura draws on Richard Hofstadter's classic book on the subject going back to the nineteenth century "Know Nothing Party" to contextualize the awarding of the "Bad Writing Prize" to Judith Butler by the Johns Hopkins–based journal *Philosophy and History* in 1998.[3] As she points out in that chapter, there were any number of poststructuralist theorists whose prose were more difficult than Butler's, and plenty of other winners of the award whose selection failed to bring any notice from the mass media. But these two facts together suggest that what was at issue was not so much the fabled difficulty of Butler's prose but the challenge it posed to fiercely guarded "commonsense" notions about gender and sexual norms, notions that were themselves rooted in deep currents of good old-fashioned American anti-intellectualism.

For Takemura herself, Butler's prose was not difficult, but a "thrilling" and clear articulation of ideas that she herself had been groping toward as a way to fight against the violence and injustice of misogynist and heteronormative ideology in Japan.[4] *Gender Trouble*, she wrote in her translator's afterword, spoke "directly, unerringly, and penetratingly of *our* reality."[5] She encouraged her Japanese readers not to be discouraged by the difficulty of Butler's language, to read her work slowly and to savor it, "*yukkuri, jikkuri*" (slowly, and with relish).

Why all this about American literature and Judith Butler in a volume about "Japanese feminism"? I could respond by stating the obvious: the fact that Takemura translated Judith Butler and worked on American literature does not make her any less of a "Japanese feminist." But rather than brushing the larger implications of this question aside in this way, I want to take them seriously, because I know that Takemura did. What does it mean to be a Japanese feminist working on American literature? Or, more broadly, what does it mean to do queer or feminist work with a focus on a culture other than one's own? This question is, of course, just as relevant for my own work as it was for Takemura's (although, of course not perfectly symmetrically so, given the imbalance of power between the United States and Japan). It is also relevant for the work of many of the readers of this volume. In offering the beginning of an answer here, I move from the personal to the textual: first explaining something about the context in which I first met Takemura, and then closing with a reading of one of her essays that addresses the question head-on.

*   *   *

In the early 1990s I was fresh out of the closet and living in Tokyo, officially doing research for my dissertation but spending most of my time working with a group called "OCCUR: The Japan Association for the Lesbian and Gay Movement" (Akā: Ugoku Gei to Rezubian no Kai). OCCUR was involved on a number of fronts in the struggle for the rights and recognition of sexual minorities in Japan and it was a privilege and a joy for me to work with them. They provided anonymous telephone counseling for gays and lesbians, and queer-friendly English conversation classes. They were also the plaintiffs in the first-ever legal case involving gay rights in Japan, in which they sued the Tokyo Metropolitan Government for excluding homosexuals from its youth hostels. They worked both at the community level and with the Ministry of Health on HIV prevention and treatment issues, and they were the Asian representative in the International Lesbian and Gay Association.

But OCCUR's work did not stop with its activism. This was the 1990s—the early, heady days of queer theory coming out of the United States—and my friends in OCCUR and I were eager for more theoretical tools with which to strategize, and to better understand and theorize the structure of Japanese heteronormative society. To that end, for several years we had a monthly seminar called the "Identity Research Group" (Aidentiti Kenkyūkai)—eventually, affectionately abbreviated as the "IDken"—in which we read and discussed work in feminism and the emerging field of queer theory, including that of Monique Wittig, Luce Irigaray, Gayle Rubin, Judith Butler, Eve Sedgwick, Leo Bersani, D. A. Miller, Lee Edelman, and others. Most of this work remained untranslated at the time, and it was often my job, with the help of those members of OCCUR who were also able to read the texts in English, to attempt to convey the arguments in Japanese. I was discovering queer theory for the first time myself—indeed it was brand new at the time, and there was something doubly exciting about encountering these works and then immediately trying to find a way to translate, paraphrase, or otherwise share them in Japanese. It made me understand them better and care about them even more, because they seemed so crucial to the struggle in which we were all engaged.

It was in this context that I first met Takemura. I think it was around 1996. I cannot remember the exact occasion of our first meeting, but I do remember very clearly a trip to her apartment near Tsukuba University, where she was teaching American literature. I went with several other OCCUR members including Kawaguchi Kazuya and Niimi Hiroshi—all gay men—and we spent the day eating pizza on the floor, chain-smoking cigarettes, and talking for hours about how to make queer theory matter in Japan, and in Japanese. This was a serious issue for us because queer theory was just starting to become a sort of fad in academic publishing in Japan, but this was happening in almost complete isolation from the queer activist community. Takemura was one of the only academics in Japan who was not only conversant with queer theory and its feminist roots, but saw it, like my friends in OCCUR and I did, as a sort of lifeline—a mode of resistance and a form of cultural activism. So we were thrilled to have her come to our *kenkyūkai* (research group) from time to time and eventually to get her help as we began to publish our own translations of queer theory into Japanese.[6] She was already an accomplished translator, having just published a translation of Trinh T. Minh-ha's *Woman, Native, Other: Writing Postcoloniality and Feminism* in 1995.[7] In 1999 she published her flawless translation of Judith Butler's *Gender Trouble* and would go on to bring out many more important translations, including Butler's *Antigone's Claim: Kinship Between Life and Death* in 2002, *Excitable Speech: A Politics of the Performative* in 2004, and Butler and Gayatri Spivak's *Who Sings the Nation State? Language, Politics, Belonging* in 2008.[8]

But Takemura was not only a gifted translator. Or rather, Takemura *was* a gifted translator, *and* for her, I think, translation of U.S. feminist and queer theory was very much part of a larger project—namely the fight against misogyny and heteronormativity within Japan. Her work as a translator was perhaps not unlike Yamakawa Kikue's translation of the work of Edward Carpenter that Sarah Frederick writes about for this volume: it was a natural outgrowth of her work as a feminist and an integral part of her scholarship. When I first met her she was also in the midst of publishing a groundbreaking six-part essay on "The Possibility of Lesbian Studies" in the journal *Eigo seinen*, despite well-meaning advice from other academics that to write about such things was "vulgar" (*hin'i o otosu*).[9] And she would go on to publish much more brilliant work right up until, and indeed even after her tragic death on December 13, 2011.

Takemura's 2012 book *The Challenge of the Power of Literature: Family, Desire, Terrorism* (*Bungakuryoku no chōsen: Famirī, yokubō, terorizumu*) is an extraordinary work about which there is much to say, but I want to focus here on the final chapter, titled "Renaissance of a Discipline? On Researching Anglophone Literature in Japan Today." In this chapter, Takemura directly addresses the question "What does it mean to study literature written in English while living in Japan? And what does it mean to do this *as a feminist*?" As I suggested above, this is something that feminist and queer scholars of Japanese literature writing in the United States could stand to think about more as well, and I hope my discussion here of Takemura's approach might serve as an impetus for further inquiry.

*   *   *

If Japanese studies in the United States has as its "original sin" its Cold War origins in area studies, English literature in Japan has its own checkered past.[10] It emerged in the early twentieth century, as part of a woefully uncritical identification with Britain and British imperial culture, even as Japan was in the process of becoming an empire itself. The postwar period, moreover, saw the emergence in Japan of an American studies with a similarly problematic origin. Takemura points out the interesting fact that the Japanese institutional structure for the study of both British literature in the early twentieth century and American literature in the postwar period did not follow, but was at least coeval with, or even *prior to* the institutionalization of these disciplines in Britain and the United States. Thus Tokyo University had a program in English literature starting in the 1890s (famously taught first by Lafcadio Hearn, then by Natsume Sōseki, and later by Yone Noguchi), while Oxford only started teaching it in 1894. English literature was not offered at Cambridge until 1911. Similarly, the Japanese American Studies Association was founded in 1946, five years earlier than anything like it would exist in the United States. In pointing this out, Takemura is not making a claim for Japan's admirable precocity. For her, what is readable in this historical chronology is a powerful mimetic desire on "Japan's" part toward these dominant Western powers, a desire to get *closer* to them, to "befriend" Britain and America, and in embracing that friendship—a kind of male homosocial friendship, in fact—to avoid having to think about its own subject position either as pseudo-colonial subject or as an imperial subject in its own right.

"What has prevailed then," writes Masao Miyoshi in an essay about the history of English literature in Japan,

> is the ongoing doctrine of equivalence, which, by emphasizing identification minimizes the significance of difference. The problems of English literature as they are faced in England are transplanted to become the problems of the Japanese study of English literature. There is nearly total indifference to the Japanese context in which such naturalization of alien perspectives must continually occur.[11]

Miyoshi does not mince words in this essay. He talks about the "intellectual vacuity," of English literature in Japan, about its tendency to "merely celebrate in reverence," and at one point he describes how, "[t]he journal *Eigo Seinen* (literally, English-language Youths, translated as *The Rising Generation*) was launched in 1898 to serve—despite its ghastly title—as the central organizing paper of the English establishment of Japan to this day."[12] As is often the case with Miyoshi, his critique here is incisive, albeit somewhat vitiated by a desire to establish himself as the one who knows better.

It was in this same journal, *Eigo seinen*, despite its "ghastly title" and its complicity with Japanese and British imperialism, in which Takemura published her six-part essay on lesbian studies I mentioned earlier. Unlike Miyoshi, who left Japan soon after the war and whose professional identity was very much tied up in that departure, Takemura stayed in Japan and did work within English and American studies there. She was certainly in agreement in many ways with Miyoshi's critique of the ideological foundations of her own discipline and its complicity with imperialism. Indeed, she quotes liberally from it and from other recent books in Japanese making similar arguments. At the same time, however, she was committed to articulating and theorizing her own particular position as a Japanese feminist who had chosen to work in this field.[13]

This question of her own positionality, she writes, is one that she only began to think consciously about in the early 2000s. She mentions three incidents in her life that provoked this serious thinking. The first occurred during a panel that she moderated at a conference in 2003 of the Tokyo branch of the American Literature Association. The topic was "Chaos and Violence of the Post-Family Era: Feminist Readings of American Literature in Late 2003." The papers were wonderful, and the panel was a great success. But during the question and answer period, "a certain sociologist" in the audience (Ueno Chizuko tells me it was she) asked the following question: What does it mean to have this kind of discussion of American literature in Japan, in Japanese, in front of a Japanese audience?[14]

Takemura writes that her first reaction was to think that in this post-poststructuralist age such a question was at best naive and at worst unnecessarily provocative. I imagine that she felt a lot like I did when, at the Association of Japanese Literary Studies conference at Rutgers

University in 2009—on a panel for which Takemura was supposed to be the discussant, had illness not prevented her from coming—I gave a paper on Eve Sedgwick and Natsume Sōseki, only to be asked, "What possible relevance can Eve Sedgwick have to Japanese literature? She writes about British literature, doesn't she?"

Takemura responded to this sociologist's question in the same spirit that I am afraid I did to that question at the AJLS, although no doubt much more elegantly. In the book, she reproduces her answer—I think intentionally—as a kind of parody of ludic postmodern theory. Marshaling the heaviest of theoretical guns—quoting Jacques Derrida and Homi Bhabha, and reader response theory, she writes,

> As readings multiply and we move further and further away from the original, the text only becomes richer, reproducing itself in ever more productive ways, as these manifold readings circle back into the text, enabling the production of new texts. Therefore there is absolutely nothing unproductive about discussing American literature in Japan, in Japanese, to an audience made up exclusively of Japanese people.[15]

While she felt good about this answer at the time, Takemura writes that she became increasingly dissatisfied with it. She began to ask herself more critical questions about her own status as a Japanese scholar of Anglophone literature. This did not mean, she insists, that she came to think that American and British literature should only be discussed by Americans and Brits, but rather that she began to take seriously what she at first thought was a naive (or just an annoying) question: What *does* it mean to read Anglophone literature in Japan? What does it mean to do that *as a feminist*?

The second factor that got her to start thinking differently about her identity as a Japanese scholar of English literature was her attendance at a number of international conferences in Asia in the early 2000s, where she began to meet other Asian scholars working on Anglophone literature. For the first time, she found herself discussing American and British literature with other scholars whose native language was not English and who came from countries that each had their own local institutions devoted to the study of English and American literature. She describes the collective impact of these encounters as constituting something like a "body blow" to her own self-understanding. As a result of this "body blow," she describes, "a dawning awareness that even as English literature existed in each country as an institutionalized system, something was deviating from these institutions, something was wriggling up and crawling out from in between them. What sort of professional identity," she asks herself, "should I have in such a context?"[16]

The verb that Takemura uses here and that I have translated as "wriggling up" is "*ugomeku*." This is not a very appealing term, and quite a frightening-looking *kanji* (蠢). It brings to mind a nest of worms or maggots all squirming in different directions. Hardly a vision of pan-Asian solidarity (Takemura was, I think, quite free of such sentimentalism) but rather a striking metaphor for a radically diverse set of reading practices. If English literature as an institution in these Asian countries could be said to be part of the apparatus of a sort of postcolonial cultural imperialism, organized in order to bring the subaltern into closer, more intimate contact with the metropole (as Miyoshi would argue), it was also true that countless acts of actually reading literature, and reading it closely, were producing a different sort of energy—less an organized collectivity with a single purpose (such as coming closer to England and America) but a kind of swarm of difference.

"The third reason," she writes,

> is even more individual, more about myself. I started to write about sexuality in the early 1990s. Or rather, I first became able to write about sexuality at that time. As I did so, I began to ask myself how to think about the connection between my being a scholar of Anglophone literature and my writing on sexuality. What does it mean for me to be a scholar of English literature? What is it that underwrites my professional identity as such?[17]

Having listed these three factors that she says caused her to reevaluate her own professional identity as a scholar of English literature, Takemura recalls the one figure in the history of English literature in Japan who thought about this most carefully, who remained outside of its blind adoration of England and "doctrine of equivalence" and struggled to find a different relation to it. For Takemura, as for Miyoshi, this figure is Natsume Sōseki, perhaps Japan's most canonical novelist who also happened to be the first native Japanese professor of British literature at Tokyo Imperial University.

* * *

Sōseki studied in England for the first two years of the last century, and seems to have hated every minute of it. As Miyoshi puts it, "Sōseki had no one to talk to and was desperately lonely. He persisted nevertheless in pondering what literary studies meant and, what was more important for him, what it could mean for a Japanese to study English literature. He read, wrote, and collected books in nearly total isolation until he had a severe nervous breakdown."[18] Sōseki, like Takemura, persisted in questioning his own positionality, and yet, "The critical issues Sōseki confronted were never vigorously discussed [by those who succeeded him], but rather were deliberately avoided, and the institutionalization of English literature continued on."[19]

What Miyoshi calls the "institution" of British (or American) literature in Japan is about bringing two nation-states, two empires into a relation of "friendship." Sōseki saw the beginning of Japan's "friendship" with Britain up close: he was living in London when the Anglo–Japanese Alliance was signed in 1902, a crucial step in the advance of the Japanese Empire across Asia. The friendship extended to literary study as well. By being good boys and studying hard, by looking up every word in the *OED*, scholars of English literature in Japan strove to get closer to the text, to reduce as far as possible the distance between themselves and Britain.

But such an approach, for Takemura, as for Sōseki, has nothing to do with what happens in the encounter of an individual subject with a literary text. Here I recall the title of her book, so hard to translate, *The Challenge of the Power of Literature*, or *The Defiant Power of Literature*. It is a book that problematizes rather than assumes group belonging. It rejects the quasi-familial, usually heteronormative gender relations that go with national identity and argues instead for a kind of queer cosmopolitanism. Takemura quotes Sōseki in his famous speech "My Individualism," where he argues against groupthink.

> More simply stated, individualism is a philosophy that replaces cliquism with values based on personal judgment of right and wrong. An individualist is not forever running with the group forming cliques that thrash around blindly in the interests of power and money. That is why there lurks beneath the surface of his philosophy a loneliness unknown to others. As soon as we deny our little groups, then I simply go my way and I let the

other man go his, unhindered. Sometimes, in some instances, we cannot avoid becoming scattered. That is what is lonely.[20]

Takemura then reads Sōseki's critique of this "cliquism" and his recognition of the inevitable "loneliness" of his kind of "individualist" alongside Gayatri Spivak's recent book on comparative literature, *The Death of a Discipline*. In this book, Spivak critiques both the "old" comparative literature for its humanism and the "new" cultural/ethnic studies for its identity politics. In a move that Takemura describes as an uncanny echo of Sōseki, Spivak critiques both forms of comparative literature for their "unexamined politics of collectivity."[21]

Sōseki and Spivak may seem like unlikely bedfellows here. First of all, Sōseki was not exactly a feminist. He did not stand outside the male homosocial world that he so faithfully described in his fiction, even if his descriptions were so finely wrought as to constitute an implicit critique. In the same lecture on "My Individualism," he shows himself to be unsympathetic to the cause of women's suffrage in Britain. And yet, like Spivak, he is a relentless critic of "unexamined collectivities."

Not only that. There is something queer about the way Sōseki related to the institutionalization of British literature in Japan. By this I mean to say that he saw literature not as a means of accessing or even calling into being some larger community, but as a critical disruptor of such notions. This is why, as Takemura argues, Sōseki was able to maintain a critical stance toward the "unexamined collectivity" at the heart of the institution of English literature in Japan, despite his position as one of its founding fathers. In a similar way, Sōseki remains perhaps Japan's greatest critic of nationalism, *and* its most revered national author (*kokumin sakka*). Think of the famous scene in *Sanshirō*, one the most beloved novels in the modern Japanese canon, when the title character first meets the enigmatic bachelor Hirota-sensei on the train on the way from Kumamoto to Tokyo: "Tokyo is bigger than Kumamoto," Hirota explains to the naïve Sanshirō, "And Japan is bigger than Tokyo. And even bigger than Japan . . . is the inside of your head. Don't ever surrender yourself—not to Japan, not to anything."[22]

Takemura was clear about Sōseki's queerness because she shared it. She explains that the title of her essay ("Renaissance of a Discipline?") is a sort of hybrid. It is partly a rejoinder to Spivak's book *Death of a Discipline*, in which Spivak argues for a new form of comparative literature that would be consonant with a feminist and postcolonial politics. Such a comparative literature would not begin with the friendship of nations—not with Japanese people studying British or American literature, and *vice versa*—as a way of entering into a homosocial bond to cement their national collectivities. Instead, it would hold the promise of a more radical democracy. And yet Spivak asks, with Derrida, "Can democracy—invariably claimed as a politics, or perhaps *the* politics of friendship—function without a logofratrocentric notion of collectivity: With the sister allowed in rarely, and only as an honorary brother?"[23] The "Renaissance" in Takemura's title is a reference to F. O. Mathiessen's 1941 book *American Renaissance*.[24] Mathiessen's book founded the field of American literary studies in the United States and established as its canon the works of Melville, Thoreau, Emerson, Hawthorne, and Whitman.

As Henry Abelove explains in a powerful essay, a certain queerness is readable in this choice of works, and indeed throughout this founding work of American studies. I quote from Abelove's *Deep Gossip*, a book that I am not sure that Takemura read, but that I feel certain she would have liked very much.

> Matthiessen's explicit theme is the culture of democracy in mid-nineteenth-century America. What is inexplicit, what is merely suggested, is the question the book frames without asking: what was the erotic meaning of that democracy, the erotic dynamic, the ties, affections, affiliations, that bound together those white men, supposititiously equal, supposititiously brothers, who were the privileged subject of the old republic? And if we could know that erotic dynamic, would we know something pertinent to the tasks of improving and deepening and expanding and advancing and even reconstructing democracy in the present? Whitman had long before described the old democracy as "boys, together clinging, fulfilling our foray." What was that "clinging?" Was the old democracy distinguishable from white male homosexuality as Matthiessen knew it, and if so, how?[25]

"Queer studies," Abelove goes on to say, was thus always there at the start of American studies as part of its "unconscious." If the sister is only "allowed in rarely" to the "logofratrocentric" collective of democracy, the queer man is excluded, while also being inscribed at its very heart. Mathiessen was a distinguished professor at Harvard who was harassed for his leftist politics and his homosexuality. He killed himself by jumping from a hotel window in 1950. Matthiessen's story—like the queer unconscious of American studies—was ignored and repressed as the institution grew. And yet the future of American studies, Abelove writes, "will depend in large measure on whether or not that unconscious is permitted to return."[26] As a founding father of English literary studies in Japan, Sōseki occupies a similar position to Mathiessen in the United States. Like Mathiessen's, Sōseki's work raises questions about the central place of male–male eroticism in each nation's understanding of democracy. Sōseki wrote his senior thesis, it bears remembering, on Walt Whitman as "the literary representative of democracy."[27]

To sum up, Takemura's title asks three questions. The first is Spivak's, in *Death of a Discipline*, about how to find a place for women in a democracy too often imagined as a band of brothers. The second is Mathiessen's and Sōseki's unasked, but no less pressing, question, about the male homoerotics of democracy. The third question is more straightforward: "Can there be a renaissance of the discipline of English literary studies in Japan?" She writes that she explained this to Spivak in an email and the latter fired back a response, saying, "There can be no renaissance of English literary studies in Japan. That's not the kind of comparative literature I was writing about." Takemura wrote back:

> No, that's not what I mean. I'm not talking only about comparative literature. I mentioned Mathiessen only because I wanted to say that the kind of English literary studies that I am hoping for has not yet been born, so it can hardly be reborn. I mean something else with the term "renaissance." Something else, that has to do with "friendship."[28]

* * *

What does it mean, then, to write about Anglophone literature in Japan, as a feminist, as a queer theorist? What does it mean to write about Japan from the United States or elsewhere? Takemura mentioned three things that got her thinking about this question seriously. First, being asked at that conference in Tokyo, What does it mean to study American texts inside Japan? Second, asking *herself* at conferences in Asia, What does it mean to study American or British texts with other scholars outside of America or Britain? Both of these questions, it is fair to say, are about destabilizing both one's own subject position and the putative "object" of one's study. If that object is "attractive," is it intrinsically so? Or are there external forces that have made it so? Or both?

The answer to this last question is clearly "both." And this is why the third factor that Takemura wrote about is so important: her own increasing focus on questions of sexuality since the early 1990s. When I mentioned this earlier, its significance may not have been clear. But let me spell it out here at the end. For Takemura, it was her work on sexuality that saved her from the institutional inertia of English literature in Japan. To study sexuality is to study the forces or the glue—the powers of "love" or "libido" or whatever you might call them—that draw us both toward and away from each other and the various objects we cathect. It is to take seriously questions like these: "What does it mean to love what we study? Or to hate it? How much of this is about individual taste, and how much of it is about structural forces outside our control? How do the institutional histories of the disciplines that we work within shape, enable, and limit this?"

The full title of Takemura's book that I have been discussing is *The Challenge of the Power of Literature: Family, Desire, Terrorism*. When I first saw these words on the cover I read them paratactically, as a simple list of keywords that the book treats. But as I read the book itself, I realized that the title is not just a list of terms covered in the various chapters. Rather they represent a kind of spectrum of different forms and intensities of the libidinal and social "glue" that connects all kinds of groups from the romantic couple, to the family, to the community of English literary studies in Japan, to the nation, and even, at its most extreme, the terrorist cell. Taking that "glue" seriously means recognizing how the lines distinguishing the bonds of family, friendship, and erotic desire are always shifting. This is what it takes to write about sexuality seriously. And this is why sexuality was key to Takemura's ability to confront and think through those questions about her own positionality among the world historical forces that shaped the "American literature" that she studied. This is what makes her work feminist and queer at once. And this is why it is worth reading for feminist and queer scholars in Japan studies, even if it is not "about Japan."

But what is most thrilling about Takemura's work, and the reason, I think, that she and I were friends, is that it does not stop with this

question of "positionality." It is also, at its core, about what makes literature literature. It was in her close and loving readings of literary texts that
Takemura Kazuko found room for something other than nation, institution, and identity—something unexpected and queer—to "crawl up and
wriggle out" from between the lines.

Notes

An earlier version of this essay appeared online on the "Women's Action
Network" website. Thanks to Professor Ueno Chizuko for publishing it there,
and to Naoko Uchibori, for translating it into Japanese. The Japanese translation can be found here: http://wan.or.jp/article/show/1278.

1 Takemura Kazuko, *Bungakuryoku no chōsen: Famirī, yokubō, terorizumu*
  (Tokyo: Kenkyūsha, 2012).
2 See Kate Millett, *Sexual Politics* (Garden City, NY: Doubleday, 1970);
  and Eve Kosofsky Sedgwick, *Between Men: English Literature and Male
  Homosocial Desire* (New York: Columbia University Press, 1985).
3 Richard Hofstadter, *Anti-Intellectualism in American Life* (New York:
  Vintage Books, 2012).
4 Takemura describes her encounter with Butler's work in "Kiki-teki jōkyō
  no naka de bungaku to feminizumu o kenkyū suru imi," in *Kenkyū suru
  imi*, ed. Komori Yōichi (Tokyo: Tokyo Tosho, 2003).
5 Takemura Kazuko, "Yakusha kaisetsu," in *Jendā toraburu: Feminizumu
  to aidentiti no kakuran* (Gender trouble: Feminism and the subversion
  of identity) by Judith Butler, trans. Takemura Kazuko (Tokyo: Seidosha,
  1999), 295 (emphasis mine).
6 The culmination of this work was a special issue of the journal *Gendai
  shisō* 25, no. 6 (May 1997), titled "Rezubian/gei sutadīzu" (Lesbian/
  gay studies). The issue included an essay by Takemura on bisexuality:
  "Bōkyaku/torikomi no senryaku: Baisekushuariti josetsu."
7 Trinh T. Minh-ha, *Josei, neitivu, tasha: Posutokoroniarizumu to
  feminizumu*, trans. Takemura Kazuko (Tokyo: Iwanami Shoten, 1995).
8 Judith Butler, *Antigonē no shuchō: Toinaosareru shinzoku kankei*,
  trans. Takemura Kazuko (2000; Tokyo: Seidosha, 2002); Judith Butler,
  Shokuhatsu suru kotoba: Gengo, kenryoku, kōitai, trans. Takemura
  Kazuko (1997; Tokyo: Iwanami Shoten, 2004); Judith Butler and Gayatri
  Chakravorty Spivak, *Kokka o utau no wa dare ka? Gurōbaru suteito ni
  okeru gengo, seiji, kizoku*, trans. Takemura Kazuko (2007; Tokyo: Iwanami
  Shoten, 2008).

9 Takemura, *Bungakuryoku*, 319. The articles on lesbian studies appeared as "Rezubian kenkyū no kanōsei," *Eigo Seinen* 142, nos. 4–9 (July–December 1996).

10 Masao Miyoshi has memorably described the situation of area studies in the United States: "More than fifty years after the war's end, American scholars are still organizing knowledge as if confronted by an implacable enemy and thus driven by the desire either to destroy it or to marry it." See Masao Miyoshi and Harry Harootunian, eds., *Learning Places: The Afterlives of Area Studies* (Durham, NC: Duke University Press, 2002), 5.

11 Masao Miyoshi, "The Invention of English Literature in Japan," in *Japan in the World*, ed. Masao Miyoshi and Harry Harootunian (Durham, NC: Duke University Press, 1993), 284.

12 Ibid., 283.

13 The other two books she mentions are Saitō Hajime, *Teikoku Nihon no eibungaku* (Kyoto: Jinbun Shoin, 2006), and Miyazaki Yoshizō, *Taiheiyō sensō to eibungakusha* (Tokyo: Kenkyūsha, 1996).

14 Takemura, *Bungakuryoku*, 289.

15 Ibid.

16 Ibid., 290.

17 Ibid.

18 Miyoshi, "The Invention of English Literature in Japan," 281.

19 Ibid., 283.

20 Quoted in Takemura, *Bungakuryoku*, 302. I have cited the text from Jay Rubin's English translation. See Natsume Sōseki, *Theory of Literature and Other Critical Writings*, ed. Michael K. Bourdaghs, Atsuko Ueda, and Joseph A. Murphy (New York: Columbia University Press, 2009), 259–260.

21 Gayatri Chakravorty Spivak, *Death of a Discipline* (New York: Columbia University Press, 2003), 28.

22 Natsume Sōseki, *Sanshirō*, trans. Jay Rubin (New York: Penguin, 2009), 16.

23 Spivak, *Death of a Discipline*, 32.

24 F. O. Mathiessen, *American Renaissance: Art and Expression in the Age of Emerson and Whitman* (New York: Oxford University Press, 1941).

25 Henry Abelove, *Deep Gossip* (Minneapolis: University of Minnesota Press, 2005), 62–63.

26 Ibid., 69. Abelove's appointment in 2012 as the inaugural appointee to the F. O. Mathiessen Visiting Professorship in Gender and Sexuality Studies at Harvard is one positive sign in the right direction.

27 Natsume Sōseki, "Bundan ni okeru byōdōshugi no daihyōsha Uorutu Hoittoman," *Sōseki zenshū*, vol. 12 (Tokyo: Iwanami Shoten, 1967).

28 Takemura, *Bungakuryoku no chōsen*, 321.

CONCLUSION

~

On Rethinking Japanese Feminisms

AYAKO KANO

Why We Need to Rethink Japanese Feminisms Now

The first word of the title of this volume, "rethinking," points toward moments of reflection and reconsideration. The second word, "Japanese," raises the question of national boundaries, and the third signals multiplicities in the plural "feminisms." Why *feminisms* rather than feminism? What is the plurality that must be attended to? Why *Japanese*, what does the modifier mean, and what is the status of the national as a modifier? And why is there a need to rethink Japanese feminisms? Why now? And how? To answer these questions, this chapter begins by considering the present moment, and then weaves together the insights of three feminist scholars, Ueno Chizuko, Vera Mackie, and Barbara Molony, whose keynote addresses originally inspired this volume.

Why rethink Japanese feminisms now? In the wake of the massive earthquake, tsunami, and nuclear meltdown of March 2011—a disaster that shook the nation and its people's faith in government—the Liberal Democratic Party returned to power after ousting the Democratic Party of Japan. The new prime minister, Abe Shinzō, was a distressingly familiar face to feminists in Japan because he had spearheaded a conservative backlash against them in the late 1990s to early 2000s, as discussed in Tomomi Yamaguchi's chapter in this volume.[1] Cleverly, and initially a little confusingly, this time he proposed a series of measures highlighting women's roles in boosting national confidence and economic growth, while at the same time seeming to expect them to remain "good wives and wise mothers" in the conventional sense. Under the term "womenomics," Abe made a number of eye-catching feminist gestures.[2] At one point, his cabinet contained five women, roughly 30 percent of the total number of ministers, thus fulfilling a "quota" set as a national goal. Increasing the number of women in leadership positions was a highly visible gesture, although most of the women handpicked by Abe were known to have conservative views.

That Abe Shinzō, who less than a decade earlier had espoused strongly anti-feminist rhetoric, now found it politically expedient to perform such gestures can perhaps be read as a sign of the tectonic shift that has occurred during this time. It is striking that Abe's public announcements on "womenomics" were made initially in international contexts where it was necessary to project Japan's bona fides as a nation leading the world in women's rights. These were strategically crafted at a moment when the Japanese government faced severe criticism from multiple sectors, for failing to atone for the violation of women's human rights during World War II, especially on the so-called "comfort women" issue.[3] As such, the very fact that this international pressure was strong enough to motivate Abe's feminist speech acts might be interpreted as a hopeful sign.

One also senses this shift when surveying the pages of conservative news outlets such as the *Sankei shinbun*. Even while its op-ed pages continue to be filled with rhetorical statements to the effect that men should be strong and defend the nation and that women should stay at home and raise healthy babies, making one doubt that the last seventy years have existed for some of these pundits,[4] news articles in the paper also describe women juggling career and family, and men stepping up to shoulder more housework and childcare. While much of this coverage is still oriented toward the national and nationalist goals of boosting economic productivity as well as the birthrate, it is nonetheless a change from the celebration of conventional gender roles that one saw in the same pages in the 1990s and 2000s. Thus, it is not outside the realm of the possible that Japanese feminists have survived the backlash, and that at least some of their ideas have become embedded in what could be called national common sense.

A tentative voicing of such a possibility, however, is immediately muffled by doubts. Some propositions may now be shared by conservative leaders and feminist activists alike, but this is surely not enough, and the divisions are just as important. Yes, the conservatives might agree, *some* women can be good leaders. And yes, under *some* circumstances, if it does not hurt their role as mothers, women should participate in society beyond the home, especially if it helps the economy and the nation. But soon the points of contention arise: Are numerical quotas for women and financial incentives for promoting women the right answer? How far is the political leadership willing to take the dismantling of conventionally gendered divisions of labor? And how far is it willing to take the blurring of sexual and gender differences? Can we—*should* we—be "gender free"?[5] In other words, have Japanese feminists won? Or only some feminists? In the second decade of the twenty-first century, we face all of these questions and more, suggesting that the definition of feminism, never unambiguous in the first place, is facing a particular kind of pressure right now.

And what about the adjective "Japanese" to modify feminisms? This volume was initially conceived at an international conference, which itself was an outgrowth of several panels at major academic conferences that had initiated the process of "rethinking" the history of Japanese feminism in English. The very nature of this multiyear scholarly project calls the meaning of Japanese-ness into question. All of us participants are interested and academically invested in the study of Japan, but our degrees of affiliation and identification vary widely, and that is a good thing: it allows us to question the "assumed isomorphism of race, space, and culture"[6] according to which Japanese ethnicity is coterminous with Japanese territory, the Japanese nation-state, Japanese culture, and Japanese language. Some of us are Japanese citizens but reside elsewhere, and some of us have different citizenships but are long-term residents of Japan. Some of us reside elsewhere but have a longtime engagement with Japanese studies. Some of us have Japanese ancestry or family members. Some of us work in Japan, and many of us collaborate with colleagues there. Some of us feel more strongly interpellated by the term "Japanese" than others, and some of us identify or dis-identify more strongly.[7] Our diverse subject positions and modes of address reflect the diversification of Japanese studies as a field, as well as the internationalization of Japanese academia—both are ongoing phenomena, fraught with difficulties and limitations, but also allowing us to shake loose some of the assumptions of knowledge production: assumptions about who "we" are, and for whom and about whom we write.

Both the need to question what it means to advocate feminism as a state policy at this historical juncture, and the need to question the assumed isomorphism of "Japanese" ethnicity, nation-state, and language, lead us to rethink Japanese feminisms at this moment in time. The remainder of this chapter organizes this questioning around the following three issues that emerged out of the 2013 conference: *canonization* vs. *contention*, the *national* vs. the *transnational*, and the *optimistic* vs. *pessimistic* arcs in narrating the history of feminism in modern Japan.

Canonization vs. Contention

Among those who joined us in our project of rethinking Japanese feminisms, there were three prominent scholars who have shaped the field. Vera Mackie is the foremost English-language scholar on Japanese feminism, and has published the most comprehensive monograph on the topic, *Feminism in Modern Japan* (2003). She also has written and edited a number of other important books on the history of gender and sexuality in Japan from the Meiji period (1868–1912) to the present, including *Creating Socialist Women* (1997) and *Gender, Nation and State in Modern Japan* (2014).[8]

Barbara Molony has been an important advocate for scholarship on Japanese feminism and gender history in North American academia as associate editor of the *U.S.–Japan Women's Journal* and as co-editor with Kathleen Uno of the groundbreaking volume *Gendering Modern Japanese History*, as well as author of many important articles on Japanese women's history. As a manuscript reviewer of many book projects, she has also enabled the careers of numerous young scholars in the field.[9]

Ueno Chizuko is one of the most prominent feminist scholars in Japan and has published a long list of groundbreaking books, spanning an astonishingly wide range of topics and disciplines. As of this publication, two are available in English translation: *Nationalism and Gender* and *The Modern Family in Japan: Its Rise and Fall*.[10] She mentored a generation of feminist sociologists as a professor at the University of Tokyo and remains a high-profile public intellectual.

These scholars hailed from different parts of the globe—Japan, Australia, and the United States—and from different disciplines—literature, history, and sociology. Their keynote speeches on the history and current situation of Japanese feminism articulated commonalities but also instructive differences.

On the one hand, it is indeed remarkable that one can speak of a canon of Japanese feminist writing. As described in the introduction to this volume, Japanese feminism at this point has a long history, and many names that appear in these pages have become iconic figures. And yet, as the chapters by Elyssa Faisson and by Sarah Frederick show about Yamakawa Kikue, and the chapters by James Welker and by Setsu Shigematsu suggest about Tanaka Mitsu, these are also contentious figures. Meanwhile, the chapters by Kathryn Hemmann and by Barbara Hartley focus on authors such as Kirino Natsuo and Sono Ayako, who hitherto have not been considered feminist, certainly not in any simple definition of the term. It makes sense to ask: Who is included in a history of Japanese feminism, and who is excluded? How are the lines drawn?

Ueno, who herself has been in many ways an iconic figure of Japanese feminism since the 1980s, has recently talked about the importance of creating a feminist legacy to pass on to the next generation. In this vein, in her keynote speech in 2013, she discussed a multivolume anthology recently published in Japan, whose criteria of inclusion and exclusion were suggestive and worthy of further analysis. In the mid-1990s, the prestigious academic publishing house Iwanami Shoten had brought forth eight volumes of collected essays under the rubric *Feminism in Japan* (*Nihon no feminizumu*).[11] Edited by Ueno, Inoue Teruko, and Ehara Yumiko, the volumes were organized topically, with titles such as "Lib and Feminism," "Feminist Theory," and "Gender Roles." Fifteen years later, the editors compiled a revised and expanded series, comprising twelve volumes.[12] In all, the series now includes about two hundred and fifty articles, and a symposium commemorating the publication gathered many of the contributors, luminaries of Japanese feminist activism and scholarship. It was at this symposium, held in January 2013 at the University of Tokyo, that these principles for anthologizing, that is, choosing certain works for inclusion in the canon, were articulated.[13]

As Ueno described it, there were three principles. First, these were all works written in the Japanese language, thus indicative of "linguistic nationalism." Second, the articles were all written by biological women, hence the collection may be said to be marked by "gender essentialism." Third, they were works published in print media, and although this included informal pamphlets and small-run magazines—known as *minikomi*, for "mini communication"—they were also clearly limited to print and did not include digital media. These three principles demarcated the boundary of what counted as Japanese *feminizumu* for this anthology, and Ueno noted that all three would be difficult to maintain from this point forward, so this might become the last printed anthology with the title "Japanese Feminism."[14]

These principles that emerged from the editing of the Iwanami series raise broader issues of definition, canonization, and contention. For example, the *linguistic nationalism* of the series reminds us that language remains a barrier as much as a conduit for communication. To privilege the Japanese language, as the editors of the Iwanami series did, is to marginalize or exclude the voices of immigrant women, as well as the scholarship of those who do not publish in Japanese. It also seems to ignore the tradition and impact of feminist texts translated from other languages into Japanese (see the chapters by James Welker, Sarah Frederick, and J. Keith Vincent in this volume). On the other hand, it was a necessary strategy to stress the "homegrown" nature of Japanese feminist scholarship. By contrast, to use the English language, as we have done in our present volume and the various conferences leading up to it, is to also repeat certain kinds of exclusions and marginalizations. We hope that the choice of English as a medium of communication here will open up these conversations to a wider global audience; we must nonetheless acknowledge the dangers of linguistic imperialism entailed by this choice.

The *gender essentialism* of the Iwanami series opens up the question of who is qualified to represent feminism and to whom. The editors of that anthology defined feminist scholarship as a form of identity politics, and thus excluded male-authored texts, thereby omitting many significant contributions by male scholars specializing in feminism and related fields. One volume was set aside for "men's studies," featuring scholarship by men about masculinity, and in the second edition this volume was compiled by a male scholar.[15] But this still left the gender binary firmly in place. In our present volume, we as editors did not make such essentialist decisions, yet this does not mean that the politics of identity simply disappear.

Finally, the question of *print vs. digital* points to a rapidly shifting landscape for feminist activism, scholarship, and debate. In North American academia, the most prestigious venues for presenting scholarship remain peer-reviewed journals and books printed on paper—though often also available in digital versions. This is why our present volume is published as a book, with peer review, from an academic press. The publishing landscape may look quite different in a decade or two. It is with this in mind that a group of feminists in Japan established the Women's Action Network (WAN), a feminist Internet portal site.[16] The site includes components such as A-WAN focusing on art, B-WAN offering book reviews, and P-WAN focusing on politics. Another critically important component of the website is the archiving of ephemeral *minikomi* as well as more established publications on feminism and women's studies.[17] While maintaining a large website like this comes with many difficulties, some of which are suggested in Yamaguchi's chapter in this current volume, it is possible that the next version of a large-scale feminist anthology—as well as the next version of a book such as ours—will be fully reliant on these types of web archives.

The National vs. the Transnational

To define Japanese feminism as being forty years old, as Ueno Chizuko does in the context of discussing the Iwanami anthology, sets its beginnings in the 1970s. It associates feminism with the student movement as a kind of "global simultaneity," which embroiled young people in Paris, New York, Tokyo, and other major global cities. To locate the birth of Japanese feminism in the turmoil of the student movement is an interesting move, a clear but contentious choice. What came before is perhaps not defined as feminism, so one would not need to consider, for example, the knotty question of women's groups and women leaders who collaborated with the state during the era of Japanese imperialism and fascism, addressed by Elyssa Faison in this volume. Instead, feminism can emerge as a youth movement, an oppositional force, associated from its beginnings with a stance critically opposing the state and capital.

But one could argue that the trajectory is far messier, and one can imagine other origin stories. Barbara Molony, along with a number of other scholars,[18] points to the late nineteenth century, the era of Japanese nation-building, as another origin for Japanese feminism. This is when transnational feminist groups, especially those associated with Christian missionary organizations, began to influence Japanese discourse about women's role in society. To begin the story of Japanese feminism not in the 1970s but instead in the Meiji period—when the Women's Christian Temperance Union established its Tokyo chapter, for example—places its origins in this earlier transnational or global moment.

Vera Mackie would broaden the story of feminism even further and claim that it is an ineluctable product of modernity. Mackie's argument views modern societies as organized around structured relationships of gender and class, rather than the status-based relations of feudalism. Once there exists a consciousness of such gendered relations, it leads inevitably to feminist consciousness, as a response to, and often rebellion against, modern gendered constructions.[19] This view sets feminism in the large story of global modernity—any society that goes through the transition to modernity will make use of gender as a category of social organization and analysis, and this will give rise to feminism.

These three types of "origin stories" can certainly be substantiated through different types of evidence. They also potentially signal three different ways of defining "feminism," and when taken together, can help us see multidimensional stories of feminisms. For example, in Ueno's view, it is important to stress the continuities between "women's lib" and feminism and also women's studies in Japan—a narrative that she knows to be disputed but also wants to defend. This narrative presents itself in opposition to those who would see *ribu* as separate from *feminizumu*, the former associated with the countercultural youth movement of the 1960s and 1970s, and the latter emerging in the 1980s and 1990s. *Joseigaku*, or women's studies, is also often criticized for being cut off from women's lib consciousness and activism, so to stress the continuity between lib, feminism, and women's studies in Japan is to stress connections and alliances where others have claimed dissociation and tension.

Molony reminds us of the uneasy connection between transnational feminisms, Christian missionary zeal, and Western imperialism, a legacy that must be recognized in order to be overcome. It would also mean that the history of Japanese feminism includes a number of decades, from the late nineteenth century to the end of the Asia-Pacific War, in which Japanese women were excluded from formal electoral politics, and during which they had to interact with the state on vastly unequal terms. This was an era in which dissent from state policy could be punished by imprisonment, even death—one thinks of the feminist activist Kanno Suga, and many others who were silenced.[20] The alternative was various degrees of cooperation with the state and its organizations. This era came to a formal end with the defeat of the nation in a disastrous war, and Occupation by a foreign government eager to promote the ideals of gender equality as part of its larger agenda to win hearts and minds. As shown in the chapters by Julia Bullock and by Elyssa Faison in this volume, American imperialism and Cold War politics enter the picture here, and as Molony reminds us, transnational feminism "does not have clean hands." To include this longer history is to include questions of collusion with and mobilization by these forces, and to admit that various kinds of feminist projects have served on many occasions as tools of national and imperial policies.

Mackie sees feminism as part of a global modernity and thereby challenges us to see the larger picture, returning us to the question of what—if anything—is specifically Japanese about Japanese feminisms. Indeed, Mackie prefers the phrase "feminisms in Japan" to "Japanese feminisms," because not all feminist activities in Japan are carried out by those of Japanese nationality or ethnicity. She also calls our attention to the pioneers of transnational feminism, whose activities crisscross the national frame. The earlier generation included the suffragettes and socialist women of the early twentieth century who engaged with transnational networks of communication.[21] The later generation especially noted by Mackie included Akiyama Yōko—also discussed in Welker's chapter—who was involved in multiple directions of translation, between Japanese and English but also between Chinese and Japanese; Atsumi Ikuko, a poet and professor of English literature who created the mass-market feminist magazine *Feminisuto*, which published translations and English-language editions; and Matsui Yayori, who started the Asian Women's Association and brought to Japanese readers' attention many of the gender issues of the Asian region. These women, and the publications and group activities that they catalyzed, grappled not only with contemporary issues but also with history, especially the troubled relationship between Japan and women in other parts of Asia.

In this regard, it is also important to remember the Women's International War Crimes Tribunal that took place in 2000. This was organized by many grassroots Asian women's organizations, including the Violence Against Women in War Network, Japan (VAWW-Net Japan) and the Korean Council for the Women Drafted for Military Sexual Slavery. As Mackie points out, this tribunal was built on preexisting transnational connections, extending them in new ways, and creating a forum in which the victims' voices could be heard, translated, and amplified. These transnational connections are also examined in Akwi Seo's chapter in this volume. At the same time, the comfort women controversy is a topic in which the tension between nationalism and feminism has become the most acute and seemingly intractable. It is an issue in which Japanese and Korean ethnic nationalisms seem to feed on each other to exacerbate tension. The situation has arguably worsened since 2000, despite recent attempts at resolution between the governments of Japan and Korea.[22]

The question of the national and transnational, of local and global processes, also raises the question of what has happened since the 1990s. This was the moment when a particular vision of a "gender-equal society" became national policy, was fiercely contested by conservatives, and eventually became the orthodoxy of the neo-liberal/neo-conservative administration of Prime Minister Abe, albeit in transmogrified form. Writing a history of Japanese feminism to include these messy episodes would not be easy, but it would expand our understanding of what Japanese feminism has meant, and could mean in the future. And it would lead us to think of *feminisms*, rather than one unified feminism. If feminisms can include all of these things, we have a complex picture, full of contradictions and paradoxes.

Narrative Pessimism vs. Optimism

Should one be optimistic or pessimistic about the future of Japanese feminisms? On this question, the three scholars were split: Ueno Chizuko was clearly pessimistic, Barbara Molony was optimistic, and Vera Mackie was neutral. To pose the question of narrative optimism vs. pessimism is, on one level, to simply acknowledge that any attempt to narrate a history will consciously, or unconsciously, follow a particular rhetorical genre. As Hayden White reminds us, historical situations are not inherently tragic or comic, triumphant or deflating—it is the historian who makes it so through her narrative choices.[23] But in the case of a narrative about feminisms, there is an additional twist in that the *scholar of feminisms* might also often be a *feminist scholar*. Ueno has taken this situation as axiomatic, claiming that knowledge is most fruitfully pursued by members of a group who are directly and gravely affected by a problem (*tōjisha kenkyū*). While this does not mean that scholarship equals activism, it does mean that a scholar's choice of narrative genre and tone can become inter-twined with her prognosis of social and political afflictions.

Ueno's pessimism stems, at least in part, from the recent return of Abe Shinzō to power, as well as the rise of populist politicians whose sup-port base suggests a widespread disillusionment with progressive poli-cies. Ueno's recent writings and public speeches, for example the lecture commemorating her retirement from the University of Tokyo,[24] express a sentiment of powerlessness in the face of political and environmental calamities, but then connect that to the idea of feminism as a philosophy for the survival of the weak. Ueno's pessimism might be described as that of a sociologist who has her eyes trained unflinchingly on the difficulties of society in the present.[25] Yet, it is possible that her definition of femi-nism as a philosophy for the weak also allows her to regard these predica-ments as opportunities to deepen feminist practice.[26]

By contrast, Mackie is careful to be descriptive rather than prescrip-tive, and thus her tone comes across as neither pessimistic nor optimis-tic. In the long-term view that is the hallmark of historians, one can point to rights and freedoms that have been fought for and won: to voice opinions, to organize in collectives, to vote and to stand for office, to be employed on equal terms with men, to have paid maternity and child-care leave, to have access to decent childcare, health care, and eldercare. These are issues that Mackie notes in *Feminism in Modern Japan*, and in her authoritative overview, Japanese feminism comes across as a long and winding road, with significant detours and obstacles, but eventually lead-ing to greater rights and freedoms.

It is with this in mind that Molony expresses the greatest tone of hope among the three keynote speakers. Like Mackie, she is a historian con-scious of the *longue durée* of women's progress, but Molony chooses to express her optimism for the future even more consistently. Her keynote remarks at the 2013 conference ended by quoting the words of Martin Luther King Jr.: "[T]he arc of the moral universe is long but it bends toward justice."[27]

It is always tempting to end a conference, a lecture, or a book on an optimistic note. One would like to believe that hope springs eternal, espe-cially from the energy of the next generation of activists and scholars, including our junior colleagues and our students. Yet, it is also difficult to ignore the troubling signs or to misread what is a clearly emerging global structure that will challenge feminist solidarities in the years to come. As a shorthand for challenges on the horizon for Japanese feminisms, let us turn to an image from Kanai Yoshiko's essay from about two decades ago. In the introductory essay to *Voices of the Japanese Women's Movement*, published in 1996, Kanai asks: "Is it better to eat a steak in the smog, or eat a rice ball under a blue sky?"[28] She posed this question at the very end of the bubble economy period, when the choice presented to feminism seemed to be between a polluted and exploitative capitalist prosperity and an ecologically and ethically attractive frugality.

What are our choices now, two decades later? These choices may have accrued new meaning in the post-Fukushima landscape. Is it even possible to wish for blue skies under which to eat a rice ball? Is our air, our soil, our water, and what grows out of these elements ever going to be clear of contamination, or the threat of it, the fear of it? The fear might be the most insidious, the most difficult to clean up. Will the Japanese archipelago be a place where people can hold on to a sense of hope for the future? Clearly some will be eating steaks, and the ones who can afford to eat steaks are also the ones most likely to be globally mobile, who can pick up their laptops and smartphones and move to where the skies are bluer, the grass greener. In a further twist of irony, those who can afford to eat steaks under a blue sky are also likely to be the ones who can afford to eat organically grown rice balls. The image of capitalist prosperity vs. ecological frugality has become fragmented and mashed up. It may now be the precarious poor who are trapped under smoggy skies eating toxic hamburgers, and optimism may come at a price that is too heavy to pay.

The growing gap between the rich and the poor within Japan makes it more difficult to imagine a single vision of feminist utopia that is shared by all.[29] For elite women, this goal may be envisioned in terms of the ability to move between different localities, seeking optimum happiness, leveraging difference to extract profit. For the non-elite, it may mean strengthening the social safety net, so that one does not descend into abject poverty. In the medium term, is it possible to keep both groups happy? Or to actually come up with a shared picture of happiness? Supporting individuals, or supporting families? Inspiring the best to excel or offering security to all? Feminism for the strong or the weak? Or different feminisms for different ends?

Challenging questions indeed. It is because of such questions that rethinking Japanese feminisms *now* is timely, fruitful, and also absolutely necessary.

Notes

As the organizers of the 2013 conference, we invited four prominent figures in Japanese feminist scholarship as keynote panelists. Mizuta Noriko, who in the end could not participate due to health issues, is a pioneer in the field of feminist literary criticism and higher education in Japan—having earned a PhD in American literature from Yale University and having become one of the first female presidents of a major Japanese university (Jōsai University, later Jōsai International University). The journal that she co-founded, *U.S.–Japan Women's Journal*, has been an important venue for publication of scholarship on feminism and gender issues, and Jōsai International University was one of the first institutions in Japan to offer a graduate degree in women's studies. Her many books on literature and feminist criticism include: Noriko Mizuta Lippit, *Reality and Fiction in Modern Japanese Literature* (White Plains, NY: M. E. Sharpe, 1980); *Feminizumu no kanata: Josei hyōgen no shinsō* (Tokyo: Kōdansha, 1991); *Joseigaku to no deai* (Tokyo: Shūeisha, 2004). *U.S.–Japan Women's Journal* was initially published in Japanese, as *Nichibei josei jānaru*, with English-language supplements.

1   See also Ayako Kano, "Backlash, Fight Back, and Back-Pedaling: Responses to State Feminism in Contemporary Japan," *International Journal of Asian Studies* 8, no. 1 (2011).
2   Ayako Kano and Vera Mackie, "Is Shinzo Abe Really a Feminist?" *East Asia Forum*, November 9, 2013, http://www.eastasiaforum.org/2013/11/09/is-shinzo-abe-really-a-feminist/.
3   As noted in the introduction to this volume, the terminology is itself contentious. See also note 22 below.
4   See for example, the controversy incited by conservative commentator Sono Ayako's statements to this effect: *J-Cast News*, "'Shussan shitara o-yamenasai': Sono Ayako kikō de netto mo daigekiron," September 8, 2013, http://www.j-cast.com/kaisha/2013/09/05183030.html?p=1. On Sono, see also Barbara Hartley's chapter in this volume.
5   Kano, "Backlash." See also Tomomi Yamaguchi, "'Gender Free' Feminism in Japan: A Story of Mainstreaming and Backlash," *Feminist Studies* 40, no. 3 (2014).
6   The phrase is from Akhil Gupta and James Ferguson, "Beyond 'Culture': Space, Identity, and the Politics of Difference," *Cultural Anthropology* 7, no. 1 (1992): 7.
7   On modes of identification and non-identification, see Naoki Sakai, *Translation and Subjectivity: On "Japan" and Cultural Nationalism* (Minneapolis: University of Minnesota Press, 1997), 44–48.

8 Vera Mackie, *Creating Socialist Women in Japan: Gender, Labour and Activism, 1900-1937* (Cambridge: Cambridge University Press, 1997); Vera Mackie, *Feminism in Modern Japan: Citizenship, Embodiment and Sexuality* (Cambridge: Cambridge University Press, 2003); Andrea Germer, Vera Mackie, and Ulrike Wöhr, eds., *Gender, Nation and State in Modern Japan* (London: Routledge, 2014); Vera Mackie, "Feminism," in *The Sage Handbook of Modern Japanese Studies*, ed. James Babb (London: Sage, 2015); Mark McLelland and Vera Mackie, eds., *The Routledge Handbook of Sexuality Studies in East Asia* (New York: Routledge, 2015).

9 Barbara Molony and Kathleen Uno, eds., *Gendering Modern Japanese History* (Cambridge, MA: Harvard University Asia Center, 2005). See also Barbara Molony, "Equality Versus Difference: The Japanese Debate over 'Motherhood Protection' 1915-50," in *Japanese Women Working*, ed. Janet Hunter (London: Routledge, 1993); Barbara Molony, "Japan's 1986 Equal Employment Opportunity Law and the Changing Discourse on Gender," *Signs* 20, no. 2 (1995); Barbara Molony, "Women's Rights, Feminism, and Suffragism in Japan, 1870-1925," *Pacific Historical Review* 69, no. 4 (2000).

10 Chizuko Ueno, *Nationalism and Gender*, trans. Beverley Yamamoto (1998; Melbourne: Trans Pacific Press, 2004); Chizuko Ueno, *The Modern Family in Japan: Its Rise and Fall* (Melbourne: Trans Pacific Press, 2009).

11 Inoue Teruko et al., eds., *Nihon no feminizumu*, 6 vols. (Tokyo: Iwanami Shoten, 1994-1995).

12 Amano Masako et al., eds., *Shinpen Nihon no feminizumu*, 12 vols. (Tokyo: Iwanami Shoten, 2009-2011).

13 See Inoue Teruko, "Nihon no feminizumu o tewatasu tame ni," http://wan.or.jp/reading/?p=2146, accessed February 23, 2015.

14 According to the records of the commemorative Symposium held January 30, 2013, at the University of Tokyo, these three principles were the target of critique by Kitamura Aya, Saitō Keisuke, and Myōki Shinobu, respectively.

15 Amano Masako et al., *Shinpen Nihon no feminizumu*, vol. 12.

16 Women's Action Network (WAN) is located at http://wan.or.jp.

17 For example, the important feminist journal *Agora* and the women's studies journal *Joseigaku kenkyū* (Women's studies research), as well as the important compendium of women's lib documents, Mizoguchi Akiyo, Saeki Yōko, and Miki Sōko, eds., *Shiryō Nihon ūman ribu shi*, 3 vols. (Kyoto: Shōkadō Shoten, 1992-1995) are accessible and downloadable in part or in whole via this website.

18 Sharon L. Sievers, *Flowers in Salt: The Beginnings of Feminist Consciousness in Modern Japan* (Stanford, CA: Stanford University Press,

1983); Marnie S. Anderson, *A Place in Public: Women's Rights in Meiji Japan* (Cambridge, MA: Harvard University Asia Center, 2010); Elizabeth Dorn Lublin, *Reforming Japan: The Woman's Christian Temperance Union in the Meiji Period* (Vancouver: UBC Press, 2010); Mara Patessio, *Women and Public Life in Early Meiji Japan: The Development of the Feminist Movement* (Ann Arbor: Center for Japanese Studies, University of Michigan, 2011).

19 See also Mackie, *Feminism in Modern Japan*. In this view, the Freedom and People's Rights Movement of the 1870s and 1880s would be considered a crucial moment for the emergence of gender and feminist consciousness.

20 Mikiso Hane, *Reflections on the Way to the Gallows: Voices of Japanese Rebel Women* (New York: Pantheon, 1988); Hélène Bowen Raddeker, *Treacherous Women of Imperial Japan: Patriarchal Fictions, Patricidal Fantasies* (New York: Routledge, 1997).

21 See for example, Rumi Yasutake, *Transnational Women's Activism: The United States, Japan, and Japanese Immigrant Communities in California, 1859–1920* (New York: New York University Press, 2004).

22 Yamashita Yeong-Ae, "Revisiting the 'Comfort Women': Moving Beyond Nationalism," in *Transforming Japan: How Feminism and Diversity Are Making a Difference*, ed. Kumiko Fujimura-Fanselow (New York: The Feminist Press, 2011). See also C. Sarah Soh, *The Comfort Women: Sexual Violence and Postcolonial Memory in Korea and Japan* (Chicago: University of Chicago Press, 2009); and Ueno, *Nationalism and Gender*.

23 Hayden White, *Metahistory: The Historical Imagination in Nineteenth-Century Europe* (Baltimore: Johns Hopkins University Press, 1973). See also Ann Curthoys and John Docker, *Is History Fiction?* (Ann Arbor: University of Michigan Press, 2005).

24 Ueno Chizuko, *Ikinobiru tame no shisō: Tōkyō Daigaku taishoku kinen tokubetsu kōen: Tokubetsu kōen & tokuten eizō*, DVD (Tokyo: Kōdansha, 2011).

25 Ueno Chizuko, *Onnagirai: Nippon no misojinī* (Tokyo: Kinokuniya Shoten, 2010).

26 Ueno Chizuko, *Ikinobiru tame no shisō: Jendā byōdō no wana* (Tokyo: Iwanami Shoten, 2006); see also her *Onnatachi no sabaibaru sakusen* (Tokyo: Bungei Shunjū, 2013).

27 This quote is from Martin Luther King Jr.'s sermon at Temple Israel of Hollywood, Los Angeles, California, February 26, 1965.

28 Yoshiko Kanai, "The Women's Movement: Issues for Japanese Feminism," in *Voices From the Japanese Women's Movement*, ed. AMPO, *Japan Asia Quarterly Review* (Armonk, NY: M. E. Sharpe, 1996), 21.

29 See Frank Baldwin and Anne Allison, *Japan: The Precarious Future* (New York: New York University Press, 2015). On the emergence of the *kakusa shakai* (disparity society), see also Seike Atsushi, "Japan's Demographic Collapse," in *Examining Japan's Lost Decades*, ed. Yoichi Funabashi and Barak Kushner (London: Routledge, 2015).

Contributors

Julia C. Bullock is Associate Professor of Japanese Literature and Culture at Emory University. Her first book, entitled *The Other Women's Lib: Gender and Body in Japanese Women's Fiction* (University of Hawaiʻi Press, 2010), analyzes the 1960s boom in literature by Japanese women as a precursor to the "women's lib" discourse of the following decade. She is currently working on two book projects, one that explores the reception of the feminist theory of Simone de Beauvoir (1908–1986) in postwar Japan, and another that analyzes the controversy surrounding the introduction of coeducation as part of post–World War II Japanese educational reforms. Her contribution to this volume is part of this second research project.

Elyssa Faison is Associate Professor of History at the University of Oklahoma. She is the author of *Managing Women: Disciplining Labor in Modern Japan* (University of California Press, 2007), and co-editor with Ruth Barraclough of the volume *Gender and Labour in Korea and Japan: Sexing Class* (Routledge, 2009). She is currently working on a monograph about the legacies of atomic bombings and nuclear testing in the United States, Japan, and the Pacific Islands; and a biography of Yamakawa Kikue (1890–1980) that will also be a social history of twentieth-century Japan.

Sarah Frederick is Associate Professor of Japanese in the Department of Modern Languages and Comparative Literature at Boston University. She is the author of *Turning Pages: Reading and Writing Women's Magazines in Interwar Japan* (University of Hawaiʻi Press, 2006), which explores the literary, visual, commercial, and political texts of three women's magazines of the 1920s, *Fujin kōron*, *Shufu no tomo*, and *Nyōnin geijutsu*. She is currently working on a book on the life and work of author Yoshiya Nobuko (1896–1973) and is translator of her story "The Yellow Rose" (Expanded Editions, 2016).

Barbara Hartley is Senior Lecturer and Discipline Director of Asian Languages and Studies in the School of Humanities at the University of Tasmania. With doctoral studies in representations of motherhood in twentieth-century narrative in Japan, she has a background in feminist analysis of modern Japanese literature and has published a range of material on women writers in Japan. She also has a strong interest in representations of China and East Asia in Japanese narrative and visual art and is currently completing a book examining these representations in the work of the postwar writer, Takeda Taijun (1912–1976).

Kathryn Hemmann is Assistant Professor in the Department of Modern and Classical Languages at George Mason University. She earned her PhD at the University of Pennsylvania, and she is currently working on a manuscript titled "Writing Women Readers: Manga Cultures and the Female Gaze." Kathryn's work covers material ranging from fiction to manga to video games. She is interested in how women interpret texts that are usually understood as being targeted at a male audience. She also has a blog called "Contemporary Japanese Literature," where she reviews recent translations and posts essays on gender issues in Japanese popular culture.

Ayako Kano is Professor in the Department of East Asian Languages and Civilizations, and core faculty member in Gender, Sexuality, and Women's Studies at the University of Pennsylvania. She is the author of *Acting Like a Woman in Modern Japan: Theater, Gender, and Nationalism* (Palgrave, 2001), and *Japanese Feminist Debates: A Century of Contention on Sex, Love, and Labor* (University of Hawai'i Press, 2016).

Hillary Maxson is a doctoral candidate studying women and gender at the University of Oregon, where she completed her master's degree in Modern Japanese History in 2012. Her research focuses on social constructions of motherhood in the twentieth century. She is currently working on her dissertation, which is tentatively titled "Kakeibo Monogatari: Women's Consumerism and the Postwar Japanese Kitchen."

Chris McMorran is Senior Lecturer in the Department of Japanese Studies at the National University of Singapore. He researches mobility, labor, and tourism, especially in contemporary Japan. He is working on a book on Japanese inns (*ryokan*), which analyzes the intense physical and emotional work necessary to produce these relaxing places and reproduce the families that own them. He has also researched the geographies of learning, focusing on student field trips and online courses.

Akwi Seo is Associate Professor of Sociology at Fukuoka Women's University. Her research interests are in migrant women's organizations and transnational feminist activism in Japan and Korea. Her particular focus has been on the processes through which women who belong to socially marginalized groups participate in politics and construct active citizenship through activities that transcend ethnic and national boundaries. She is the author of *Creating Subaltern Counterpublics: Korean Women in Japan and Their Struggle for Night School* (Melbourne: Trans Pacific Press, 2017), the original Japanese version of which was awarded the 32nd Yamakawa Kikue Prize and the 7th Words and Gender Prize. Her recent work covers the (multi)cultural representation of foreign women who immigrate to Korea to marry Korean men.

Setsu Shigematsu is Associate Professor in the Media and Cultural Studies Department at the University of California, Riverside. She is the author of *Scream from the Shadows: The Women's Liberation Movement in Japan* (University of Minnesota Press, 2012) and the co-editor of *Militarized Currents: Towards a Decolonized Future in Asia and the Pacific* (University of Minnesota Press, 2010). She is also the director of *Visions of Abolition* (2011), a documentary film about the prison industrial complex and women's activism in the prison abolition movement.

Nancy Stalker is Associate Professor at the University of Texas at Austin in the Departments of Asian Studies and History, and a core faculty member of the UT Center for Women and Gender Studies. Her focus is on cultural history in modern Japan, including popular religion, traditional arts, and cuisine. She is the author of *Prophet Motive: Deguchi Onisaburō, Oomoto and the Rise of New Religions in Imperial Japan* (University of Hawai'i Press, 2008). She is currently completing a book on the growth and globalization of flower arranging (ikebana) in the twentieth century, *Budding Fortunes: Ikebana as Art, Industry and Cold War Culture* and is editing a volume entitled *Devouring Japan: Global*

Perspectives on Japanese Culinary Identity, which will be published by Oxford University Press.

J. Keith Vincent is Associate Professor of Japanese and Comparative Literature and Women's, Gender and Sexuality Studies at Boston University. He was instrumental in introducing and translating U.S. gay and lesbian studies to Japan in the 1990s and has striven since then to create a dialogue between Japanese queer scholarship and U.S. queer theory. His publications include *Perversion and Modern Japan: Psychoanalysis, Literature, Culture* (Routledge, 2009), co-edited with Nina Cornyetz; a translation, with Dawn Lawson, of the Lacanian critic Saitō Tamaki's groundbreaking study, *Beautiful Fighting Girl* (University of Minnesota Press, 2011); and *Two-Timing Modernity: Homosocial Narrative in Modern Japanese Fiction* (Harvard University Press, 2012). He is currently at work on two edited volumes, both with Alan Tasman and Reiko Abe Auestad, on the novelist Natsume Sōseki (1867–1916), and a monograph on the haiku poet Masaoka Shiki (1867–1902).

James Welker is Associate Professor of Cross-Cultural Studies at Kanagawa University in Yokohama, Japan. His research focuses on women and girls' culture in late twentieth-century Japan—with an emphasis on the women's liberation (*ūman ribu*) movement, the les- bian community, and the queer girls' comics sphere. In addition to vari- ous book chapters and journal articles on these topics, he is co-editor and translator for *Queer Voices from Japan: First-Person Narratives from Japan's Sexual Minorities* (Lexington, 2007) and co-editor of *Boys Love in Japan: History, Culture, Community* (University Press of Mississippi, 2015). He is the author of *Transfigurations: Feminists, Lesbians, and* Shōjo *Manga Fans in Late Twentieth-Century Japan* (University of Hawai'i Press, forthcoming).

Leslie Winston is Adjunct Assistant Professor of Japanese at UCLA. She is currently at work on a manuscript entitled *Second Sexes: Uses of Intersexuality in Meiji–Taishō Japan*. Her contribution to this volume derives from that project.

Tomomi Yamaguchi is Associate Professor of Anthropology at Montana State University, specializing in feminism, nationalism, and social movements in contemporary Japan. She has published a co-authored book in Japanese, entitled *Social Movements at a Crossroads: Feminism's "Lost Years" vs. Grassroots Conservatism (Shakai undō no tomadoi: Feminizumu no 'ushinawareta jidai' to kusanone hoshu undō*; Keisō Shobō, 2012), on the anti-feminist backlash in Japan since the mid-1990s. She is also a co-editor of the eight-volume collection, Takagi Sumiko et al., eds., *Women's Action Group Documents Collection (Kōdō-suru onna-tachi no kai shiryō shūsei: Henshū fukkokuban*; Rikka Shuppan, 2015–2016); and co-author of Saito Masami and Tomomi Yamaguchi, *On Tajima Yōko (Tajima Yōko-ron*; Seidosha, forthcoming), and Tomomi Yamaguchi, Tessa-Morris Suzuki, Nogawa Motokazu, and Emi Koyama, *The "Comfort Woman" Issue Going Overseas: Questioning the Right-Wing "History Wars" (Umi o wataru "ianfu" mondai: Uha no 'rekishisen' o tou*; Iwanami Shoten, 2016).

Index

Page numbers in **boldface** type refer to illustrations.

Greater Japan Federated Women's
Association (Dai Nihon Rengō
Fujinkai), 5
Greater Japan National Defense
Women's Association (Dai Nihon
Kokubō Fujinkai), 5
Grewal, Inderpal, 207, 231
Grotesque (*Gurotesuku*; Kirino), 171,
172, 175–179, 183n.26
Group Chame, 244
Group of Fighting Women (Gurūpu
Tatakau Onna), 52, 220

Hani Motoko, 3
Hantongryun (Korean Democratic
Reunification Union), 235, 240,
249n.24
Hara Minako, 50, 51
Harding, Sandra, 156, 164
Hartley, Barbara, 141
Hendry, Joy, 122
hermaphrodites, 134, 137, 138
heterosexual feminism *vs.* lesbian
feminism, 50–51. *See also* lesbian
(*rezubian*) feminism
High Treason Incident (1910), 191,
202n.17
Hiratsuka Raichō: child of, 44, 45;
creation of Mother's Congress
by, 34, 36–37, 41; New Women's
Association by, 4; opinions of, 16,
41, 47n.30, 94; in roundtable on
state feminism, 26; and *Seitō*, 3;
Suzuki on, 155
home work (*naishoku*), 74, 104,
122. *See also* "good wives, wise
mothers" (*ryōsai kenbo*); *ryokan*
work
homosexuality. *See* lesbian
(*rezubian*) feminism; male
homosexuality; same-sex
sexuality
hooks, bell, 156, 245

Howl of the Loser Dogs (*Makeinu no
tōboe*; Sakai), 170–171
Ichikawa Fusae, 4, 16, 23, 24–25,
33n.33, 155
ikebana: and educational reforms,
105–108; as female employment
opportunity, 95, 103–105, 115–
116; *iemoto* system in, 114–115;
rise of postwar programs on, 6,
103, 116, 117n.10; *Sogetsu Ikebana
Notes*, 110; styles of, 107, 111;
teacher recruitment in, 109–112;
U.S. interest in, 103–104; in the
workplace, 113, 118n.34
Ikenobo (*ikebana* school), 103, 105,
109, 111, 112
Ikuta Kizan, 147, 153n.41
individualism, 91–92, 260–261
infanticide, 210
Inoue Teruko, 218, 271
The Intermediate Sex (Carpenter),
190, 192, 201n.5, 203n.25
International Feminists of Japan
(IFJ), 59
intersectionality, 166n.19, 217, 230–
231, 239–241, 245
Ishihara Shintarō, 167n.30
Ishikawa Sanshirō, 191
Itō Kei (Itō Megumu), 191, 192,
202n.16, 202n.23
Itō Noe, 3, 191, 196–198
Iwanami Shoten, 218, 271
Izumo Marou, 57, 62n.7

Japan Communist Party, 18, 20, 76,
83n.20
Japan Conference. *See* Nippon Kaigi
Japanese American Studies
Association, 256
Japanese feminisms: canonization
vs. contention in, 270–273; a case
for rethinking, 42–44, 267–270;